Operation Oyster

Dedication

This book is dedicated to all who took part in Operation OYSTER, or who were affected by the raid, on the ground or in the air. It is especially in remembrance of those, both military and civilian, who were killed.

Royalties

Royalties from the sale of this book will go to the Royal Air Force Benevolent Fund.

Operation Oyster

The Daring Low Level Raid on the Philips Radio Works

Kees Rijken, Paul Schepers and Arthur Thorning

Pen & Sword
AVIATION

First published in Great Britain in 2014 and reprinted in this format in
2022 by
Pen & Sword Aviation
an imprint of
Pen & Sword Books Ltd
47 Church Street
Barnsley
South Yorkshire
S70 2AS

ISBN 978 1 39901 976 7

Typeset in Ehrhardt by
Mac Style Ltd, Bridlington, East Yorkshire

Printed and bound in the UK by
CPI Group (UK) Ltd, Croydon, CR0 4YY

Pen & Sword Books Ltd incorporates the imprints of Pen & Sword
Archaeology, Atlas, Aviation, Battleground, Discovery, Family
History, History, Maritime, Military, Naval, Politics, Railways, Select,
Transport, True Crime, and Fiction, Frontline Books, Leo Cooper,
Praetorian Press, Seaforth Publishing and Wharncliffe.

For a complete list of Pen & Sword titles please contact
PEN & SWORD BOOKS LIMITED
47 Church Street, Barnsley, South Yorkshire, S70 2AS, England
E-mail: enquiries@pen-and-sword.co.uk
Website: www.pen-and-sword.co.uk

Contents

Maps

Introduction: Eyewitness Accounts and Acknowledgements

Kees Rijken's words

My interest in aeroplanes dates back from 1932, when the airfield at Eindhoven was opened and my grandad offered me a flight in the single-engine Fokker F.7A PH-ACT above the city of Eindhoven (this aircraft was destroyed on 10 May 1940, when hangared at Schiphol, by a German bombardment during the invasion of The Netherlands). Through the magazine *De Vliegwereld* I was able to follow the development and production of all new aircraft. This enabled me on 10 May 1940 to recognize the German Heinkel 111s, which were flying in great numbers across Eindhoven on a Western heading. This was the invasion of The Netherlands and the beginning of the war in our country.

During the war years, the only possible way to gain knowledge about participating aircraft from the countries at war was via German publications. However, this proved rather satisfactory and I never had difficulty in instantly recognizing any particular type of plane during the war. Whenever it was reasonably possible, I tried to see as much as possible of the aerial movements above and around Eindhoven during these years. My favourite spotting place was the roof of my parents' house along the Sint Rochusstraat. This was also the case on 6 December 1942.

It was noon, half-past twelve. We were all having dinner, when suddenly an enormous amount of noise interfered, originating from aeroplane engines, anti-aircraft guns, exploding bombs and machine guns. Up to the roof!

From the rooftop I could see a number of Douglas Bostons approaching from the west, flying in the direction of the Philips factories. As seen from my vantage point, some of them started the bomb drop ahead of the St Rochusstraat. Explosions and clouds of smoke were clearly visible. Several minutes after the Bostons' departure, from a somewhat more northerly direction, another group of aircraft followed which I immediately recognized as Lockheed Venturas, producing a terrific coffee-grinder like noise. They were being hailed by the now fully alert German anti-aircraft guns. Suddenly the right wing of one of the attacking Venturas was enveloped in fire. It pulled up sharply, stalled and dropped like a stone to crash in open terrain near the Schoolstraat (Ventura I, AE702 SB-Q, 464 Squadron). All the crew perished, as I was informed later. I also saw a Ventura, apparently hit, lose height and disappear in an easterly direction. It crashed at the Nieuwe Dijk; all the crew perished.

After the departure of the Venturas huge clouds of smoke were filling the sky above Eindhoven, and the blazing inferno of many fires could be seen and heard. Curious as I was, I took to my bike and cycled to the city centre. Stratumseind and the Wal were already sealed off. At the Bergstraat I was ordered to reverse. At that moment a lone Mosquito raced over the city to photograph and film the results of the bombardment as I was told by one of the spectators who had been forced to work in Germany for a while and had seen this happen before. On my way home I saw two not-yet-exploded bombs lying on the Dommelbrug in de Jan Smitzlaan.

After the war my interest in this raid never left me and I tried to gain an overall picture of it by buying books in which, albeit mostly on just one or two pages, an anecdote about this bombardment could be found. This has led to overcrowded bookshelves but still no clear picture of what happened on 6 December 1942. It was not until my son-in-law Paul and I started to really investigate the history of Operation OYSTER, by means of repeated visits to the UK Public Records Office, Imperial War Museum, London and RAF Hendon that most (still not all) of the puzzle could be recovered. There followed many discussions and an extensive correspondence with participating veteran airmen and multiple visits to former airfields involved. We reported our findings in one document, so as to have all Operation OYSTER related information at hand at once. This is the result.

C. L. J. M. Rijken (1928 – 2020),
Eindhoven, 12 April 1998

Paul Schepers' introduction to the two-volume research document 'RAF No 2 Group Operation Order No.82 – Operation OYSTER' follows:

This document is written to be of use to relatives of aircrew and existing RAF Squadron associations who participated in Operation OYSTER (RAF Operation Order No. 82), in researching the whereabouts of particular crews and planes. The authors do not have the intention of reproducing the booklet commercially, unless advised otherwise by any of those mentioned above.

Our keen interest in this particular RAF operation is, apart from being aviation enthusiasts above all, twofold. For my father-in-law, because he had a grandstand view of the whole raid from the rooftop of his parental house, guarded against shell-fragments falling on his head by wearing a cooking-pot (!), being fourteen years of age and knowing by type all participating aircraft. He was hooked on retrieving every single bit of information published about this raid since then. For myself, being a Philips employee who works in one of the knocked-down buildings on the Strijp complex, is the reason.

The trigger for the document was to combine as much information as possible regarding aircrew and aircraft, plans and results in relation to Operation OYSTER in one single booklet. One can find numerous books and articles which reveal part of the operation, but we found it difficult to get the complete overview by reading them separately. So it was decided to gather the available pieces of the puzzle, gradually filling in the missing ones.

Both the authors have collected quite some material over the years; that has all been included. However, not until we started our research at the UK Public Records Office in Kew did we gain an in-depth knowledge of the tremendous effort conducted by the RAF. It was rather amazing to us as to how much authentic information could be retrieved from the PRO, keeping us busy for a much longer time than anticipated, I can tell you (beside providing the first-ever hands-on experience of computers for my father-in-law).

By writing to squadron associations, numerous contacts were established with surviving aircrew who actually took part in Operation OYSTER and were very willing to share their experiences. Though people who have contributed to this document are numerous, I would like to thank especially RAF crew members Freddie Deeks, Peter Mallinson, Jim Moore, Stan Moss, Albert Ricketts, George Shinnie, Jay Snow, Tony Valle-Jones, Edith Wagner (widow of late Reg Wagner) and Arthur Wheeler. Furthermore, Jim Taylor (who was an air gunner on Avro Manchesters), John Younge from Methwold for his *tour d'historique* of the Methwold aviation area, Thérése Eke of Little

Barford Power Station for her kind assistance in obtaining unique photo material, the personnel of the Imperial War Museum, London, Philips Company Archives, Eindhoven, Public Records Office, London and the RAF Museum, Hendon, for their kind assistance and invaluable patience. Without the cooperation of the following people this book could never have reached the current stage: Martin Bowman, Jackie Gaylor (daughter of T. J. Cross), Arno de Greef, Lionel Hastings, Dennis van Hoof, Ad Louwers, Henny Munsters, Squadron Leader Sandeman (RAF Marham), Stuart Scott, Alistair Payne, Ad van Zantvoort and A. C. van Zunderd. Many, many thanks to all of them.

A special 'mention in despatches' goes to my wife, Jeanne, for the endless stream of sandwiches and cuppas during the time I virtually lived in my study room. She had to suffer many a lonely day and night over a couple of years.

Paul Schepers
Eindhoven, 26 June 2002

It should be noted at this point that the above document is not in a form convenient for a general readership. A copy is held by the Library of the Royal Air Force Museum at Hendon. Thus this book has been produced to condense the principal points into a narrative, supported by selected items from British and Dutch archives for those readers who want a flavour of the source material.

English Co-Author

I must explain how I came to join my Dutch colleagues, Kees Rijken and Paul Schepers, as co-author of this work. After a career as an aeronautical engineer and scientist, mainly in civil aviation R&D, I found myself writing a biography of Melvin 'Dinghy' Young, one of the Dambuster pilots who had studied at the same Oxford College as myself – this exercise released a long, but slumbering, interest in aviation history.

A much respected neighbour, Norman Roche, now sadly dead, had told me about his brother Stephen who had died in 1943 while serving as a pilot in the RAF, and of some interesting letters which Stephen had written telling of his wartime experience. When I was shown these letters by Mrs Enid Roche I was fascinated by one in particular, in which Stephen Roche recounted in some detail a low-level raid on which he had flown to attack the Philips factory at Eindhoven – Operation OYSTER.

This led me to further research at the Royal Air Force Museum at Hendon, where I was shown two comprehensive research documents compiled by Kees Rijken and Paul Schepers, which are described in Paul Schepers' words above. Kees and Paul kindly agreed to work with me to produce this book as a tribute to all involved, both in Britain and The Netherlands. I must also record my indebtedness to my wife Valerie for her patience and encouragement during the prolonged process of preparing this book, for accompanying me on trips to meet Kees, Paul and their families and (not least) for drawing several maps.

The authors would also like to thank our editor, Richard Doherty, and Laura Hirst, Pen & Sword's Aviation Imprint Administrator, for their support and help in the preparation of this book.

Arthur Thorning
Hitchin, England
July 2013

Also as a further introduction, some personal recollections of aircrew involved follow.

In their own words – aircrew accounts of the raid

Before the raid (Account of John Beede, role unknown, from Gavin Lyall's *War in the Air 1939-45*):

'I looked at the faces of these young airmen who were about to be blooded. They were serious and generally quiet. As each crew got out [of the crew transport] the rest wished them luck.'

Approaching enemy coast (John Beede):

'Two tremendous splashes that tossed water over our heads marked the passing of two crews.'

Over the Dutch coastal land, Sergeant Albert Ricketts, pilot 21 Squadron (personal recollection):

'Not long after the Dutch coast we were in the area of 'dykes' and of course there were roads on some of these. It came as a bit of a surprise to see a fellow on a bike some 10ft or so higher than our aircraft riding along one of them.'

Over The Netherlands, towards the target (Sergeant Peter Mallinson, air gunner 487 Squadron – in a letter to his sister, Connie):

'As we hopped over trees and roofs there were people waving like mad, handkerchiefs, even flags.'

Over The Netherlands (Sergeant Stephen Roche, pilot 226 Squadron – in a letter to his sister Margaret):

'The Dutch people were marvellous, they held up their arms in the shape of a V … by the way we saw a peach of a girl running after a boy on a cycle and everyone spoke about her! Mmm!!!'

Over the target (Sergeant Peter Mallinson):

'As I looked back from my turret I saw two German machine gunners still on the roof.'

Leaving the target (Sergeant Stephen Roche):

'It was terribly exciting of course, but the only thing that frightened me was all the other machines milling around all over the place! Two Fw190 fighters came after us, but being so close to the ground they couldn't attack me! … We came out so fast my engines were nearly red hot.'

On return (Sergeant Peter Mallinson):

'The only casualty [on his aircraft] was the remains of a stork which was stuck in the port engine air cooler … I'm sorry I didn't manage to get you a genuine pair of Dutch clogs, Con, but we didn't stay very long.'

On return (Sergeant Stephen Roche):

'That same evening we had a marvellous concert … So, it was a perfect end to a perfect day, what?!'

Chapter One

Eindhoven and the Philips Company

Eindhoven

Eindhoven, which has its origins in the middle ages, is now a growing industrial centre in the Dutch province of Noord-Brabant and is the fifth largest city of The Netherlands after Amsterdam, Rotterdam, The Hague and Utrecht – it lies in the south of the Netherlands near the Belgian border. In the second half of the nineteenth century the town had about 3,000 residents and covered only 140 acres, but there was already developing industrial activity. Textile, cigar and match factories had developed in the nineteenth century but by 1900 they had been supplanted by the Philips electrical works as the main industry, and later (1928) the vehicle manufacturer van Doorne's Aanhangwagen Fabrieken started in the city (in 1938 the company started producing lorries and was renamed van Doorne's Automobiel Fabrieken: DAF). Because of its industrial importance Eindhoven was bombed several times during the Second World War and, so, few historic buildings survived. It was this strategic industrial importance which gave rise to the gallant operation described in this book. Eindhoven has subsequently been redeveloped with a modern urban plan including attractive pedestrian precincts.

Philips

Eindhoven owes its spectacular expansion mainly to Philips which grew from a simple electric light bulb factory – giving rise to the popular reference as 'The City of Light' – into an international electronics giant. Philips now makes audio, video and medical equipment, household appliances and all kinds of electronic components (and still bulbs, or rather lighting in general).

In 1891 Gerard Philips set up a light bulb assembly plant on the Emmasingel. The young engineer, Ir Gerard Philips, who had just graduated from the Glasgow College of Science and the University of Delft, bought a 1,200 square metre piece of ground upon which was a factory building measuring eighteen by twenty metres. Within the factory there was a 45bhp steam engine and boiler with matching chimney. It was in this former woollen mill that Gerard Philips started the production of an American invention by Thomas Alva Edison: the electrical incandescent lamp. Setting up such a factory in The Netherlands was at that time very attractive because foreign patents were not recognized. During the first year of its existence the company Philips & Co. manufactured about 11,000 incandescent lamps (a technically more accurate description than 'light bulb') with a workforce of thirty employees. At the time electric lamps were mainly sold for the illumination of factories, major shops, government agency buildings and the slowly emerging civic street lighting. Widespread domestic use was to come later but, in spite of this, the new product was very successful. Just four years later the production reached 200,000 incandescent lamps and at the end of the year 1900 (barely nine years after foundation) the lamp factory already had four hundred employees.

The popularity, rapid acceptance and international spread of electric lighting resulted in the explosive growth of the Philips Gloeilampen (incandescent lamp) factory. In parallel to this growth and the increasing number of employees came the need for more housing. The small city of Eindhoven was not prepared for house-building on the necessary scale. Thus the Philips Company took the initiative to study possibilities including consideration of the surrounding villages. This resulted in the company acquiring a leased farm complete with surrounding pastures in 1909. The goal was to build a modern housing complex providing all necessary facilities. This was modelled after the British factory village Port Sunlight (Wirral, Merseyside), following the example of the famous soap-making business Lever Brothers. Consequently a pretty and modern factory village was built in a short time span. In 1923 five surrounding villages were acquired by the city of Eindhoven, among them the village Strijp and the new 'Philipsdorp' (Philips village), after which Eindhoven was now officially referred to as Greater Eindhoven.

After the first five difficult years Gerard's brother Anton (whose statue stands at the railway station) came to his aid, and from then onwards the business took off in a big way. The factory began making radio valves, X-ray tubes and medical equipment, exporting across Europe. In 1914 Gerard set up the natural sciences laboratory Natlab, which has since been responsible for many important new technologies, including the video recorder and the Compact Disc (CD). Later, in collaboration with DAF, Philips established a Technical College, now Eindhoven Technical University.

By 1929 Philips had 20,000 employees and provided jobs for 70 per cent of the local workforce. It opened new factories and offices on the Emmasingel and Mathildelaan, with names like De Witte Dame (The White Lady), De Bruine Heer (The Brown Man) (remark: the name De Bruine Heer was never an official name for this building, and has never been associated as such by citizens of Eindhoven. It seems that the name originated from recent project development to give each large building in Eindhoven an official name) and De Lichttoren (The Lighthouse). Philips provided medical care for its employees, as well as transportation to and from their work. The company also set up its own sports club, Philips Sport Vereniging, whose football club (PSV Eindhoven) is one of the country's best known.

The close ties between Philips and Eindhoven were reduced when the company moved its headquarters to Amsterdam in 1998. New uses were sought for many of its buildings. However, the small light bulb factory where it all began is now open to the public as a museum.

The Netherlands, Philips and the War

It is worth putting the situation in The Netherlands in 1942 into perspective, as a background to this book. Officially the country is the Kingdom of The Netherlands although it is often conveniently, but incorrectly, called Holland. Strictly, North and South Holland are two provinces in the northwest part of the kingdom, but Dutch people themselves, especially in those provinces, often use Holland for the whole country. The reason behind this originates from the era of the Dutch *Vereenigde Oost-Indische Compagnie* (VOC, United East Indies Company) sailing ships. These ships departed from the province of Holland, and since they travelled all across the globe the name of Holland has stuck ever since. The sailors introduced themselves as coming from Holland rather than from The Netherlands. To add to the confusion, the whole region of mostly low-lying country including Belgium and Luxembourg has traditionally been known as the 'Low Countries', which is another way of saying the 'Netherlands'. The Low Countries are situated within the delta of the Rijn/Rhine, Maas/Meuse and Schelde/Sheldt rivers, and much of the land is below sea level.

Before the German invasion in 1940 The Netherlands had maintained its neutrality for over a century and was one of the most prosperous countries in the world. The expectation of life was among the longest and the average real income per head was among the highest in Europe; indeed The Netherlands was one of the few countries able to lend money abroad. With a population of about eight and a half million it was one of the most densely populated in Europe. The Dutch were, and still are, one of the most highly educated peoples in the world. As a small nation surrounded by larger ones they are among the best linguists, in the sense that a large proportion of them read, speak and write foreign languages. They regard their universities and other institutions of higher education with well-founded pride – the Philips Company made a notable contribution in the technical field.

At dawn on 10 May 1940 the Germans invaded The Netherlands, Belgium, Luxembourg and France by land and air. The Dutch resisted bravely but they were overcome by the large and well-equipped German Army. Eventually, after the bombardment of Rotterdam, the main Dutch forces had no choice but to surrender. Queen Wilhelmina and her Government evacuated to London from where they could direct the war effort of the Dutch Navy and free Dutchmen around the world.

At first the German occupation offered a pretence of mildness, but from the beginning the press was controlled and there were widespread requisitions of goods and property. The Dutch people may never have had much love for the Germans but soon they began to hate them. Some bold spirits organized resistance and executions began. Thus the Dutch people were encouraged when they saw British aircraft on their way to attack their mutual enemy, even if they sometimes caused harm to their country – they still hold the sacrifices of Allied airmen over their country close to their hearts and hold remembrance services each May on their Liberation Day, in Eindhoven and many other places.

At the outbreak of the Second World War the original Philips lamp factory had grown as 'Philips Electronics' into one of the leading electronic factories in the world with 22,000 employees. Philips meanwhile had establishments in a large number of countries worldwide.

During the German occupation the Philips factories in the Netherlands were forced to contribute to the German war industry, ample reason for the Allies to eliminate the factories as soon as possible. Accordingly the Germans established an extensive network of searchlights and anti-aircraft batteries surrounding the factory buildings. For the inhabitants of Philipsdorp, directly adjacent to the factories, this meant that during the war they had to live with continual fear that sooner or later the Philips factories would become a bombing target. To take the best possible care for its employees and the people living in the Philipsdorp, shelters were constructed and pupils of the schools within the Philipsdorp were sent to classes in – it was hoped – less dangerous areas of the city.

Chapter Two

Choice of Target

Main Targets in Occupied Countries

The sixty-first meeting of the Bomb Targets Information Committee, held at the Air Ministry in London on 9 April 1942, requested that consideration should be given to the selection of a limited number of objectives of *outstanding importance* in enemy occupied countries. Accordingly a memorandum, with the above title, was prepared. (National Archives AIR40/232 – note that this document is quoted as written, with Holland instead of The Netherlands and Stryp compared with the Dutch spelling Strijp.)

Information with regard to the economic and industrial importance of various objectives was compiled in collaboration with the Ministry of Economic Warfare, who suggested eight possible targets as the most important in occupied countries within reach of the RAF. The eight targets were:

NORWAY – Aluminium, magnesium, nitrates and fertiliser plants at Heroya, approximately 600 miles from the RAF bases.

DENMARK – Shipyards and diesel engine works near Copenhagen, some 550 miles from base.

HOLLAND – two targets:
Rotterdam, port area and shipyards, 170 miles from base.
Eindhoven, Philips wireless valve and radio works, 230 miles from base

BELGIUM – four targets:
Liège, heavy engineering works, blast furnaces and chemical plants, 240 miles.
Tertre, coke ovens, chemical plants, 190 miles.
Gent-Terneuzen Canal and adjacent works, 160 miles
Antwerp, Ford and General Motors plants, 190 miles.

The memorandum concluded that only the two Dutch targets compared in economic importance with targets of the first priority in Germany.

Given the increasing importance of electronics in the development of communications and weapon systems, especially radar, it is understandable that plans were put in train for an attack on the Philips factories at Eindhoven. An appendix to the memorandum gave more details of the two Philips works, namely:

The STRYP (Northern) block of factories, the larger of the two, making all types of material for lamp and valve manufacture (as well as wireless sets) and includes some experimental laboratories.

The EMMASINGEL (Southern) block of factories, smaller and some 500 metres from STRYP, comprises the lamp and valve manufacturing plant, rare gases department, offices etc.

The memorandum continued:

The PHILIPS concern is the largest producing radio valves in Europe and in spite of decentralisation since 1929 by the establishment of

The Strijp Complex from the air in 1934. *(Aviodrome Ref 13377)*

The Emmasingel site in 1939. The 'Light Tower', at the extreme left of the photograph, is still a prominent feature in Eindhoven with the 2011 Memorial adjacent. In 1942 the tower had a flak battery on top. *(Aviodrome Ref 2055)*

subsidiary manufacturing plants abroad, the EINDHOVEN WORKS still remained the largest plant of its kind in Europe and in 1939 Dutch employees numbered 15,000.

Since the occupation the Dutch plants have been under German management and in view of the large demand for radio valves and of the fact the less important valve factories in France are known to be working to capacity on German orders, the Germans are doubtless utilising the extensive production facilities of the EINDHOVEN factories. The EINDHOVEN Works produce components for other smaller factories at HILVERSUM and DORDRECHT.

The EINDHOVEN WORKS are in close proximity to the town of EINDHOVEN and the bombing of this target would inevitably be attended with considerable risk of casualties to the civilian population unless some prior steps are taken to avoid this. The Works are not situated adjacent to any particular landmark such as water, but the size of the Works should render them reasonably easily distinguishable.

The most vital part of the Works [is] in the EMMASINGEL BLOCK which should prove very vulnerable to bombing owing to the special natures and extreme delicacy of the plant.

This appreciation, written in London, was necessarily based on a combination of pre-war information and rather limited current intelligence. In his book *45 jaar met Philips* Frits Philips, the Director General of the Philips factories during the war years, states that the company had to report to a German commission in Berlin with monthly production figures. He proudly states that these figures were never achieved. By means of carefully prepared graphs the Germans were misled. However, with hindsight, Frits Philips admitted that if these figures had found their way to British Intelligence they might have encouraged the bombardment. It is notable that Frits Philips was imprisoned by the Germans in the period 1 May to 20 September 1943 in an attempt to break strikes at Philips. These strikes were caused by a German order for all former Dutch military personnel to report

Frits Philips statue in Eindhoven city centre. *(Arthur Thorning)*

to the German authorities. Many feared that they would be made prisoners of war and national strikes broke out.

The book gives an insight into the goods produced by the factories:

> Communication equipment, radio receivers and transmitters, radio valves, telephones and cabling, some for civil use, but some for delivery to important German electronics companies such as Telefunken and Siemens, undoubtedly for military purposes.

On the development side the Germans tried to utilize the Philips research facilities, an example being making radio equipment able to withstand desert sand, no doubt with the Panzerarmee Afrika in mind. Generally the Philips researchers were reluctant workers during the occupation – as Frits Philips said, 'With unwilling dogs it is difficult to catch rabbits'. Unknown to the Germans batches of radio valves were treated chemically to shorten their operating life.

In planning the raid, the British were very conscious of the risk of civilian casualties in a raid on the Philips factories. The British suffered some 60,000 civilian deaths due to German aerial bombardment in the Second World War, mainly in 1940 and 1941. Accordingly they were concerned to minimize the risk to their Allies under occupation but, in total war, 'needs must when the devil drives'.

Chapter Three

Forces Available for the Attack

Operation OYSTER, the daring low-level raid on the Philips valve and radio factories at Eindhoven in The Netherlands was the first large-scale operation mounted by the medium bombers of 2 Group, RAF Bomber Command, from their bases in Eastern England, principally in the county of Norfolk. No. 2 Group had already mounted numerous smaller-scale raids on targets in the near continent of Europe and strikes on German coastal shipping. Sometimes they took part in 'Circus' operations designed to draw the enemy fighter forces into action with escorting British fighters. Other typical targets included power stations, railway viaducts and ships in harbour. The headquarters of 2 Group were at Bylaugh Hall, near Swanton Morley, a large country house (now in ruins).

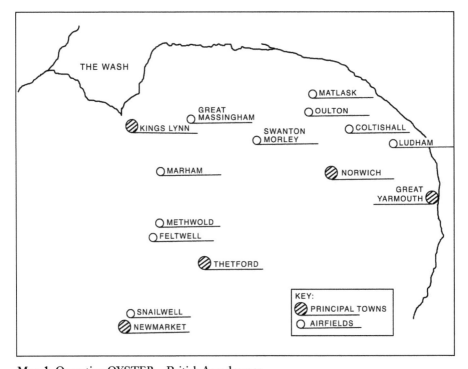

Map 1. Operation OYSTER – British Aerodromes.

The Bases

Ten aerodromes were involved in Operation OYSTER (see Map 1) – six for the bombers (Feltwell, Great Massingham, Marham, Methwold, Oulton and Swanton Morley) and four for the escorting fighters (Coltishall, Ludham, Matlaske and Snailwell). The term aerodrome is used in this book rather than airfield, since by the 1940s grass fields were becoming inadequate for the heavier aircraft increasingly in use. Indeed the word aerodrome (literally a course for the running of aeroplanes) is defined as 'Large tract of open level ground, including all buildings and fixtures, for the operation of aircraft' (Concise Oxford Dictionary) and as such covers sites with either grass- or hard-surfaced aircraft movement areas.

These aerodromes varied in character depending on their history. Some were established RAF bases with fine permanent buildings, the product of the expansion of the RAF's infrastructure in the late 1930s in the light of the gathering threat of war. The leading architect of the time, Sir Edwin Lutyens, was employed to provide designs for the more prestigious buildings. Coltishall, Feltwell and Marham (which is still in operation as a base for Tornado jets) were examples of this 'Expansion Period'. Occasionally a country house in the locality was taken over for use by the RAF – an outstanding example was the use of nearby Blickling Hall as the officers' mess for RAF Oulton. Blickling Hall is one of the finest Jacobean mansions in England, built in the seventeenth century with splendid gardens and an extensive park, it is now in the care of the National Trust and is open to visitors – one of the attractions is an RAF Museum in the harness room.

Sometimes an aerodrome started with grass surfaces and was later provided with hard runways and taxiways – some, like Swanton Morley, continued with grass but were thus limited in the aircraft they could handle and were susceptible to wet conditions. Many aerodromes were built hastily during the war – some 600 were constructed in Britain during the Second World War, one of the greatest civil engineering operations in the nation's history – and these had functional, but more basic, buildings. Although most of these wartime constructions have been ploughed up (the hardcore being used for motorway construction in the 1960s and 70s) there are a great many still visible and a few remain in use for aviation purposes.

The Bomber Squadrons

At the time of Operation OYSTER the bomber squadrons involved were located thus:

21 Squadron – Lockheed Ventura (Mks I and II) – Methwold
88 Squadron – Douglas Boston III – Oulton
105 Squadron – de Havilland Mosquito IV – Marham
107 Squadron – Douglas Boston III – Great Massingham
139 Squadron – de Havilland Mosquito IV – Marham
226 Squadron – Douglas Boston III – Swanton Morley
464 (RAAF) Squadron – Lockheed Ventura I/II – Feltwell
487 (RNZAF) Squadron – Lockheed Ventura I/II – Feltwell.

Each squadron was typically equipped with about sixteen aircraft, although not all would be serviceable at any one time.

No. 21 Squadron (squadron code: YH)

No. 21 Squadron was regularly part of 2 Group Bomber Command from 1938, being based at various aerodromes in England and occasionally at Lossiemouth in Scotland. Its wartime letter code was YH – each aircraft had a three letter designation, in large letters on the sides of the fuselage, beginning YH and followed by an individual letter for each aircraft. At the end of 1941 and into the beginning of 1942 the squadron, like many others, took its turn operating from Malta, that 'most bombed place on earth', as part of the epic struggle to deny the Panzerarmee Afrika the supplies it needed to threaten Egypt, the Suez Canal and the Middle Eastern oilfields. However, by the end of September 1942 the squadron had arrived at Methwold with its new, as yet untried, Lockheed Venturas. It took several weeks for them to reach operational efficiency and they performed their first daylight raid in November, so were still relatively inexperienced with the Ventura for Operation OYSTER. The squadron served throughout the war from the UK and the continent until disbanded in 1947 – they made many daylight raids on shipping and coastal land targets.

No. 88 Squadron (RH)

No. 88 Squadron joined 2 Group in July 1941 and operated from numerous aerodromes in England, Scotland and Northern Ireland until they moved to Oulton in September 1942. They were then soon engaged in operations over northern France, especially le Havre where the large German vessel

Neumark was the object of their attention. They also did several night operations over Belgium and The Netherlands, dropping leaflets giving the news of the Allied victory over the Panzerarmee Afrika at El Alamein. The CO of 88 Squadron, Wing Commander Pelly-Fry, led Operation OYSTER and his was the first aircraft to attack. The squadron continued to serve with distinction until it was disbanded in 1945.

No. 105 Squadron (GB)
No. 105 Squadron became part of 2 Group at Honington in June 1940, and subsequently operated Blenheim aircraft from various places in UK, interrupted by the not uncommon detachment to Malta. In September 1942 the squadron moved from Horsham St Faith (now Norwich International Airport) to RAF Marham, south-east of Kings Lynn, with their newly acquired de Havilland Mosquito bombers. The Mosquito had a two-man crew, who sat in very close proximity in a narrow fuselage, and relied for protection on its very high speed and altitude capability – its existence had yet to be announced to the public, but this was soon to change. The squadron was commanded by Wing Commander 'Hughie' Edwards who had won the Victoria Cross, Britain's highest military award, when serving with the squadron earlier at Swanton Morley. He had recently returned from a tour of the USA promoting the British war effort. One of 105 Squadron's earliest Mosquito raids involved a raid on the Gestapo headquarters in Oslo, attacking at roof-top height with delayed action bombs. Although the defenders were taken by surprise one of the four aircraft was shot down, emphasizing the hazards of low-level operations. In 1943 the squadron moved to 8 Group, the Pathfinders.

No. 107 Squadron (OM)
No. 107 Squadron had been in 2 Group since 1936 (with a short period in 1 Group) and had operated from a typical range of RAF stations, mostly with the Bristol Blenheim bomber, which, although already outdated by 1939, was required to put in heroic service. Throughout 1940 the squadron was engaged in hazardous operations – Sylt, Bremen, Dunkirk and power stations near Cologne – and losses were heavy. A detachment to Malta also proved costly to 107 Squadron and, on its return, it was reformed and re-equipped with the much more capable Douglas Boston. With this new aircraft the squadron had a distinguished record, attacking airfields, docks, power stations and railway marshalling yards in northern France and The Netherlands. It ended the war operating from continental aerodromes.

No. 139 (Jamaica) Squadron (XD)

No. 139 Squadron joined 2 Group in 1937 at Wyton and subsequently served at various places in the UK and (from December 1939 to May 1940) in France. As with many other squadrons they sent a detachment to Malta for a few months in 1941. In December 1941 they moved to Oulton and re-equipped with Lockheed Hudson aircraft before leaving for Far East service and merging with 62 Squadron. The squadron was reformed at Horsham St Faith in August 1942 and, along with 105 Squadron, then moved to Marham and were re-equipped with Mosquitos. From Marham they mounted numerous low-level, daylight sorties, in company with 105 Squadron, leading up to Operation OYSTER. In January 1943 the Marham-based Mosquitos took part in two notable raids. Firstly (27 January) nine aircraft attacked the Burmeister and Wain factory in Denmark which was making U-boat components. The second (30 January) was a famous occasion when two raids, each by three Mosquitos of 139 Squadron, arrived over Berlin just as the Nazi leaders were making notable speeches; the first three aircraft caused a speech by Göring to be delayed and the second trio arrived at 16.00, just as propaganda minister Goebbels was about to address an open air rally, thus sending the party faithful running for cover – one of this second group of Mosquitos was shot down. In June 1943 the squadron was transferred to 8 Group for Pathfinder duties.

No. 226 Squadron (MQ)

No. 226 Squadron joined 2 Group at Wattisham in May 1941 and, after detachments to Manston and Northern Ireland (for army co-operation training), moved to Swanton Morley, where it re-equipped with the Douglas Boston III and took part in numerous raids on shipping and targets in the near continent. In June 1942 nine American crews from the USAAF Eighth Air Force joined 226 Squadron to gain experience before receiving their own Boston aircraft – several joint British/American raids were conducted attacking marshalling yards, power stations and aerodromes. After Operation OYSTER they served at various aerodromes in Scotland, England, France and The Netherlands (at the famous Gilze-Rijen airbase) before being disbanded in 1945.

No. 464 (RAAF) Squadron (SB) and 487 (RNZAF) Squadron (EG)

In August 1942 Feltwell, one of the pre-war Expansion Period aerodromes which had had distinguished use as a Wellington bomber base in 3 Group, was transferred to 2 Group and became for a few months the home for two Australasian squadrons, newly formed and equipped with the Lockheed

Ventura medium bombers. First came the New Zealanders (487 Squadron) followed on 1 September by the Australians of 464 Squadron. Necessarily these two squadrons spent most of the time leading up to Operation OYSTER getting used to their new aircraft and bringing themselves up to operational efficiency – in this they succeeded although their losses on the Eindhoven raid were heavy, probably because they were the last type to attack, when the defences were alert and smoke obscured the target area. Indeed this billowing smoke most likely caused two Venturas to crash into buildings which they were attacking. Both squadrons moved to Feltwell's satellite aerodrome Methwold in April 1943 and thereafter both squadrons served at various bases in Britain and on the continent before being disbanded in 1945 (although 487 was renumbered as 16 Squadron).

The Bomber Aircraft

Since this book is fundamentally about a bombing operation it is worth taking a look at the characteristics of the bombers used for Operation OYSTER – the fighters, performing escort and diversion duties, are adequately described in many other books. Although the North American Mitchell (B-25) medium bomber had been delivered to the RAF there had been insufficient time to bring them to an adequate state of operational efficiency, so they were not used on Operation OYSTER. This is no reflection on the design of the Mitchell which served with great distinction and had already won its place in history on the famous 'Doolittle Raid'. On Saturday 18 April 1942 a force of sixteen B-25 bombers commanded by Lieutenant Colonel 'Jimmy' Doolittle, operating from the carrier USS *Hornet*, made a surprise daylight raid on Tokyo and other targets in Japan, a reprisal for the attack on Pearl Harbor and a warning of aerial devastation yet to come. The removal of the Mitchell left three medium bomber types on Operation OYSTER – the Douglas (DB-7) Boston III, the Lockheed (Vega 37) Ventura (Marks I and II) and the de Havilland Mosquito B. Mark IV.

These three bomber types were all designed around 1940, but from different starting points. It was an era of rapidly developing aeronautical technology and the industry was led by talented engineers, some of whom gave their names to famous companies – Geoffrey de Havilland, Donald Douglas, Jack Northrop all had a hand in the design of the three types in this story. The Lockheed Vega Ventura, so called because it was made by the Vega Division of Lockheed at Burbank, California, was developed from the L18 Lodestar airliner in response to a requirement from the British Government

– its civilian origin with a wide fuselage and limited manoeuvrability gave it a relatively poor performance despite excellent, powerful engines.

The Douglas Aircraft Company, of Santa Monica, California, had already produced the very successful DC-3 airliner and designed the DB-7 series of bombers for Britain and France. It was specifically designed as a military aircraft, performed well by the standards of the time and was popular with its pilots.

The third type was the de Havilland Mosquito, from Hatfield, England; this was a quite new and radically different concept. It was of wooden construction (de Havilland had considerable experience with this very efficient material), was unarmed and had a crew of only two (pilot and navigator/bomb aimer), relying on its speed and high altitude capability to elude the enemy defences. The Mosquito became one of the most successful and versatile aircraft of the Second World War.

(Data relating to aircraft are quoted in the units in use at the time, in particular airspeeds in miles per hour (1mph = 1.609 kilometres per hour), weights in pounds (1lb =0.454 kg) and engine power settings in pounds per square inch (psi).)

Douglas Boston aircraft in RAF service. *(Authors' collection)*

Douglas Boston

The Douglas DB-7 was given the name Boston by the British (the American version was known as the A-20 Havoc). The model designed for the British, the DB-7b, was given the mark number III to distinguish it from DB-7a aircraft designed for the French but delivered to the UK, and known as Marks I and II. One of the most noticeable innovations was the adoption of a tricycle undercarriage layout, which has subsequently become almost universal since it provides greater stability on the ground, especially during the critical take-off and landing phases of flight. The other types with their tail-wheel undercarriage layout, which had some advantage on bumpy grass aerodromes (keeping the propellers well clear of the ground), suffered from having the centre of gravity behind the main weight-bearing wheels with a consequent tendency to swing out of control (ground loop).

The Boston had a crew of three or four – pilot, navigator/bomb-aimer, wireless operator/air gunner and often another air gunner. The pilot sat centrally in the fuselage in a relatively comfortable seat (American aircraft were often good in this regard). Although the control and instrument layouts were less than ideal ergonomically, this was the norm in those times and the Boston was generally well regarded by its pilots. The pilot had control of four fixed, forward-firing Browning .303-inch machine guns which gave the aircraft a useful ground attack capability. There were two more machine guns mounted on the top of the fuselage and another below for defensive purposes. The bomb load could be up to 4,000lb and the maximum weight of the aircraft was 27,000lb (12,250 kg). The aircraft was powered by two Wright R-2600 Double Cyclone engines of 1,600 horse power (hp) each.

All the powerful twin engine aircraft of the Second World War were difficult to control in the event of one engine failing – there were many accidents, especially on take off when the engines were at maximum power. The Boston was typical in this respect and it is worth taking the aircraft as an example of the challenge posed to relatively inexperienced pilots. The handling notes[1] suggest a lift-off speed in the range 100-110mph indicated air speed (IAS); however the safety speed (above which control can be maintained in the event of engine failure) is quoted as 160mph IAS at 20,000lb weight and 170mph IAS at 23,700lb, and ten mph higher with half flap. Clearly there was always a dangerous period as the aircraft accelerated near the ground. The recommended climbing speed was 160mph (presumably for best rate of climb), so pilots would have needed to stay alert.

The stalling speeds at 24,000lb weight were approximately 125mph IAS with flaps and undercarriage up (with a warning buffet at 145mph) and around 110mph with flaps and wheels down, but with little stall warning. If manoeuvring hard at 2g (60-degree bank) the stalling speed at 24,000lb was about 175mph – it was reported that crews took some while to adapt after flying lower performance aircraft. In the case of a missed approach to landing the pilot was advised to 'open the throttles slowly' and climb (flaps and undercarriage down) at about 135-140mph IAS. Various maximum speeds are quoted in reference publications, but it would be conservative to suggest that it was difficult to exceed 250mph IAS in level flight. The aircraft was reported to be slightly unstable longitudinally (i.e. in pitch) but stable laterally (roll) and directionally (yaw) and that it tightened up in steep turns, and thus needed sharp handling skills if manoeuvring near the ground. In all this the Boston was unexceptional. On the positive side the control during landing was good: 'a normal tricycle undercarriage landing should be made with the nose wheel clear of the ground'.

In summary, the Douglas Boston medium bomber was a tough, dependable combat aircraft with good speed (if not the fastest of its class) and manoeuvrability. In a report to the Aeroplane and Armament Experimental Establishment (A&AEE) at Boscombe Down test pilots stated that it 'has no vices and is very easy to take off and land … The aeroplane represents a definite advance in the design of flying controls … extremely pleasant to fly and manoeuvre'. It was extremely adaptable for different roles and was popular with pilots – in all over 7,000 were built. Wing Commander A. F. Carlisle, who took part in the raid in Ventura AJ491 SB-P of 464 Squadron but later flew Bostons, commented, 'Whether the Boston was operationally suitable for the European Theatre is questionable but it filled the gap between the Blenheims and Mosquito IVs and was immensely popular with the crews who flew in it.'

Lockheed Vega Ventura

At the outbreak of the war the British Purchasing Commission set about finding sources of military aircraft to supplement Britain's own aircraft building capacity. The USA was the principal source of such aircraft. The RAF was already satisfied with the Lockheed Hudson which it had ordered for RAF Coastal Command and the Commission was receptive to a proposal from Lockheed for a bomber version of their Model 18 Lodestar airliner and placed an order. The aircraft were to be built at Lockheed's new Vega plant at Burbank, California. The new aircraft was named the Ventura – in appearance it was like a larger Hudson – and the first aircraft flew on 31 July 1941. The British were pleased with the flight test data and ordered 650; deliveries commenced in 1942 but, in the end, only 394 were delivered.

Lockheed Vega Ventura. *(IWM CH8259)*

By contrast with the Boston, the Ventura was larger all round and heavier (31,000lb maximum loaded weight, 14,000kg) and slower, despite powerful 2,000hp Pratt & Whitney engines. It was also less manoeuvrable, a legacy of its civilian airliner origins. Overall, the performance of the Ventura was disappointing and it suffered heavy losses in action. In one attack on a power station at Amsterdam on 3 May 1943 by 487 Squadron (RNZAF), twelve aircraft set out, one returned early and of the remaining eleven, nine were shot down – the leader, Squadron Leader Leonard Trent, won the VC for his leadership on this raid, having succeeded in bombing the power station but got home despite suffering heavy damage to his aircraft. The Ventura was phased out in the summer of 1943, being replaced by the de Havilland Mosquito.

de Havilland Mosquito
The DH98 Mosquito was conceived in 1938 by Geoffrey de Havilland as a small bomber which was to rely for its safety on its speed rather than armament. It was to be built predominantly of wood – in wartime metal and metalworkers were expected to be in short supply whereas there were significant numbers of woodworkers in the construction and furniture industries. The British Air Ministry were initially sceptical of such a radical design concept, but de Havilland persisted and the prototype was first flown on 25 November 1940, having been built in secrecy in the grounds of a historic house near the main de Havilland factory at Hatfield. This prototype

DH Mosquito of 105 Squadron.
(Authors' collection)

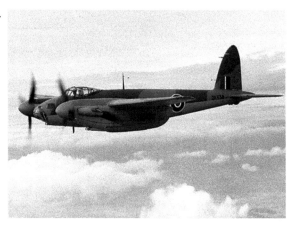

may still be viewed in its birthplace at the de Havilland Heritage Museum, Salisbury Hall.

The Mosquito fuselage was a plywood-balsa-plywood laminate built round spruce stringers – it might be said to be one of the first aircraft of 'composite' construction. The fuselage was built in two halves, moulded on concrete formers. When the electrical, hydraulic, pneumatic and mechanical systems were in place the two halves were glued together. The wings were plywood skins formed around two deep section spars. The control surfaces were of light alloy metal, with metal skin on the ailerons and fabric on the tail surfaces. The aircraft was of the then conventional tail-wheel undercarriage layout, with the third, small, wheel under the tail. The engines were Rolls Royce Merlin, liquid-cooled V-12s, similar to those fitted in the famous Spitfire fighter. Overall the Mosquito was a notably sleek design, with room, just, for its two crew and bomb load. The normal maximum weight of the aircraft was 21,000lb (9535 kg)

In February 1941 the first official test flight took place over Boscombe Down. The Air Ministry sceptics were soon persuaded of the Mosquito's potential, when it achieved a top speed of 392mph, rather faster than the 374mph of the contemporary Spitfire Mk V. Many variations of the Mosquito were built – photo-reconnaissance, fighter-bomber, night-fighter – but the initial pure bomber version was the B.Mk IV, which was the type used on Operation OYSTER; this model had made its operational debut on the famous 'Thousand Bomber Raid on Cologne' on 31 May 1942.

The *Pilot's Notes* for the Mosquito[2] tell us that the aircraft was stable directionally, but unstable laterally and longitudinally; the notes do not indicate the severity of this instability, but do remark that the aircraft was difficult to trim accurately, especially under bumpy conditions. The rudder and elevators were light and effective throughout the speed range but the ailerons became progressively heavy as speed increased. On take off the pilot was warned to open the throttles slowly, the travel of the throttle levers being very short for the power obtained so that coarse use of the throttles could aggravate any tendency to swing. The aircraft 'should be eased off the ground at 120mph at full load' and there was a tendency for the port wing to drop, this tendency being increased if the pilot pulled the aircraft off the ground positively. The take-off safety speed at full power (3,000rpm and +18psi boost) was 184mph, reducing to 172mph at climb power (2,850rpm and +12psi boost) – so climb power was recommended as soon as possible after take off, albeit there was still a considerable period of hazard while accelerating.

The power-off stalling speed at maximum weight (21,000lb) with undercarriage and flaps up was 120mph, reducing to 110mph with wheels and flaps down. With power on for a typical landing approach the stall speed was some 20mph lower. The stall was not very well defined, but with a warning buffet about 5mph before the stall; however, at the stall the nose dropped gently and there was little tendency for a wing to drop and recovery was 'normal and easy'. The recommended final approach speed was 125mph, engine assisted and with flaps down. In the case of a 'mislanding' (going around again) it was recommended to apply only climb power (+12psi) and climb at 140mph, increasing to 170mph as soon as possible. Clearly the Mosquito was relatively demanding to fly and disaster could come quickly near the ground. However, its superb performance made up for such shortcomings and the loss rate on bombing operations was the lowest in Bomber Command – all in all it was one of the most versatile and admired designs of all time.

Notes

1. A.P.2023D-P.N., Douglas DB-7 Boston Handling Notes.
2. A.P.2653Q-P.N., de Havilland Mosquito Handling Notes.

Chapter Four

Planning and Training for the Raid

'Group Captain Denis Barnett, Station Commander at Swanton Morley, summoned me from Oulton,' recalled Wing Commander Pelly-Fry. 'There's to be a big show soon, Pelly, and it needs a lot of practice. It's to be a low-level affair, but I don't know where the target is. The big problem will be getting a large group of aircraft to arrive at very precise times, and we shall be using different types of aircraft of varying speeds. You'll all need a lot of practice.'[1] This call set in motion a period of intense activity, training the squadrons for the most ambitious daylight raid by the RAF so far.

No. 2 Group RAF was ordered to commit almost its entire strength to one operation, using four aircraft types. Speed, range and manoeuvrability were different for each type. The Mosquito was the fastest and the Ventura the slowest, with the Mitchell and Boston in between. It was clearly going to need careful planning to bring these diverse types over the target in a short period

Wing Commander Pelly-Fry, centre of group. *(J.E. Pelly-Fry)*

of time to saturate the defences. Also, the need for surprise dictated that the operation should be carried out at very low altitude to minimize the chance of detection by the enemy radar. Much thought went into the planning of the raid.

Operation Order No. 82 detailing the plan was sent to 2 Group stations on 17 November 1942.[2] The main plant (Strijp complex) was to be bombed by twenty-four Venturas at Zero Hour, twelve Mitchells at Zero plus two minutes and twelve Mosquitos at Zero plus six minutes. The valve and lamp factory (Emmasingel complex) would be hit by twelve Venturas at Zero Hour, and thirty-six Bostons at Zero plus four minutes. All aircraft were to fly in pairs in company echelon to starboard, no formation exceeding six aircraft. Route from base to target was to be flown at very low level, all aircraft except Venturas climbing to release bombs from 1,000 to 1,500 feet, after which they would dive to low level as fast as possible. Suitable weather for the operation was a cloud base of not less than 1,500 feet. This plan called for the Venturas to be loaded with the maximum number of 30lb incendiary bombs plus two 250lb delayed action general purpose (GP) bombs for release at low altitude. All other types were to carry the maximum load of high explosive (HE) bombs with a near instantaneous time delay (0.025 seconds), to be dropped from approximately 1,000 to 1,500 feet.

The experience level of the crews varied considerably. Some squadrons had not flown operationally, although they included a core of experienced leaders. Others, particularly the Bostons and Mosquitos, had already seen action. The Ventura squadrons had been working up for some weeks, practising formation flying and bombing; however, the Mitchell squadrons had hardly got started on their training. All the crews needed plenty of practice in low-level formation flying and this started immediately, leading up to the first large-scale practice, which was flown on 17 November, on a route simulating that to be taken on the raid. The town of St Neots (Huntingdonshire, now Cambridgeshire) was to act as the large target (Strijp Complex Main Factory) and the nearby Little Barford Power Station, on the River Great Ouse just outside the town, was to represent the smaller Emmasingel valve and lamp factory. (Author's note: The power station retained its wartime camouflage, rather faded, for many years – it was used as a landmark by raiding German aircraft and could easily be found by following the river from the coast – even today its successor gas-fired station shows up well from the air.) St Neots was to be 'bombed' by twenty-four Venturas at Zero Hour, twelve Mitchells at Zero plus two minutes and twelve Mosquitos at Zero plus six minutes. Little Barford Power Station would be 'hit' by twelve Venturas at Zero Hour and thirty-six Bostons at Zero plus four minutes.

Little Barford power station,
near St Neots, practice target for
Emmasingel complex. *(English
Heritage Aerofilms Collection, ref.
A53356, taken 7 April 1954)*

After getting airborne from their bases the squadrons got into pre-arranged formations and then attempted to follow the route for the practice which was:

Base to British Coast:
Spalding (on the River Welland just inland from The Wash) – Goole (where the Yorkshire River Ouse meets the River Humber) – across Yorkshire to the coast at the prominent Flamborough Head

Sea Crossing:
Direct to Cromer on the Norfolk Coast

Run over enemy territory:
Cromer – Newmarket – Targets

Homeward Run:
Targets – Kimbolton (a small town about four miles from St Neots) – Digby (an aerodrome near the RAF College at Cranwell) – squadron bases.

(See map 2 – shown as an example starting from Oulton where the attack leader Wing Commander Pelly-Fry was based.)

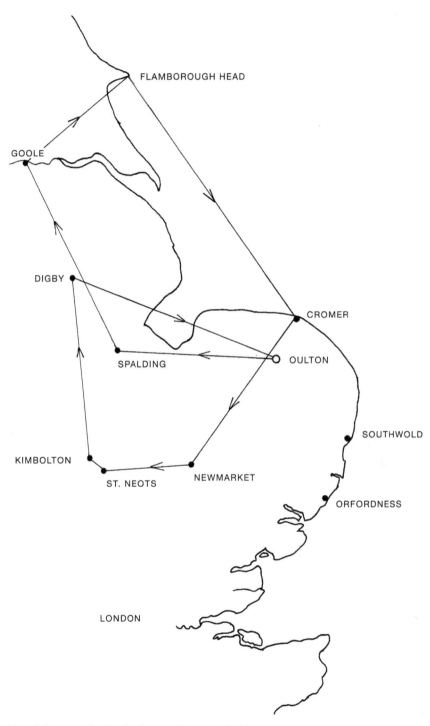

Map 2. Eastern England – Route of Practice Flight.

Various factors resulted in this practice being less successful than it might have been – the brief time in which the exercise was mounted, unfavourable weather and the presence of North Sea convoys which called for re-routing. Assembling nearly one hundred aircraft into a stream that would pass quickly over the estimated weakest spot in the enemy flak defences on the Dutch coast was no mean task. The need for early take off in order to assemble the force became apparent and it was essential that all crews understood clearly which 'plant' they had to aim for to avoid confusion over the target. Unsurprisingly, many mistakes were made – in navigation, accurate timing, evasive action and keeping close formation. Some aircraft were slow to climb to the bombing height over the 'targets' and also slow to dive back down to low level for their escape run – thus putting themselves at risk to flak and fighter attack for longer.

A major problem was soon identified with the original plan, in that the Mitchell force was not ready for operations; partly lack of time to 'work up' and partly because some basic items were yet to be fitted to the aircraft, in particular clear vision panels and the standard British Sutton seat harnesses for the pilots. Equally important, it was also realized that if the Venturas attacked first at low level the smoke from their incendiary bombs would obscure the target for following waves. Another important feature missing from the first practice was the lack of intercepting fighters.

For all these reasons it was clear that another large-scale practice would be necessary, with fighters from 12 Group Fighter Command acting as 'enemy' interceptors. To test the new arrangements a further major practice at operational speed was organized, with the targets changed to Godmanchester and Huntingdon (two small towns close together, not far from St Neots) with similar routing to the first exercise. This trial was a definite improvement over the first and lessons were learned. Interceptions by 12 Group fighters showed that beam and three-quarter attacks would probably have been ineffective, which was encouraging since the bombers would need to rely on their own defences over enemy territory. Also it was decided that the first two aircraft over each target (these would be Bostons in the new plan) would attack at very low level with 11-second delay bombs to divert the defenders' attention while the remaining Bostons climbed to about 1,500 feet to attack with near instantaneous fusing on their bombs thus reducing any tendency for the weapons to career along the ground before exploding.

Sergeant S. C. 'Stan' Moss RAAF, 464 Squadron, has left the following recollection of this practice (perhaps inaccurate in detail but included here to give a flavour of the exercise):

We flew east beyond the English coast then turned north, a tightly packed formation of Venturas at almost nought feet. But the 'tail-gating' effect meant we were flying in each other's slipstream and this caused one's aircraft to twist and yaw with the fearsome danger of hitting the water or another aircraft. One sweated at the controls like a navvy. At Flamborough Head, where we turned inland to the supposed 'target' we became entangled with Bostons and Mosquitos in a frightening shambles, exacerbated by a simulated attack by Spitfires which dived amongst us with amazing daring. Surprisingly, there were no collisions, even though more than 100 aircraft were involved. In the scattering of our formation, I

Sergeant S. C. 'Stan' Moss, RAAF, of 464 Squadron. *(Stan Moss)*

managed to hang on to my number one until reaching base, but jibbed at following him under high-tension wires!

Next day, a frank post-mortem took place, which much relieved everyone's anxiety about the slipstream hazard. Then came the announcement: target Philips' Radio Factory at Eindhoven, The Netherlands, seventy miles from the coast. The extensive factory supplied essential radar equipment for the German military. Bostons were to go in first and bomb from a medium height, followed by Venturas carrying a mixture of incendiaries and delayed action bombs, and finally the Mosquitos would sweep in to distract the fire fighters. To bluff enemy defences, three diversionary sweeps would be made by our fighters and there would be top cover for us as well. It all sounded foolproof.

Sergeant Stan Moss piloted Ventura II, AJ213 SB-N, of 464 Squadron. The other crewmembers were Sergeant (Nav) R. A. Wagner, Sergeant (WO/AG) J. A. Wallis and Sergeant (AG) F. C. Lindsay. They were shot down over Walcheren, belly-landed near Vrouwenpolder and taken prisoner by the Germans.

Eventually a significantly revised plan of No. 2 Group Operation Order No. 82 was issued, dated 23 November (see Appendix 1). This order called for a force of thirty-six Venturas, thirty-six Bostons and twelve Mosquitos. These would be loaded with the same bombs as in the earlier order; again the Venturas would attack at low level. The schedule was for the Bostons to attack at Zero hour (twelve on the main factory, twenty-four on the valve and lamp factory, the twelve Mosquitos to attack the main factory at Zero plus two minutes and the Venturas at Zero plus six minutes (twenty-four on the main factory and twelve on the valve and lamp works). This order also specified the indicated airspeeds (IAS) to be flown by the various aircraft types; in the range 200–240mph for the Bostons, 210–260 for the Mosquitos and 180–220 for the Venturas, with the proviso that all aircraft were 'to approach, attack and leave the target area at the maximum speed consistent with good formation flying'.

In the meantime training continued. On 18 November some thirty Venturas carried out simulated attacks on the same training routes and their performance improved. The emphasis on extremely low-level flying inevitably brought up the problem of bird strikes. Birds will dive to escape a hazard, since this enables them to gain speed quickly – however, when aircraft are already very low the risk of a strike is increased. The risk is also increased in coastal regions where there are many sizeable birds (gulls etc.) and this would indeed prove to be a problem over the Dutch coast. Pilot Officer R. A. J. (Reggie) Goode of 21 Squadron reported:

It was clearly illustrated to the crew of which I was a member very early in our training, although it was not then regarded as of any significance. This was the action of pigeons smashing through the window of our Ventura which, apart from covering the pilot's face with pigeon's blood, necessitated the navigator reporting to the MO (Medical Officer) upon landing to have small pieces of Perspex removed from his face.

In a personal account Pilot Officer J. W. 'Dinty' Moore recalled:

Low flying means skipping over hedge-rows, climbing to avoid trees, high tension cables, telephone wires and so on, a truly exhilarating experience. We all appreciated the advantages of flying low as it made it virtually impossible to be picked up by German radar and we were also a very difficult target for enemy anti-aircraft gunners.

Squadron Leader L. H. Trent thought:

> Low-level flying is always exciting. But over enemy territory it is also very dangerous, particularly if aircraft are flying in formation and therefore are unable to take evasive action. For any alert ground gunner they offer an easy target.

Flight Lieutenant E. F. Hart DFC was the Leading Navigator of the Ventura formation. In his undated report 'Low level navigation to Eindhoven' (see Appendix II) he wrote that, in the interest of security, the target was kept a close secret. Nevertheless he had prior warning. He and other lead navigators were able to acquaint themselves with route details by a series of sessions during which a map of the route was projected, together with photographs that had been recently filmed by a reconnaissance Mosquito. He later declared, 'I had a complete picture in my mind's eye of the whole trip'.

For the benefit of all the navigators a plan was provided detailing prominent ground features against distance, with bearings to towns and features close to the route, enabling the preparation of maps marked with waypoints that could be identified as the flights progressed.[3]

Thus, by the first week in December 1942, the stage was set for a major attack on the Philips works at Eindhoven.

Notes

1. Bowyer, *2 Group RAF – A Complete History 1936-1945*.
2. See Appendix I. NA Kew, AIR 25/35, Vol 1, pp.38-53.
3. See Appendix II, Flight Lieutenant Hart's comments, in NA Kew AIR14/523 and 'Low Level Navigation Landmarks' in Operations Record Book No. 2 Group RAF, AIR 25/35 [D27].

Chapter Five

The Raid

Weather Delay: The raid was originally scheduled for Thursday 3 December but the weather conditions required a delay. The following terse but factual comment appeared in the No. 2 Group HQ Operations Record Book for Sunday 6 December.

OPERATION OYSTER - EINDHOVEN
After being cancelled for two or three days running owing to unsuitable weather conditions, No. 2 Group 'Blitz' on the above target, in accordance with No. 2 Group Operation Order No. 82, took place today, Zero hour time on target being 1230 hours, a total of 94 aircraft being airborne, but of these thirteen failed to return.

(See also Appendix III regarding this delay.)

Flight to Eindhoven

A principal navigational challenge in Operation OYSTER was the need to get concentration of attack on the target with three types of aircraft of different speed capabilities. The speeds and routes had been laid out in detail (see Appendix I; Operation Order No. 82, 23 Nov 1942) The first priority was thus to arrange for the three types, thirty-six Bostons, twelve Mosquitos and forty-seven Venturas to take off, form up, follow the prescribed routes and arrive at Eindhoven in a six-minute period starting at 12.30, Bostons leading and Venturas coming in last for their low-level bombing. The aircraft took off in the period 11.15 to 11.30 from their various bases, formed up in groups by type and set off for the English coast, Southwold for the Bostons and Mosquitos, and Orfordness for the Venturas. The forty-seven aircraft formation of Venturas, which had set course from overhead Feltwell led by Wing Commander R. H. 'Bob' Young, CO of 464 Squadron, made an impressive sight. Both coasting out points had prominent lighthouses.

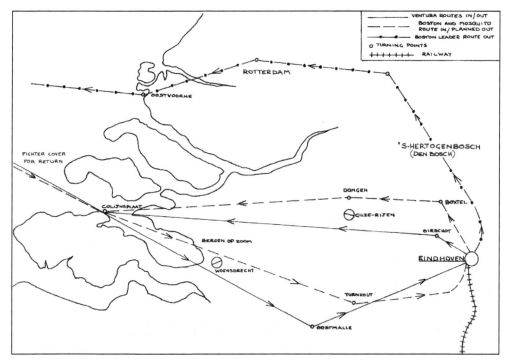

Map 3. Operational Routes to and from Eindhoven.

One aircraft, W8293 RH–Z of 88 Squadron, flown by Flight Sergeant A. B. Wilson, had to abandon the flight before reaching the English coast owing to cutting of the starboard engine and AL755 OM–P of 88 squadron, Flying Officer R. A. Bance, returned to base with bombs owing to the failure of a hatch.[1]

Navigators were instructed to use the distance between the Norwich-Stowmarket railway and the coast as a check on the accuracy of their ground speeds. Accurate navigation, both in terms of track keeping and times over waypoints, was of critical importance. Wing Commander J. E. Pelly-Fry DSO (Pelly), in the lead Boston, and thus the leader of the raid, recorded afterwards that:

It was absolutely vital that we made a very accurate landfall between the Dutch islands of Schouwen-Duiveland and Walcheren, then keep hull down up the thirty-mile long Schelde estuary before flying between Bergen op Zoom and Woensdrecht … the problem was that at zero height the Dutch coastline is no better than a thin line on the horizon …

The flight over the sea was conducted at very low level, often below 100 feet – this is evident from the films taken from camera-equipped aircraft. Care was needed not to get too low and there were some reports that propeller wash could be seen disturbing the sea surface.

For all the aircraft the initial landfall was planned to be by a small village called Colijnsplaat on the north coast of the island of Beveland, on the south side of the Oosterschelde estuary. After following the Oosterschelde to a main landfall near Bergen op Zoom the routes then took them into Belgium close to Oostmalle (Ventura track) and Turnhout (Bostons and Mosquitos) where

Orfordness Lighthouse – in its solitary position on the coast. *(Arthur Thorning)*

they turned to approach Eindhoven from the south using a lake and a railway line (now removed) to guide the final run to the target. Again, the films from the raid show that the aircraft were flying only just above the trees and sometimes level with the banks of canals, with the numerous chimneys of greenhouse heating plants adding to the hazard (one aircraft returned with brick debris from, possibly, a chimney strike).

As well as the obvious hazards of flight close to the ground the close formation required alertness on the part of the pilots to guard against collision. Other hazards were both natural, especially bird strikes over the coast, and enemy fire – the coast was heavily defended with anti-aircraft guns, although the route had been chosen to minimize this risk. The diversionary raid by the USAAF B-17s at Lille (Circus 241) had drawn away many German fighters but the route took the raid close to a fighter aerodrome at Woensdrecht (near Bergen op Zoom). The defences were also occupied to some extent by a low-level 'Rhubarb' operation in the Alkmaar area of North Holland by eight Mustang aircraft of 268 Squadron from Snailwell.

The official evaluation of Operation OYSTER is to be found at the National Archives.[2] This gives much detail and is reproduced as Appendix

An actual sortie photograph showing Boston AL749 RH-R, 88 Squadron, Pilot Officer Jack Peppiatt, and several other Bostons flying low over the North Sea. *(IWM CH7844)*

III – for the purposes of this narrative only the salient points are included. The speeds to be flown by the various types to and from the target were specified with the intention that the Bostons should arrive at the target at Zero hour (Z, 12.30), the Mosquitos at Z + 2 and the Venturas at Z + 6. This meant that the attacking force crossed the coast (nominally at Colijnsplaat, depending on accuracy of overwater navigation) in a three-minute period, Z – 19 (12.11hrs) for the Bostons and Z – 16 (12.14hrs) for the Venturas.

This was the point at which enemy and natural hazards met the crews. The natural hazards came in the form of wild fowl, which rose in alarm at the sound of the engines. This had been anticipated but, in the event, was worse than expected. It was later found that, of those aircraft which got back, no fewer than twenty-three had been damaged by bird strikes, some seriously. Some birds penetrated cockpits spreading blood, feathers and carcasses everywhere. Others penetrated wings and bent fuel pipes and other components. In one Ventura the observer (navigator) was hit in the face by a large duck which came through the windscreen; the observer held a tin hat (shell helmet) against the damaged Perspex for the remainder of the flight. Two gulls came through the nose of Pilot Officer Philip Burley's aircraft (Boston III, W8330, O-ME of 107 Sqdn), injuring his navigator, Pilot Officer Herbert Besford, in the legs, while at the same time the draught

Crew of 226 Squadron Boston AL678 MQ-R, Flight Lieutenant Yates-Earl, examining remains of a seagull which penetrated the leading edge of the wing of their aircraft. *(RAF Museum)*

whisked his maps away. Besford directed his pilot from then on by memory, which showed the value of the careful pre-flight preparation. To this day, gulls remain the most commonly struck bird species, both inland and at coastal sites!

The first encounter with enemy fire came at the Dutch coast. The intended route aimed to minimize this hazard by routing along the Oosterschelde but some, at least, of the Venturas had drifted too far south-west and made landfall over the well-defended island of Walcheren. Two Venturas were lost at this point. According to Chorley's 1942 *Bomber Command Losses*,[3] at 12.17 Flight Sergeant Paterson's aircraft, AE701 EG-F of 487 Squadron, was hit by flak and crashed into the sea off Oostkapelle. However, the Feltwell ORB says the aircraft dived into the sea twenty-four miles off Orfordness and the 487 Squadron ORB attributes this loss to birds. Whatever happened, the crew all perished and are commemorated at the Runnymede Memorial for aircrew with no known grave.

One minute later Sergeant Moss's aircraft, AJ213 SB-N of 464 Squadron was also hit by coastal flak and belly-landed at Vrouwenpolder on the

Walcheren peninsula. The crew survived, although injured by the flak, and were made prisoners of war. Sergeant S. C. 'Stan' Moss, Royal Australian Air Force, had a mixed crew – two Australians and two Londoners. He had joined 464 Squadron just two months previously and has left a graphic account of the busy time leading up to the raid. He described the flak impact

> like a flash of lightning, the right side cabin window exploded almost noiselessly below the roar of the engines. Instantly and involuntarily I doubled up in my seat in reaction to being hit by pieces of exploding flak shell … my sudden movement had lifted the aircraft several hundred feet. One thought dominated my mind, namely, that I must get the machine on the deck before blacking out.

Stan Moss then did well to belly-land the aircraft in a ploughed field. Three of the crew had been injured but they succeeded in escaping from the wreckage. They were captured almost immediately and given first aid and later hospital treatment by the Germans before being sent to PoW camp.

Runnymede Air Forces Memorial. *(Arthur Thorning)*

The flight plan then called for the Bostons and Mosquitos to run down the northern coast of the Oosterschelde passing very close to Sint Maartensdijk, reaching the mainland proper just south of Bergen op Zoom, and then pass just north of the well-defended aerodrome at Woensdrecht, heading for the turning point at Turnhout. The Venturas' track should have taken them along the southern shore of the Oosterschelde and to the south of Woensdrecht. Having made their landfall further south than intended they passed close to Woensdrecht, and Wing Commander Seavill's aircraft, AJ196 EG-C of 487 Squadron, was hit by flak from the defences at 12.25 and crashed at Schaapskooi on the aerodrome. All the crew perished and are buried at Bergen op Zoom. In return, Squadron Leader Leonard Trent in EG-V succeeded in bringing his forward firing guns (two .5-inch and two .3-inch calibre) to bear on the crew of a flak tower on the aerodrome. Also over Woensdrecht aerodrome, AE854 SB-J of 464 Squadron, piloted by Pilot Officer S. B. Abbott RAAF, was hit in the port engine, but was able to continue to bomb the Strijp target and return safely to base.[4]

Francis (Frankie) Seavill, the CO of 487 Squadron, was on his first operational flight. He had worked hard leading his crews, taking part in all the training exercises and was a popular and successful squadron commanding officer. He was a New Zealander who had served with the RAF since 1930.

Ventura II AJ213 SB–N at Vrouwenpolder. *(Bevrijdings Museum, Zeeland)*

Seavill and Flying Officer J. A. W. Withers RCAF (Navigator) are buried in the Allied Plot at Bergen op Zoom Cemetery; the other two crew members are in the Canadian section, (Flight Sergeant F. E. King RCAF (WO/AG) and Sergeant T. M. Richings RAFVR (WO/AG), although the latter was from the UK rather than Canada.

Shortly afterwards the Ventura piloted by Pilot Officer H. T. Bichard (AE707 YH-N of 21 Squadron) was attacked by a Fw190 fighter of II/JG1 Staffel flown by Unteroffizier Rudolf Rauhaus and returning from the B-17 diversion at Lille. Pilot Officer Bichard succeeded in making a belly-landing at Rilland-Bath (on the Zuid-Beveland peninsula). The navigator, Sergeant R. C. Lamerton was killed (buried at Bergen op Zoom Allied War Cemetery) but the other three crew members survived to be made PoWs.

Meanwhile the Bostons led by Pelly-Fry had 'swept up the estuary ... streaking along in ships-of-the-line fashion'. As already described, the first hazard was from bird strikes but this was soon replaced by enemy action. 'Pelly' recounts:

No sooner had we passed the mudflats than we aroused a hornets' nest of Fw190 fighters from nearby Woensdrecht aerodrome. We could actually see them taking off and curving round to meet us. Not only

Ventura I, AE707 YH-N, 21 Squadron crashed 12.29 at Rilland-Bath. *(Dennis van Hoof)*

Unteroffizier Rauhaus in Fw190. *(www.luftwaffe.be)*

that, all the aerodrome defences opened up furiously, the Venturas in particular getting the brunt of cannon and machine-gun fire …

Most pilots managed to continue despite flak and fighters, although one Ventura (AE695 SB-B of 464 Squadron flown by Canadian Sergeant A. M. Swan) lost five feet of its outer wing and had to turn back, jettisoning its bombs which were seen to burst on a gun emplacement. Three of the Mosquito pilots, Squadron Leader D. A. G. 'George' Parry, Flight Lieutenant W. C. S. 'Bill' Blessing RAAF and Pilot Officer J. G. 'Jimmy' Bruce were intercepted by Fw190s. They then used the speed of their aircraft to draw off the fighters in a gallant and aggressive manner. The fighters attacked for some ten minutes but were eventually eluded. Flight Lieutenant Blessing abandoned his bombing task at 12.40 to the north of Turnhout and brought his bombs back to Marham. Bruce was forced to jettison his bombs but escaped and made it back to base although damaged by cannon fire. Parry was able to rejoin the attack. Although there were relatively few Fw190s at Woensdrecht, due to the diversionary raids, these gallant actions by the Mosquitos probably saved some of the main force.

The Bostons having passed these hazards on time at 12.16hrs, 'Pelly' continued to lead them on the same course to their next turning point at

Turnhout, a town just inside the Belgian border. Pelly noted that this crossing of a border 'was of no consequence at the time, the map reading by Jock was what really mattered'. In his aircraft (Boston III, Z2236 RH-G, 88 Squadron) Pelly had as his master navigator Flight Lieutenant T. H. J. 'Jock' Cairns DFC DFM, and Flying Officer C. A. 'Buster' Evans DFM as air gunner. It cannot be emphasized too much how difficult visual navigation can be over flat terrain, flying at 220mph and fifty feet above the ground. It is interesting to note that Jock Cairns was a brother of 'Tubby' Cairns, navigator to Hugh Edwards who was leading the Mosquitos.

Pilot Officer J. C. 'Jack' Peppiatt (pilot of Boston AL748 RH-R, 88 Squadron) recounted the experience thus:

> We slid about, keeping sight of our leader and watching to avoid airfields. The other hazard was overhead cables, etc., and the trick was to look out to the sides ahead so that you could spot the lines of pylons, which could reveal where the invisible cables might be. Although there was a lot of apprehension, there was also a great thrill in it. Talk over the intercom went on the whole time between the navigator and myself, discussing where we were, where the leader was going, and did you see that railway or canal, etc.? I saw the landscape flying by with brief flashes of recognition; a house, some people, vehicles and every now and then a blink as I thought we had gone too near an airfield.

The original flight plan required a direct route from Turnhout to Eindhoven. However, Pelly-Fry and his navigating team decided that it would be sensible to route somewhat further south to acquire a line feature leading to the targets over the last few miles – without such track guidance a small error could have led to last minute turns and a spread of the bombers as they passed over the target, and there would only be one chance to get it right. Such a line feature (in this case a railway track) would at least provide a guard against going too far and missing Eindhoven.

It seems from Pelly-Fry's subsequent recollection that this amended plan was in the forefront of his, and his navigator's, mind, although analysis of the films taken by the second Boston (AL738, OM-Z), which attacked the Strijp target, shows that in the event they were able to turn directly towards the targets, on a north-easterly heading, before they reached the railway, although having seen locomotive steam they were confident that they had not passed it. Further evidence for this manoeuvre comes from author Kees Rijken, who was an eyewitness and is sure that no aircraft approached the

Emmasingel complex from the south, as they would if they had followed the only likely railway line. The film shows that the large buildings of the Strijp complex were clearly visible and thus would have confirmed the line of approach.

Thus they decided to follow a track somewhat to the south until they were sure of the position of the targets. The railway line which was to be their final guide was known as the *Bels lijntje* (literally translated 'Belgian line', Dutch dialect expression for this particular railway track as it linked Eindhoven direct to Belgium); it ran from Eindhoven to Valkenswaard (five miles south of Eindhoven) and on to Hasselt in Belgium. The modern reader will search in vain for this railway on the map since it has long since been removed – the later replacement is further east and this seems to have misled other authors who did not have local knowledge. There was also a wartime railway branching off north-west to Eindhoven aerodrome but this would not have been chosen as track guidance since it was both quite a short track and not across their routing, making it very easy to miss it altogether. The Beatrix Canal harbour, to the south-west of the city, would have made a useful last checkpoint for aircraft on their bombing runs, and certainly the film from the second Boston shows that it must have passed close by.

The Emmasingel complex, roughly a triangular site, lay close to the city centre and just to the right of the railway as it curved around to the east in Eindhoven. The larger Strijp complex lay to the left of the railway in the north-west sector of the city and contained some distinctive, large buildings.

As they approached Eindhoven, Pelly-Fry and Cairns, his navigator, were clearly concerned with the problem of picking out the railway line in time to avoid the rest of his force overshooting it and making an untidy turn. Pelly-Fry summed the problem up thus: 'Success depended on seeing the railway in sufficient time to begin a gentle turn and so avoid the pitfall of the long crocodile getting into a pendulum swing from which it would be difficult to recover.' Fortunately, the smoke and vapour from a railway locomotive indicated the line and the turn was made in good order. It seems from the film evidence that the turn towards the target was made before reaching the railway although Pelly-Fry's later account gives prominence to the use of this feature and such was his anxiety to hit the target that his memory may have given it emphasis; nonetheless his words are worth quoting:

If we were late in spotting it … the whole damned business would collapse within spitting distance of the target. And then it happened. I saw a thin plume of white smoke, ahead and slightly to left of our track.

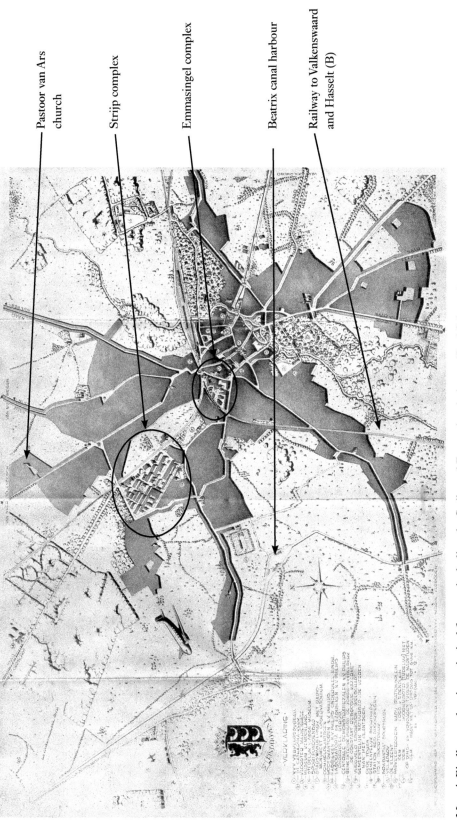

Pastoor van Ars church

Strijp complex

Emmasingel complex

Beatrix canal harbour

Railway to Valkenswaard and Hasselt (B)

Map 4. Eindhoven showing principal features including the Strijp and Emmasingel plants. *(Paul Schepers)*

It could only be a providential locomotive, very nicely placed to give me the message to begin the turn. I said to Jock 'Moving loco with smoke at 10 o'clock, turning left'. He confirmed the sighting ... we began to fly alongside the single track line, now comfortably on our right side. That fellow driving ... will never know the vital contribution he made to our cause ... the job was in the bag.

Thus the Boston force was led accurately to the targets, Pelly-Fry and the camera aircraft bombing from low altitude and the rest climbing to over 1,000 feet for their attacks. The Mosquitos were following the Bostons, aiming to be two minutes behind (and having to be careful not to overtake), pulling up for their dive attack.

The Ventura force, arriving six minutes after the Bostons for their low-level attack, had routed via Oostmalle, a few miles south-west of Turnhout, and flew directly towards Eindhoven on an east-north-east heading. Even if they did not have the Bostons and Mosquitos in sight they had the smoke from the preceding attacks as an aiming point.

The Attack on the Philips factory

The next few minutes were the essence of Operation OYSTER – the culmination of months of planning and training. The targets were in sight as were the bombers to the defences – no doubt warned by reports of low-flying aircraft crossing the coast and racing on inland. Indeed the film from the camera aircraft shows evidence of anti-aircraft fire from the factory where quick-firing guns were mounted on high points – the cameraman was Flying Officer G. W. 'Skeets' Kelly and his filming of the entire raid is a major source of first-hand evidence for the history of the operation. Also taking valuable movie-film was the leading Boston, AL738 OM-Z, of 107 Squadron, which attacked the Strijp complex from low level – pilot Squadron Leader R. J. N. McLachlan, film unit cameraman Flight Lieutenant C. Peace.

A reconstruction of the route flown overhead Eindhoven by this Boston is given in Map 5, with stills taken from the movie and referenced to a map of Eindhoven at the time (below).

Key to Map 5

1) Brick works Meerveldhovense weg
2) Brick works Kasteel weg

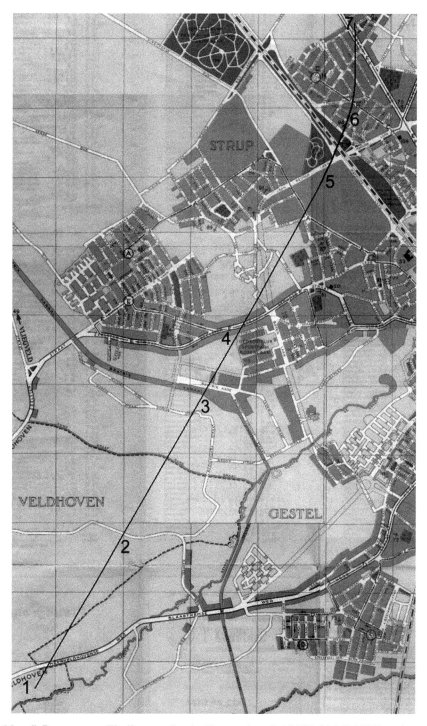

Map 5. Route across Eindhoven taken by Boston aircraft AL738 OM–Z 107 Squadron, piloted by Squadron Leader R.J.N. McLachlan. *(Paul Schepers)*

3) Beatrix canal harbour
4) Zeelsterstraat
5) Attack on Strijp complex; buildings SDM (Veemgebouw) and SBP
6) Morsestraat and Wattstraat
7) Pastoor van Ars church

The Boston formations attack

The leader, Wing Commander Pelly-Fry, and the second, camera-equipped, aircraft in the Boston wave, flown by Pilot Officer G. 'Jock' Campbell, bombed the very important Emmasingel valve plant from 100 feet, each dropping four 500lb medium capacity (MC) weapons with time delays (TD) of eleven seconds, long enough to avoid damage from the blast of their own explosions. They were, however, at great risk from the defences which they had to pass at very short range – Pelly-Fry's aircraft was hit in the starboard wing and engine and he had to fight to regain control with consequences both for his aircraft and those he was leading as this account will explain later.

With the exception of Squadron Leader McLachlan, leading 107 Squadron to the Strijp complex, the rest of the Boston force had climbed rapidly once the targets were in sight, and each aimed their four 500lb MC weapons from heights variously reported between 1,000 and 1,500 feet – the cloud base was reported as eight tenths of stratocumulus at 2,000 feet (by Pilot Officer F. J. 'Freddie' Deeks, navigator of AL693 RH-U, 88 Squadron). These bombs had near instantaneous fuses (TD 0.025 seconds). Nos. 88 and 226 Squadrons, a total of twenty-four aircraft, aimed at the Emmasingel plant, while 107 Squadron, twelve aircraft, attacked the Strijp complex. The

Stills from movie film taken by Boston aircraft AL738 107 Squadron showing the approach to the Strijp complex as seen from the cockpit. Filmed by Flight Lieutenant Charlie Peace, RAF Film Unit. *(IWM Film)*

Beatrix canal harbour

Philips Strijp target

Houses Zeelsterstr.

gunfire from aircraft

Photo from low level 88 Squadron aircraft Z2236 RH-G, seconds after delayed action bombs dropped but before they exploded; looking back to the south after Emmasingel having passed the target. *(IWM C3272)*

choice of 1,500 feet as a bombing height gave the bomb-aimers a good sight of the targets while remaining low enough to achieve good accuracy. At this point in the raid, almost exactly on 12.30 as shown by the Philips' factory tower clock photographed by a 107 Squadron navigator, there was initially no smoke and dust to obscure their aim and even for later aircraft in this group the target was less obscured than it was for the Ventura force six minutes later. The downside of bombing from this height was, of course, that it gave the defences more time and a clearer view of the Bostons as they approached the targets. The 2 Group Operational Record Book indicates that the whole Boston force attacked in the short space of time between 12.30 and 12.33, thus achieving surprise and concentration of attack as planned. The Strijp factory tower clock was stopped by the raid, showing 12.32 and stayed like this for the rest of the war.

Due to massive clouds of smoke in the photograph C5755 (p.48) it seems logical that it was taken by a 226 Squadron Boston, which was the second squadron in to attack the Emmasingel. Two more Bostons can be seen, of which one has only just dropped its bombs. To the right of the St Antonius Fellenoord Church, yet another burning housing area can be seen.

Philips clock tower at the Strijp stopped at 12.32 for the duration of the war. *(Ad van Zantvoort)*

Boston View of Emmasingel attack, from 1,000–1,500 feet. (*IWM C3266*)

Bostons attacking the Emmasingel. *(IWM C5755)*

Sergeant Stephen Roche of 226 Squadron, writing to his sister the day after the raid said, 'We bombed from a suicidal height – 1,500ft! Most of [our] machines were like sieves when we got back. We lost one machine.' (That aircraft, Z2266, MQ-S flown by Flying Officer N. J. A. Norman Paton DFM, was hit by marine flak and crashed in the sea off Scheveningen at 12.55 – the crew are commemorated on the Runnymede Memorial). After bombing, the Bostons dived back down to roof-top height to make their escape. Stephen Roche recorded:

> It was an enormous show. There were planes *everywhere*. Our squadron went in second [to the Emmasingel plant] with HEs [high explosive bombs]. The flak and machine-gun fire though was terrific, and once we bombed it was everyman for himself.

Stephen Roche had been a King's Scout and his only previous visit to The Netherlands had been to attend a scouting jamboree before the war. Stephen Roche is not recorded in the 226 Squadron ORB[5] for Operation OYSTER, but it does record that there were two reserve aircraft. His account of the operation is quite consistent with the known facts, so it is likely that he and his crew were substituted at a late moment and the record not amended. He went on to fly five more operations, culminating in the Morlaix Viaduct raid on 29 January 1943, in all cases flying AL750, MQ-Z. His usual crew was Sergeant R. A. Fretwell (Navigator), Sergeant P. Julyans (WO/AG) and Sergeant W. W. Sims (AG); tragically they were with him on the fatal accident flight, albeit in Z2261 MQ-W.

Pilot Officer F. J. 'Freddie' Deeks, navigator of RH-U, 88 Squadron, recalled:

At 12.30 hours we attacked the target, Wing Commander Pelly-Fry and his 'number two' attacking from low level, machine gunning as they went in, in order to cause a diversion, whilst the remainder of us bombed from 1,000-1,500ft just outside blast

Sergeant Stephen Roche RAFVR, 226 Squadron – killed in a flying accident on 3 February 1943, aged twenty-two. *(Mrs Enid Roche)*

range, diving back onto the deck afterwards. After the first element of surprise had passed away, the enemy flak positions on the factory itself and in the town got busy with heavy and light flak, thus more evasive action became necessary. The target was left in a cloud of smoke, but some bombs overshot and exploded in the town itself.

Pilot Officer J. C. 'Jack' Peppiatt, pilot of AL749 RH-R, 88 Squadron, recorded his impression of the attack:

In front I had glimpses of the leading Bostons and we began to pack in as we saw the buildings of the factory way ahead. The first two went in low and then we sailed up to 1,500ft – that felt very vulnerable! We seemed to suddenly stand still and hang about waiting to be shot at. By the time we were over the factory it was all smoke and explosions, with Bostons all around at different angles and at that point there was a bang. 'R for Robert' turned several degrees to port like a weather-vane, while I heard Len Dellow (air gunner) telling me there was a big hole in the

Crew of Boston AL693 RH–U of 88 Squadron. *(Jim Moore)*
Left to right; Pilot Officer (Nav) F. J. 'Freddie' Deeks, Flight Lieutenant (Pilot) John H. Reeve, Pilot Officer (Air Gunner) J. W. 'Jim' Moore.

fin just above his head, but the aircraft seemed to handle all right and at that stage I was more concerned with where to go next.'

Also hit was the pitot head, leaving Jack Peppiatt without altimeter and airspeed readings – this was of secondary importance in the low level dash back to the coast but was to have consequences on landing back at base.

The squadron ORBs give a detailed insight into the attack as seen by the crews. From the 88 Squadron ORB we have the following terse reports, given as examples (see also Appendix III for Philips plant maps from Interpretation Report S.A. 176):

Wing Commander J. E. Pelly-Fry DSO, Z2236 RH-G: 'Primary attacked. Own bombs seen in Eastern side of factory. Two large explosions from within building were followed by debris and a great cloud of smoke.'

Flight Lieutenant R. S. 'Dickie' Gunning DFM, AL289 RH-E: 'Primary attacked. Own bombs unobserved. Bombs of aircraft Z2236 [Pelly-Fry] seen to burst on South Block of Valve Factory. Bombs seen to burst on Railway Line near town, North of Office Block which was also damaged.'

Pilot Officer G. 'Jock' Campbell, Z2233 RH-K (camera aircraft): 'Primary attacked. Own bombs struck block of Valve Factory with tower, beside railway. Results unobserved.'

Sergeant C. D. 'Chas' Tyler, Z2211 RH-N: 'Primary attacked. Saw several explosions on main buildings and thick black smoke rising to 200ft.'

Flight Lieutenant J. H. John Reeve, AL693 RH-U: 'Primary attacked. Own bombs unobserved. One enormous explosion from buildings in target area, followed by smoke to 300 feet high.'

There are no records from the 226 Squadron ORB specific to the effects of the raid. However, meanwhile 107 Squadron Bostons were attacking the Strijp complex and some of their reports follow:

Flight Sergeant G. E. T. Nichols, AL754 OM-D: 'Primary target attacked from 1,500 feet at 12.30 hours with 4x500lb MC TD 0.025. Bursts were seen on Radio Erecting Block and one bomb entered top storey and exploded.'

Pilot Officer P. Philip Burley, W8330, OM-E: 'Primary target attacked … at 12.31 … Bursts seen on Machine Shop and second block from left of Radio Erecting Shops. Three bombs slightly undershot and bursts were seen on the Paper and Cardboard Stores.'

Pilot Officer J. M. Rankin, W8373 OM-F: 'Bombs thought to have burst on centre block of Radio Erecting Shops. The whole target area was covered in smoke, the largest tower was seen collapsing and the valve factory [Emmasingel] was also seen to be disintegrating. Intense light flak was encountered over the target area.'

Pilot Officer G. A. Turner, AL752 OM-G: 'Saw three bursts, one of which overshot target. Machine gunned gun on top of Bakelite Factory and strikes were observed.'

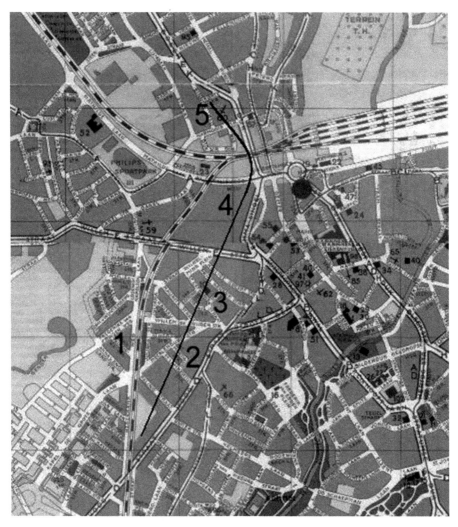

Map 6. Route of Boston Z2233 RH-K 88 Squadron; crew: Pilot Officer G. Campbell (pilot), Pilot Officer P. J. Stack (navigator), Flight Sergeant J. Robertson (air gunner) and Flying Officer G. W. Kelly. (Film Unit) *(Paul Schepers)*

Key to Map 6
1) Frederika van Pruisen weg
2) Mauritsstraat and Egmondstraat
3) Wilhelmina plein and Julianastraat
4) Emmasingel target
5) Church Fellenoord (H. Antonius van Padua)

Sergeant W. E. Burns, W8302 OM-J: 'Forced to bomb east of target area owing to slip stream from leading A/C 'E' [Pilot Officer Burley] Attacked at 12.31 from 1500ft. Bombs believed to have fallen on buildings east of target area.'

Squadron Leader R. J. N. McLachlan, AL738 OM-Z: 'Primary attacked at 12.30 hours with 4x500lb MC TD 11 seconds. Two bursts were seen on buildings on far side of Bakelite factory and on the Bakelite factory itself. Second building from left of Radio erecting Shops seen to blow up with orange glare. An Hispano type gun, mounted on this building, failed to fire and the gunner was immediately afterwards blown up with the building.'

Squadron Leader McLachlan received the DFC for his actions in this raid.

A reconstruction of the route flown overhead Eindhoven by one of the Bostons attacking the Emmasingel complex is given in Map 6, referenced to a map of Eindhoven at the time.

The Mosquito Squadrons attack

The Mosquitos were all detailed to attack the larger, Strijp, plant in Eindhoven.

The bombing tactic employed by the Mosquitos had been developed by experience and required them to climb to 1,500 feet, begin a shallow dive towards the target at full power and release their bombs from about 1,000 feet. Ten aircraft took part as bombers, eight from 105 Squadron and two from 139 Squadron; another aircraft from 139 flew over Eindhoven after the raid to take damage assessment photographs. Each attacking aircraft was armed with four 500lb MC bombs with instantaneous (0.025 second) fuses. In the event two Mosquitos (DZ367 GB-J, Flight Lieutenant W. C. S. Blessing, and DZ370 GB-Z, Pilot Officer J. G. Bruce) did not attack – as previously recorded they decoyed some intercepting Fw190 fighters and were forced to abandon the raid, but escaped back to base. The Mosquitos were in two groups, the first of six led by Wing Commander H. I. Edwards VC DFC; the second four aircraft were led by Squadron Leader D. A. G. Parry but, when the Fw190s took off from Woensdrecht aerodrome to intercept, Parry led Blessing towards the fighters to distract them from the raid, leaving Flight Lieutenant C. E. S. 'Charles' Patterson (DK338 GB-O) leading Flying Officer S. G. Kimmel RCAF (DZ372 GB-C).

Charles Patterson has left a graphic description of the attack – instead of a navigator he had with him Pilot Officer J. 'Jimmy' Hill of the RAF Film Photographic Unit who was taking 35mm moving film of the raid. Patterson recalled:

I was now leading the formation, and ahead of me I saw the front formation of Mosquitos in the distance, already climbing up to 1,500ft. So I immediately took my formation, now two short, up to 1,500ft. I went as fast as I could ... to catch Edwards up and join his formation. When we actually arrived at 1,500ft, about two or three miles south of Eindhoven, I'd practically caught Edwards up. He banked over to port and started to dive down on to the Philips works in the centre of the town.

Wing Commander Hughie Edwards remembered the moment:

With throttles fully open I climbed to 2,000ft, suddenly feeling naked and a sitting target. I put the nose down and levelled at 1,000ft. The flak was spasmodic; wrong time of day perhaps! ... we were heading for the main plant, and bombed at 1,000ft. I then pushed the stick forward to get as low as possible. A large clock face loomed up over Eindhoven; it showed 12.32 hours.

Patterson's story continues:

The moment I turned to port, I could see this factory standing out unmistakenly, very prominently, right in the centre of Eindhoven town. So there was little problem with identifying the target, and at the appropriate moment, dropped the bombs; pilot dropped [instead of a navigator he had a cameraman with him]. Then, of course, as I went across the Philips works the whole factory seemed to erupt in a cloud of smoke and flashes. Looking down on it at height, it looked as though the whole thing was completely eliminated. In the distance, I could see masses of Bostons whizzing about across the trees at low level away to port.

As with the Boston attacks, the Operations Record Books (for RAF Marham) provide an account of the attack as reported by the Mosquito crews:

Mosquito IV, DK338 GB-O, 105 Squadron flown by Flight Lieutenant Charles Patterson with Pilot Officer Jimmy Hill, a photographic unit cameraman. *(IWM CH7781)*

105 Squadron

Flying Officer Spencer Griffith Kimmel RCAF, DZ372 GB-C: 'Attacked primary (Strijp) from 1,000ft at 12.33 hrs. Pilot released 4x500lb bombs which are believed to have straddled machine shop and radio erecting shop. Own bursts not seen but numerous bursts from other aircraft seen in target area and bombs from the leading aircraft [DZ365 GB-V Wing Commander Edwards] seen to burst in centre of most northerly block of radio erecting shops. Photo taken.'

(Sadly, Flying Officer Kimmel and his navigator, Flying Officer H. N. Kirkland, were killed in a mid-air collision with another Mosquito while attacking a target at Rennes on 26 February 1943.)

Squadron Leader D. A. G. 'George' Parry DSO DFC, DK296 GB-G: 'Dropped 4x500lb MC bombs on Strijp target at 12.33hrs from 1,000ft. The first bomb was seen to burst in centre of target on building to N of paper and cardboard stores, bursts of remaining bombs not seen but they were believed to have straddled centre of target. Columns of black smoke seen rising from NNE portion of target area.'

Flight Lieutenant W. C. S. 'Bill' Blessing RAAF, DZ367 GB-J: 'Abandoned task at 51 25N 05 00E [approximately 3 miles north of Turnhout] after breaking away from formation to draw off a Fw190 which continued to attack aircraft for 10 minutes. After taking evasive action enemy aircraft was eventually eluded. Bombs were brought back.'

(Sadly, Bill Blessing, by then a squadron leader, was killed in action over France on 1 July 1944.)

Flight Lieutenant C. E. S. 'Charles' Patterson, DK338 GB-O: 'Attacked Strijp target at 12.34 from 1,000ft and believed 4x500lb bombs fell on bakelite factory. Although own bursts were unobserved bursts of other aircraft were seen in machine shop area. Weather – light fair 8/10 2,000ft visibility 5miles. Cine film 35mm was taken over target.'

Flight Sergeant K. L. Monaghan, DK336 GB-P: 'Attacked primary at 12.33hrs from 1,000ft. The pilot released bombs which were believed to have dropped on the bakelite factory. Black smoke was seen arising from glassware houses and one bomb from another aircraft was seen to explode on the southernmost radio erecting shop. Photos taken.'

Wing Commander H. I. 'Hughie' Edwards VC DFC, DZ365 GB-V: 'DZ365 reaches Strijp target at 12.32hrs and dropped 4x500lb from 1,200ft. Bombs were definitely dropped on target, and bombs from Bostons were seen to fall on radio erecting shops which disintegrated and went up in flames. Visibility was average, 8/10 cloud at 1,500ft light fair, photos taken.'

Warrant Officer A. R. 'Raymond' Noseda DFC, DZ374 GB-X: 'Bombed at 12.33hrs from 1,400ft. Pilot released bombs which are believed to have fallen on mechanical glassworks in SE end of target. Several bursts seen on and near radio erecting shops with considerable smoke and flame. Weather – light moderate, cloud 10/10 2,000ft, visibility 3-4 miles. Photos taken.'

(Warrant Officer Raymond Noseda and Sergeant John Watson Urquhart, navigator, were both killed in action on 9 January 1943 on a mission against rail sheds at Rouen.)

Flying Officer J. G. 'Jimmy' Bruce, DZ370 GB-Z: 'DZ370 did not attack target owing to interception by 2 Fw190s 10 miles W of Turnhout at 12.23hrs. Enemy successfully evaded and bombs jettisoned. Aircraft damaged by cannon fire from Fw190.'

139 (Jamaica) Squadron

Flying Officer J. E. O'Grady RCAF, DZ371 XD-A: 'DZ371 was hit by flak while bombing the Strijp target. Streaming smoke she made her way out via Utrecht and Amsterdam but crashed in the sea 30 miles off Den Helder.' (Both crew killed)

(John Earl O'Grady was twenty-one and from Saskatoon; his navigator, Sergeant George William Lewis, also twenty-one, was from Dudley, Worcestershire. Both are commemorated on the Runnymede Memorial.)

Flight Lieutenant M. M. 'Mike' Wayman, DZ373 XD-B: 'Attacked at 12.33hrs from 1,000ft. Bombs seen falling on glassworks and radio erecting works. Own bursts unobserved, but saw others on component factory, end of which collapsed causing flames and smoke. Photos taken.'

(The navigator, Flight Lieutenant Charles Kenneth Hayden DFC failed to return from a raid on le Mans on 9 July 1943 – he is commemorated at Runnymede.)

Squadron Leader J. E. 'Jack' Houlston DFC AFC, DZ314 ZD-F: 'DZ314 took off (at 11.45) to photograph the damage at Eindhoven making two runs over the target at 13.00-13.03hrs at 800ft. No bombs carried, weather light dull 9/10 cloud 800ft visibility 5 miles.' This aircraft was on loan from 105 Squadron.

(Squadron Leader Jack Edward Houlston DFC AFC and his navigator, Warrant Officer James Lloyd Armitage DFC, failed to return from a raid on railway targets in the Oldenburg/Bremen area of north-west Germany on 20 December 1942. Both are buried in the Reichswald Forest War cemetery.)

The Ventura squadrons Attack

The Ventura squadrons represented half of the total attacking force. They came in about four minutes after the Mosquitos, at low level, into the face of alerted defences and with much smoke to confuse their aim. Theirs was indeed a heroic performance, not least because this was the first operation undertaken by 464 and 487 Squadrons – they were to suffer proportionately heavier casualties than their colleagues in the Bostons and Mosquitos. Nine of the forty-seven Ventures did not return from the raid, although the crew of one was rescued from the sea. The aircraft were each armed with two 250lb general purpose (GP) bombs with time delays of either half an hour or one hour (long enough to avoid damage to later aircraft and to cause confusion to the defenders) plus forty 30lb incendiary bombs intended to burn the remains of the damaged factories. Nos. 464 and 487 Squadrons attacked the larger Strijp works while 21 Squadron went for the Emmasingel works half a mile to the east.

In the next picture very specific smoke trails of exploding incendiary bombs can be seen over the whole length of the Emmasingel target. Between the Emmasingel complex and the barracks in the foreground (built for Belgian refugees in 1914) the railway line between Eindhoven and Den

Picture from a 21 Squadron Ventura turning for home after bombing the Emmasingel target. *(IWM C3269)*

Bosch can be seen. To the right the Abonné cigar-plant is to be seen, a most famous one at that time.

In the report from Feltwell to HQ 2 Group it was stated:

> On the run-in smoke was seen coming from both targets ... on the large target the leader reported that the erecting shops were on fire. Following aircraft confirmed this ... the bakelite factory [was] well ablaze. The last aircraft reported that the laboratories and other parts of the target were also being hit. The whole target was covered by fire and smoke ... numerous incendiaries from the Venturas were seen to hit the walls of the buildings ... one of the more experienced pilots ... stated that he had never seen more concentrated and effective bombing.

Aircrew reported seeing the German gunners on the flat roofs of the buildings firing at them as they flew over.

The cost to the Ventura squadrons over the target was heavy. In the few minutes it took for them to cross the target areas four aircraft were shot down by flak. The first was AE945, SB-E of 464 squadron, Flight Sergeant Beverley Harvey RCAF, which crashed at 12.39 in the Strijp target area. All the crew were killed and are buried in the Woensel General Cemetery, Eindhoven. Then AE702, SB-Q, Flying Officer Maurice Moor RCAF, was seen by author Kees Rijken to pull up sharply after bombing the Strijp complex, stall and dive into the ground on a square in the Schoolstraat; the crew are also buried in the Woensel Cemetery. AE940, YH-T of 21 Squadron, Flight Lieutenant Kenneth Smith, crashed in flames in the Nieuwe Dijk street just north of the Emmasingel site; again the crew are buried in the Woensel Cemetery. AE902, EG-W of 487 Squadron, Flight Sergeant John

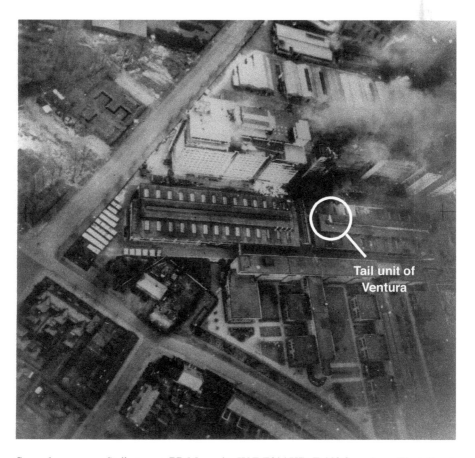

Second run across Strijp target, PR Mosquito IV DZ314 XD-F, 139 Squadron. The tail unit of Ventura EG-W visible on roof of building. *(IWM C5757)*

Greening RAF was hit by flak and crashed into the Veemgebouw building on the Strijp site; this building suffered major damage from this collision but has since been restored, the crew are also buried at Eindhoven near their comrades.

The photo above is from the PR Mosquito flying to the north-west skimming the Strijp target area just to the south at roughly 800 feet. The western extreme end of the Strijp complex can be seen with the Veemgebouw prominently showing apart (white building). It was this building into which Ventura II, AE902 EG-W, of 487 Squadron crashed. The impact marks can be clearly distinguished on the Veemgebouw to the top-right, just one floor beneath the roof. Debris from the aircraft can be seen directly in front of the Veemgebouw, while the tail-unit can be seen on a building to the right and a bit lower. The tail, together with part of the rear-fuselage is standing straight up on the fuselage part. It seems as if it has snapped directly aft of the belly-gunner's position. It is likely that the aircraft was flying in the enormous clouds of smoke and was flying blind. Consequently, they most certainly never saw the building into which they crashed.

All the crew perished, and are buried at Woensel General Cemetery in Eindhoven: Flight Sergeant (Pilot) J. L. John Greening RAF 533208, Sergeant (Nav.) E. C. Mowforth RAF(VR) 1038399, Sergeant (WO/AG) D. H. Harries RAF(VR) 1377756 and Sergeant (AG) B. H. Thomas RAF(VR) 1318061.

There were also some close escapes from disaster. Two Venturas of 487 (RNZAF) Squadron, EG-B flown by Flying Officer Coshall and EG-M by Sergeant Baker, touched wings 'with a tearing sound' but, as their speed was the same, no serious damage occurred. Another aircraft, EG-H flown by Sergeant Coutts, was hit by an explosive shell which set a Very light on fire, filling the aircraft with smoke until subdued with the aid of a fire extinguisher.[6]

The large number of Venturas in the attack, coupled with their low-level bombing tactic and the fact that the defences had been alerted by the preceding waves of aircraft, resulted in a large number of exciting anecdotes:

Sergeant Peter Mallinson, air gunner in AE811 EG-L, 487 Squadron, in a letter to his sister Connie, recorded:

we at last reached the target area where we ran into a terrific barrage, again, as we were so low it proved ineffective so far as we were concerned. Bill, the pilot [Flight Sergeant G. W. 'Bill' Lee] rose from about 20ft to about 60ft and I heard the navigator [Sergeant W. 'Burt'

Lowe] say 'Bomb Doors Open'. Then we flew into clouds of smoke and I heard 'Bombs Gone'. I saw lots of flashes and sparks rise up as our bombs and incendiaries went into the centre of the target. What a blaze! As I looked back from my turret I saw two German machine gunners still on the roof (this was confirmed later). I think it would have been impossible for them to get down and were most likely blown up by the other planes behind us.

Sergeant A. V. 'Albert' Ricketts, pilot of AE687 YH-P, 21 Squadron left a personal account:

As we were one of the last aircraft to drop our bombs it wasn't surprising that, with the bombing that had gone on before we arrived, the factory was well and truly alight. The incendiaries we were dropping were of a new [for the period] phosphor type and would explode on impact and would stick to whatever it hit and continue burning. Unfortunately the aircraft in front of me was too close to the building when its bombs exploded so that they stuck to his plane and it went down in flames after he passed over the factory [this was AE940 YH-T of 21 squadron, flown by Flight Lieutenant K. S. Smith]. Not wanting to suffer the same fate, as soon as I had released our bombs, I made the aircraft climb rapidly and so we disappeared into the smoke and levelled out at about 600ft. I continued to fly at that height blind and on instruments until we were out of the smoke and then realized how vulnerable we were. I pushed the nose of the aircraft down quickly so as not to attract the anti-aircraft fire little realizing the confusion this was causing to Bill Legg who was the air gunner in the downward facing gun position. These guns were fed by a switch-back system from the bullet panniers positioned on both sides of the aircraft. These switch-backs didn't have a cover on them and the sudden descent of the aircraft caused the bullets to come out of the switch-back and wrap themselves around Bill's neck. The expletives he used were unprintable.

Pilot Officer George M. Shinnie RAF, WO/AG in AJ466 SB-H of 464 Squadron recalled:

We successfully attacked our respective targets but the buildings appeared to be far taller than expected and they were well protected by flak batteries on the roofs. Although flying so low we did get over the buildings in our cumbersome Venturas, albeit with little room to spare. Unfortunately one of our aircraft was lost. It was in the rear of the formation and it appeared that his target was so obscured by smoke that the pilot could not see the top of the building, and tragically flew into it. [This was AE945 SB-E, Flight Sergeant Beverley Harvey RCAF, which crashed into the FITTERIJ building on the Strijp complex.] Some minutes later I was shocked to see our number two aircraft on our port side suddenly completely enveloped in flames, the aircraft dipped, flew into the side of a house and then appeared at the other side. It was all over in seconds. [This was AE702 SB-Q, Flying Officer Maurice G. Moor RCAF.]

Squadron Leader Leonard Trent, pilot AJ209 EG-V, left his story of the attack recorded in *Ventura Courageous, biography of Group Captain Leonard Trent VC DFC*, by James Saunders:

No. 464 Squadron Venturas. *(George Shinnie)*

Pressing on over the flat, open country the bomber crews could see their target clearly defined by the columns of smoke rising from the attack of the Bostons and Mosquitos. A gentle turn to starboard brought the Venturas in line for their run up and Trent had already pinpointed his target building. Climbing to clear the parapets, he let loose his stick of bombs so that they plummeted into the structure, holing it from basement to roof-top. As his aircraft cleared the top of the flaming and smoking target, Len Trent glimpsed, on the left hand corner of the building, a German machine gunner stubbornly sticking to his post and pouring a steady stream of fire at his attacker – albeit none of the bullets

Anti-aircraft gun Spandau Flak MG 08 of the Luftwaffe on the Philips Lichttoren. *(Regionaal Historisch Centrum Eindhoven, reference no. 0064142)*

damaging the Ventura. 'There,' says Trent, 'was a damned good soldier.' Trent is also reported as seeing one aircraft blow up only ten yards away on his starboard side while over the target.[7]

Pilot Officer Arthur E. C. Wheeler, pilot of AE839 YH-A of 21 Squadron left a notable account:

We flew into huge flocks of birds as we crossed over the other side but no damage was done as we turned past Oostmalle heading for Eindhoven. Smoke from the Boston attack earlier hid the target as we went in at about 100ft. For me, strange to say, it was an exhilarating experience rather than a frightening one, seeing gunners on the flat roofs of some buildings swivelling round as we flew over and dropped our incendiaries. We were at zero feet as I saw ahead a line of electrical pylons which I knew I could not climb over. However, I breathed a sigh of relief when I realized that fortunately somebody had been there first

YEAR 1942		AIRCRAFT		PILOT, OR	2ND PILOT, PUPIL	DUTY
MONTH	DATE	Type	No.	1ST PILOT	OR PASSENGER	(INCLUDING RESULTS AND REMARKS)
—	—	—	—	—	. —	—— TOTALS BROUGHT FORWARD
EC	2	VENTURA I	AE 839	SELF	CREW	AIR TEST
EC	6	VENTURA I	AE 839	SELF	CREW + CROSS SGT	OPERATIONS — EINDHOVEN
EC	17	VENTURA II	AE 892	SELF	P/O PRATT SGT DONOVAN SGT WELLS SGT MACDONALD	FELTWELL - BASE
EC	17	VENTURA II	AE 892	SELF	SGT DONOVAN SGT GERTY SGT MAY SGT MACDONALD SGT MILLIKEN	BASE - S. MORLEY - HURN - S. MORLEY - BASE
EC	20	VENTURA I	AE 744	SELF	P/O BECKMAN	FELTWELL - BASE
EC	20	VENTURA I	AE 744	SELF	P/O BECKMAN F/S DAVISON SGT DONOVAN	PRACTISE CIRCUS
EC	21	VENTURA I	AE 744	SELF	CREW F/S DAVISON	CIRCUS OPERATION - ABORTIVE
EC	22	VENTURA I	AE 744	SELF	SGT DONOVAN SGT	NF TEST
EC	23	VENTURA I	AE 744	SELF	CREW + McKENNIE	BULLSEYE EXERCISE
EC	29	VENTURA I	AE 839	SELF	CREW + F/L LORD	LOW LEVEL BOMBING

SUMMARY FOR DECEMBER						AIRCRAFT TYPES	
UNIT	21 SQUADRON	DATE 2.1.43			1	VENTURA I - II	
O.C. "A" FLIGHT					2		
O.C. 21 SQUADRON					3.		

Logbook of Pilot Officer Arthur Wheeler for December 1942. *(Arthur Wheeler)*

21 Squadron Venturas, AE839 YH-A in foreground. *(Arthur Wheeler)*

and there were no power lines between them. We flew home safely and I cannot remember if we had any bullet-holes through our aircraft but my logbook records that I did not fly AE839 again until December 29th, 23 days after the raid, so we must have had some damage from flak or birds.'

Indeed, of the eighteen Venturas in 21 Squadron, three failed to return, all had received some damage from bird strikes and no less than fifteen had been hit by light flak causing two aircraft to return on one engine. In all, the three Ventura units had incurred 20 per cent casualties on the raid.

The Flight Home

Over The Netherlands

Boston Squadrons

The stories about the raiding aircraft as they raced for home are at least as exciting as the attack itself – many aircraft had been damaged by flak and bird-strikes and they were harried by German fighters. Most got back to base with varying difficulty, not always by the planned route, but sadly some aircraft were lost in the attempt. The story of the leading aircraft flown by Wing Commander Johnny Pelly-Fry was particularly dramatic and led to some confusion among the following aircraft. It is worth recounting in some detail from his own account.

Pelly-Fry in Boston Z2233 RH-K had

barely reached the target when without warning it shuddered violently and then began a slow roll to starboard (due to being hit in the starboard engine from anti-aircraft fire of the Emmasingel target). It was only when the wings were almost vertical that I was able to employ maximum correction and the response was painfully slow .... the Boston was not behaving at all well, I could not but smile briefly when we passed over a game of football in progress – some of the players beginning to run very briskly off the pitch to take what cover was available.

The plan for the route home was to turn left onto a north-westerly heading until passing the town of Boxtel, then west passing Breda and on to clear the coast at Colijnsplaat, where Spitfires would provide fighter cover. Pelly-Fry continued his account:

The new problem, now that I had succeeded in getting the aeroplane the right way up, was that I could not make the planned turn onto a westerly heading to begin the dash back to the coast. The best that I could persuade the Boston to do was to inch its way to the left very slowly, painfully slowly. The next thing I saw after about sixty miles of difficult flying was the big dock area of Rotterdam with all the cranes sticking up like tall fingers. This was certainly no place to be in broad daylight as earlier Blenheim crews had discovered to their cost. In the meantime the other Boston pilots were still following and probably wondering why I had wandered so much off track. I called them on the radio to tell them to press on as I had problems, and one after the other they overtook me with their superior speed.

The reason for lack of effective flying control now became obvious. A large piece of the top skin of the starboard wing at the thickest part was sticking up vertically, and to add to the evidence the fabric on the starboard aileron – the one I needed most – was shredding itself into little pieces in the slipstream. To pile on the bad news further, the starboard engine began to rattle and bang alarmingly and had to be throttled well back before it quietened down satisfactorily. So now I had an almost uncontrollable aeroplane and with the engine I needed most to keep straight almost out of action ... we struggled on, but not without more hazards to come. Buster [Flying Officer C. A. 'Buster' Evans DFM, air gunner] calmly announced that we were being chased by two Fw190 fighters. They were 600 yards astern, at 7 o'clock as we say, closing. When I heard the single word 'Corkscrew' all I could do was to bob up and down and wait for the cannon shells to arrive. It seemed to work quite well during the attacks, thanks to Buster's uncanny sense of timing, and now at last out to sea the two German pilots for some reason gave up the hunt ... in retrospect they were not up to the job ... Who am I to complain?

Leaving Pelly-Fry to nurse his aircraft across the North Sea it is chronologically sensible to return to consider what the rest of the Boston force did after bombing. Notwithstanding the planned return route, it is hardly surprising that the aircraft following the leader most closely will have continued to follow his lead until it became clear that he was in trouble and had ordered them to press on. By this time they were probably approaching 's-Hertogenbosch (den Bosch), some miles north-east of the intended track. A rapid re-evaluation of the situation by the leading navigator, probably

Pilot Officer P. J. Stack in 'Jock' Campbell's aircraft (Z2211 RH-N), led to many of the Bostons routing just south of Utrecht, north of Rotterdam, and coasting out near Brielle – certainly this is how Pilot Officer F. J. 'Freddie' Deeks, navigator of Flight Lieutenant John Reeve's aircraft (AL693 RH-U), has recorded their track. It seems that some of the Bostons further back in the formation emerged from the excitement and smoke of the attack and turned north-west to Boxtel as briefed and then more or less directly to the sea in the region of Colijnsplaat. In all cases they were flying as low and fast as possible with the consequent hazards now increased by the attentions of such German fighters as had been directed to the area.

Again we are indebted to Pilot Officer Jack Peppiatt for his account of this confusing situation. He pointed his damaged aircraft (AL749, RH-R) after the gaggle of aircraft following Pelly-Fry until

> both I and my navigator [Sergeant C. F. Kirk] began to wonder why they didn't turn west toward the coast. By now we were all down hugging the ground for comfort. We made a joint decision what to do and some of the aircraft made the turn; we went with them but we were also joined and passed by Mosquitos as time went on.

But their problems were by no means over:

> After a few minutes settling down it all went up with a bang as Fw190s appeared. Without doubt the next 20 minutes or so were full of action and not a little confusion. Some 10 or 20 aircraft were screaming along, full throttle in a loose mass; no one wanted to be at the back where the Focke-Wulfs were coming in to attack and wheeling away for another go.
>
> They had one problem, which I think was that, as they dived, they had to pull out early to avoid hitting the ground because we were all at zero feet. I distinctly saw cannon shells hitting ploughed fields in front of me and moving on ahead as the Focke-Wulf began to pull out. At one point a fighter slid past us and just sat to my right as he slowed – so close I could stare at the pilot and admire the yellow spinner. Meanwhile Len [Sergeant Len Dellow, air gunner] was calling for me to jink and then shouted that he had got one. If he did I really don't know how he did it as I was sliding and diving constantly. The astonishing thing was that we didn't collide, as aircraft constantly criss-crossed in front of each other.

Sergeant Stephen Roche of 226 Squadron recounted similar experiences in his next day letter to his sister:

> It was terribly exciting of course, but the only thing that frightened me was all those other machines milling round all over the place! Two Fw190 fighters came after me, but being so close to the ground they couldn't attack me.

He tells how he eluded one by flying under a cable and concluded his account: 'We came out so fast my engines were nearly red hot!'

Another Boston, W8373 OM-F, flown by Pilot Officer Philip Burley RAFVR, is recorded in the 107 Squadron ORB as having been attacked by a Bf109 at 12.50 hours while at fifty feet. The enemy aircraft made four separate attacks from the stern but no strikes were scored. This Bf109 was claimed as damaged by a five-second burst from the rear air gunner at 400 yards range. No further attack was made so this claim may well have been justified.

The Boston aircraft which followed Pelly-Fry too far then found their way to the coast by a track passing near Rotterdam and Hoek van Holland (the Hook of Holland). They had not only a longer period over enemy territory – extended by about five minutes – but significant coastal defences to contend with. Flight Lieutenant Ronald A. 'Yogi' Yates–Earl, pilot of AL678 MQ-R 226 Squadron, remembered:

> The Hook was very heavily defended and when we got there we saw hundreds of Germans dashing out of huts and rushing up to their gun emplacements. We had very good sport shooting them with our front guns, but when we got out to sea they got their wind back and fired at us with damn big coastal guns. They didn't do much damage to us, but it looked pretty unpleasant for a while.

The attacks by German fighters during the flight from the target to the sea took its toll. The aircraft flown by Wing Commander Peter H. Dutton RAFVR, the Commanding Officer of 107 Squadron (AH740 OM-A) was shot down by Fw190s of 5/JG1 from Schiphol (now Amsterdam's international airport) and crashed in the sea at 12.59, six kilometres west of Katwijk aan Zee, which is on the coast north-east of Den Haag, the capital of The Netherlands; no bodies were recovered. Peter Hiley Dutton was twenty-nine and a married man. His crew were Flight Lieutenant

Norman H. Shepherd DFM RAFVR (navigator), aged twenty-eight, Flight Lieutenant Robert W. McCarthy DFM RAFVR, aged twenty-four, and Pilot Officer M. L. Delanchy of the Free French Forces. This was a more than usually mature crew who, apart from their Free French colleague, are commemorated on the Runnymede Memorial.

Also from 107 Squadron, Z2252 OM-M was shot down by fighters and crashed at 12.52 in the sea. The pilot was Warrant Officer Alan J. Reid RAFVR, the navigator Flying Officer Derrick R. Redbourn RAFVR and the two wireless operator/air gunners were Flight Sergeant William J. A. Spriggs RAFVR and Pilot Officer John W. Beck RCAF. Derrick Redbourn is buried at the Vlissingen Northern Cemetery; Vlissingen is on the Westerschelde estuary, south of Colijnsplaat, so it is likely that this aircraft is one which took the originally planned route home. The other crew members are commemorated at Runnymede. Although John Beck was serving in the Royal Canadian Air Force he is listed as the son of Stella Morgan Beck of Vernont, Michigan, USA; he was twenty-two years old.[8]

Indeed the 107 Squadron Boston crews suffered worse than their fellows from the attention of fighters. Another casualty was AL737 OM-U flown by Sergeant Cecil A. Maw RAFVR, with Flight Sergeant Harold E. Wilson RCAF, navigator, and Sergeant Ronald A. Barnes RAFVR, wireless operator/air gunner. Once again it was the Fw190s of 5/JG1 from Schiphol that accounted for this aircraft which fell into the sea at 12.50. Maw and Wilson, who was from Richmond Hill, Ontario, Canada, are commemorated at Runnymede and Barnes is buried at the Bergen op Zoom Allied War Cemetery.

No. 226 Squadron also lost one aircraft, Z2266 MQ-S, in this phase of the operation. The crew comprised Flying Officer Norman J. A. Paton DFM RAFVR, pilot, Flight Lieutenant James G. A. Maguire DFC, navigator and a married man aged twenty-nine and Pilot Officer James L. Fletcher RCAF, wireless operator/air gunner. The fate of this aircraft has been ascribed either to being shot down off the coast at Renesse (north-west of Colijnsplaat) by a Fw190[9] or hit by marine flak, crashing into the sea off Scheveningen, which is the seaside suburb of Den Haag.[10] All the crew are commemorated at Runnymede.

Mosquito squadrons – overland retreat

The plan for the Mosquitos was that they should each be free to return as they saw fit, using their high speed as their defence against fighters – the Mosquito and the Fw190 had a similar maximum speed at low level. Individual circumstances resulted in a variety of tracks back to the coast but several followed the same route as planned for the Bostons towards Colijnsplaat – indeed there were reports of them overtaking and, in one case, joining Bostons in doing so. Pilot Officer 'Jimmy' Bruce (in DZ370 GB-Z, with Pilot Officer Michael Carreck as his navigator) joined a gaggle of Bostons after he had evaded fighter attack and jettisoned his bombs – unsure of his exact position he spotted the Bostons and closed in, wary of their defensive guns; Michael Carreck recalled:

> we flew alongside at a safe, respectful distance. We stood on one wing – look we're a Mosquito ... see our RAF roundels ... later we crossed the Dutch coast ... naval guns opened up. Huge spouts of water erupted optimistically around us until we passed out of range. Then I'm afraid, Jimmy was just a trifle tactless. He waggled our wings – thank you – and throttles wide open, we rocketed away, leaving the Bostons standing. Showing off, yes; but we'd had a hard day.

Charles Patterson (in DK338 GB-O) decided that it would be safer to avoid the Bostons' planned route, in case the enemy fighters had congregated to intercept, and flew north up the Zuider Zee (now the Ijsselmeer) and then west out to sea around Den Helder. He was followed by Pilot Officer John O'Grady (in DZ371 XD-A, 139 Squadron). He reported that they 'whizzed' over the causeway [at the north end of the Zuider Zee] at about twenty feet. However, this turned out to be a mistake because the light flak sites at Den Helder and the southern tip of the island of Texel were close enough to put up a fierce defence. Patterson emerged unscathed but O'Grady was hit and crashed into the sea soon afterwards.

The German fighters were indeed ready further south for the returning bombers. Warrant Officer Raymond Noseda DFC (in DZ374 GB-X) was attacked by two Fw190s over Goeree-Overflakkee (one of the estuarial islands south-west of Hoek van Holland). He sustained some damage to the starboard aileron and the port engine but speed won the day; he and his navigator, Sergeant John W. Urquhart, escaped, only to be killed in action on a raid to Rouen the following month.

As on the flight to the target, flak and fighters were not the only hazard – at such low altitudes there were still bird strikes to contend with. Squadron Leader George Parry (in DK296 GB-G, with Flying Officer Victor Robson as navigator) ran into a flock of ducks which came through the pilot's and observer's Perspex and the bomb-aimer's panel. One bird shattered Parry's windscreen, fragments of which then rebounded from the armour plate behind him and embedded themselves in his back. The remains of the bird burst into the cockpit, its splintered bones ripping Parry's helmet and partially blinding him. Fortunately, he kept control of the aircraft and got home.

Ventura Squadrons leave the target area for the coast

The Ventura squadrons were now in the unenviable position of heading back to the coast as 'tail-end Charlies', with the defences fully alerted. Ideally they might have flown as a self-protecting formation using their defensive armament to discourage too close attention from fighters. Having emerged from the confused and smoking area over the target and needing to get down very low to the ground, this was easier said than done. However, they had a route which was relatively direct – north-west for a few miles clearing Eindhoven aerodrome, then direct back to Colijnsplaat, passing south of the heavily defended aerodrome at Gilze-Rijen and just north of the town of Roosendaal. From the coast they could expect support from the Spitfires of Fighter Command.

As events unfolded, the Ventura force suffered rather less on the return than on the outward flight, although some pilots had to struggle with already damaged aircraft and there was still the hazard of bird strikes. Indeed, 487 Squadron reported the return flight as 'fairly uneventful', with some low rain clouds and 'desultory flak'.[11] One aircraft was forced to ditch in the sea and another had to put down in England before it reached base.

However, for one 21 Squadron Ventura crew the return flight was distinctly eventful. Sergeant Albert Ricketts, pilot of AE687 YH-P, recalled:

Not long after leaving the target I managed to make the aircraft hit a tree. Fortunately we hit it head on about a third of the way down ... the impact did enough damage to make life quite difficult for us to keep flying ... I realized that the pitot head (that provides the air for the airspeed indicator to work) had been ripped off. Part of the underside of the wing had been ripped away so that Ron [Sergeant Thompson, navigator] was able to see the ground through the side of the aircraft. Just before we were about to leave the Dutch Coast our starboard engine packed up. I could only conjecture that the collision had damaged the pipe line to the engine and I had no alternative but to feather the prop and fly on only one ... a practice I had carried out quite often ... to reduce drag and stay airborne.

(This crew's adventures over the sea are described later in the narrative.)

As the Venturas passed Colijnsplaat they came under the protection of the covering Spitfires which had the mouth of the Oosterschelde as the rendezvous point. As planned, the presence of the Spitfire cover discouraged the German fighters from further attacks. However, there were still some hazards to be faced before reaching safety.

Back across the North Sea to landing in England

We left Pelly-Fry struggling with a badly-damaged airframe and a 'rattling' starboard engine which was throttled back to low power. By the time he was over the sea he had coaxed his Boston up to about 1,000 feet and was heading for the nearest part of the English coast. Then, in his own words 'to pile on the agony of suspense, the port engine now decided to play up and started fading. I played the throttle gently as we lost height and each time a ditching seemed imminent it picked up and we slowly got back to around 600ft.' At last they reached the English coast, still flying, and it did not take Pelly-Fry long 'to conclude that Blickling Hall had a singular attraction'. Hoping that the carefully nursed port engine would hold out, he decided to aim for Oulton – he was resigned to a 'belly landing' since he could not lower the flaps and undercarriage and only one of the ailerons was working. Pelly-Fry offered his navigator and air gunner the option of baling out before landing but they preferred to take their chance on a landing at base.

Pelly-Fry called the Oulton control tower and advised them of his predicament and so emergency services were put on instant readiness. Given immediate clearance to land, he approached at about 190mph, levelled off, throttled back, switched off magnetos and fuel and 'made a bumpy arrival and slid across the damp grass'. The crew made a hasty exit from the aircraft, which fortunately did not catch fire. The navigator, 'Jock' Cairns, needed some help to get out and it later was found that he had a cracked vertebra and was off flying for some time. Pelly-Fry recounted, after de-briefing and 'delicious bacon and eggs', that some pike fishing on Blickling's lake was a good way to wind down. The aircraft (Z2236 RH-G) was very battered but was eventually repaired and saw more service – a tribute to the designers at the Douglas Aircraft Company.

We have heard how Albert Ricketts, flying Ventura AE687 YH-P, had hit a tree while escaping from the Eindhoven area and subsequently the starboard engine stopped due to a fractured fuel line. Having lost a lot of fuel they headed for Felixstowe, the nearest point on the English coast. Ricketts was able to coax his aircraft up to 1,300 feet, although he had no

Pelly-Fry's Boston Z2236 RH-G crash-landed back at Oulton. *(IWM Film)*

airspeed indication and was concerned not to lose flying speed and stall. The wireless operator, Sergeant Bob Goddard, found that their radio was useless, probably due to the loss of the aerial when they struck the tree. The one bright spot was that some nearby fighters were part of their escort of Spitfires, one of which eventually realized their predicament and took up station on their starboard side. They encountered a Royal Navy warship and, being conscious of the Navy's hard-earned distrust of all unidentified aircraft, fired off the colours of the day and managed to pass astern of it.

So far so good, but about seven miles from the coast the fuel was exhausted and the port engine also stopped. Albert Ricketts was then faced with the tricky job of ditching an aircraft without an airspeed indication. Fortunately the sea was smooth and the wind calm. On a Ventura, part of the ditching procedure was to jettison a panel above the pilot and navigator to assist in a rapid exit. However, Ricketts was unsure how losing this panel would affect the airflow over his stricken machine and decided to release the astrodome instead – one escape route for all four men. Another problem for Ricketts personally was that, due to having to change aircraft hurriedly before take off because of a problem with their original machine, he had not strapped himself in. Nonetheless, he achieved a very good arrival on the sea and, by bracing himself at the last moment, survived with only a small scratch on his nose, while the others in his crew were unhurt.

They now escaped through the astrodome as quickly as possible, the aircraft sinking in about forty-five seconds. The American designers of the Ventura had provided the aircraft with a 'sea switch' which when in contact with sea water released the dinghy and set off its CO_2 bottle, so they were able to get into this very welcome boat without delay. While this was happening their 'guardian Spitfire' (from Coltishall near Norwich, either 411 or 485 Squadron) had found a nearby fishing trawler and indicated the direction of the survivors. Thus within fifteen minutes they were in the fishing boat and forty-five minutes later an air sea rescue launch from Felixstowe had come alongside the trawler and took them ashore.

Then came another important action (almost, but not quite, as hazardous as the raid) – in Albert Ricketts' words:

> We told the CO of the Air Sea Rescue Unit that a party had been arranged at Feltwell and he very kindly arranged for transport to take us to the party. Driving back through the dark in the blackout at a speed necessary to ensure that we did not miss the party was very frightening. Still we were determined not to miss the party. When we arrived, the party was in full swing and it surprised most of the squadron that we were there … at the end of the party we were sat on a grass verge waiting for the wagon to arrive to take us back to base [Methwold]. When it arrived I got up to run to the lorry and promptly fell over. It was only then that I realized how much the day had taken out of me and how tired I was.

Two other 21 Squadron Venturas landed at Bodney (about five miles east of Methwold). According to Arthur Wheeler's account Flight Sergeant G. H. Turcotte RCAF, piloting AE744 YH-G, put in there on one engine. He also recorded that Flying Officer D. Pratt, AE941 YH-C, force landed at Bodney with slight injuries sustained by two crew members, Flight Sergeant Hudson and Sergeant F. Morris. It is sad to record that Flight Sergeant Turcotte and his crew, Sergeant J. R. D. Jones (navigator), Sergeant R. W. Dickson (wireless operator) and Sergeant G. W. Hutton (air gunner) along with two ground staff passengers, Sergeant O. W. Woodhead and LAC T. Rutherford, were killed four days after the raid in AE759 YH-H when it crashed on a ferry flight at Methwold Hyde (north-west of Thetford) and was completely burned out.[12]

Another aircraft which did not quite make it back to base at Feltwell was AJ468 EG-A, piloted by Flying Officer Gordon A. Park. The 487 ORB records that Gordon Park did a marvellous job of work by putting his failing aircraft down on the fens, only damaging the rear oleo leg. Oil pipes on the starboard engine had been damaged by a bird strike and the aircraft landed just outside the village of Long Stratton some twenty-five miles east of Feltwell. The ORB also comments 'nice work Gordon'.

One of the 88 Squadron Bostons, Z2211 RH-N piloted by Sergeant C. D. 'Chas' Tyler, had been hit by flak in the starboard engine just after bomb release and, having lost contact with the other Bostons, made its way home independently, having a very anxious flight over the North Sea before making a belly landing in a ploughed field at Brew House Farm, Carlton Colville near Lowestoft. Sergeant Tyler hit his head and was taken to hospital, whereas his crew, Sergeant Bob Gallup (navigator) and Sergeant Ian Stewart (air gunner) enjoyed the hospitality of the local populace before being collected the following morning.[13] As earlier recorded, another 88 Squadron aircraft flown by Jack Peppiatt had been damaged over the target. Lacking both airspeed and altimeter readings, and with Pelly-Fry's aircraft blocking the aerodrome at Oulton, Peppiatt elected to land on the long concrete runway at Attlebridge, a few miles south of Oulton.

Another Boston which made an emergency landing was AL754 OM-D of 107 Squadron, piloted by Flight Sergeant G. E. T. Nichols. According to the 107 Squadron ORB the port engine had suffered from cutting out both on the outward and return trips and both engines cut on landing and the aircraft crashed, the crew being slightly injured. Another source[14] says that the aircraft had been shot up by flak and made a wheels-up landing, sliding through an aerodrome defence position and was struck off charge soon afterwards. It may be that the crash landing of AL754 at Great Massingham at 13.50 was the cause of Z2286 OM-O, Flight Lieutenant D. J. Evans, landing at Marham at 13.58.

It is worth recording that official records were not always accurate; in the case of AL754 the 2 Group ORB shows that this aircraft was flown by Sergeant Burns whereas the 107 Squadron ORB places him and his crew in W8302 OM-J, in which they were attacked and damaged by Fw190s and landed at Ipswich at 13.35, many miles short of their base at Great Massingham. There are other cases in the records where changes of crew (e.g. reserves brought in late) may not have been recorded, Sergeant Roche of 226 Squadron being a probable case in point.

All the Bostons of 226 Squadron landed back at Swanton Morley, except for Flying Officer Norman Paton and his crew who, as we have seen, were hit by flak over the Dutch coast on the way home and crashed in the sea.

Most had been damaged by flak or bird strikes. The ensuing celebration was described by Sergeant Stephen Roche in his next-day letter to his sister Margaret: 'That same evening we had a marvellous concert given by Arthur Askey, Jack Train, Pat Taylor and, believe it or not Alvar Lidell the [radio] announcer who has a lovely singing voice.' This is evidence of some official foresight in arranging for 'household names' from the radio world, then the major source of news and entertainment, to be on hand to greet the returning heroes.

Apart from the loss of DZ371 XD-A of 139 Squadron, Flying Officer O'Grady, all the Mosquitos returned safely to Marham. Pilot Officer Mike Carreck, navigator of GB-Z 105 Squadron, recalled:

> Back at Marham, the airfield was swarming with newspapermen. They took photographs of faithful DZ370 GB-Z, of the hole a cannon shell had made. It had hit us without exploding, missing the bombs by inches. Guardian Angel day. In the crew room everyone was talking over the Eindhoven operation, how the Philips plant had caught fire, trapping the flak gunners on the roof ... Next day we went on leave.

In all, the operation had cost four Bostons, nine Venturas and one Mosquito. Many aircraft had been damaged by flak and twenty-three suffered damage by bird strikes.

Notes

1. NA Kew, ORB, 2 Group, op. cit.
2. NA Kew, AIR25/35 (D28).
3. Chorley, *Bomber Command Losses, 1942.*
4. NA Kew, ORB, 464 Squadron.
5. NA Kew, AIR27/1406, ORB 226 Squadron.
6. *New Zealanders in the Air War.*
7. Ibid.
8. NA Kew, ORB, 2 Group, op. cit. and Chorley, op. cit.
9. NA Kew, ORB, 2 Group, op. cit.
10. Chorley, op. cit.
11. *New Zealanders in the Air War*, op. cit.
12. NA Kew, ORB RAF Feltwell; Chorley, op. cit.
13. Personal account, Jim Moore.
14. Chorley, op. cit.

Chapter Six

Success Achieved

Bombing results as seen from attacking bombers

Emmasingel complex

Boston attacks
The inscription on the following photo reads: 'SM6 6.12.42 "//M8" 1000ft. LX.226'. It was added by photo-processing personnel of the RAF. The date stands out, as well as the bombing height and the squadron to which this aircraft belongs. The letters LX are code-letters for 226 Squadron Boston III, Z2234 MQ-X, being flown by Squadron Leader (Pilot) J. S. Kennedy,

Emmasingel as viewed from Boston III, Z2234 MQ-X, 226 Squadron. *(IWM C3273)*

Flying Officer (Nav) R. S. 'Jack' Rutherford and Flight Sergeant (WO/ AG) E. Eric Lee. They attacked the Emmasingel target between 12.30 and 12.33hrs from 1,000 feet, dropping four 500lb MC TD 0.025 seconds and have just reached roof-top level after their dive.

The picture was taken after bomb release, viewing back in a southerly direction. It shows the Emmasingel already well ablaze. The St Antonius Fellenoord Church can be clearly distinguished. Note also the smoke billowing away nearby, which seems to be coming from the aircraft itself; on the following photographs, however, it can be seen that this smoke originates from a third housing area which was hit by overshooting bombs.

Ventura attacks

Two incendiary impacts, one in the middle the other to the right, can be seen having been dropped from a 21 Squadron Ventura in IWM photo C3268.

Clearly visible in the first picture on page 79 is the Emmasingel complex turret to the left, while the photographing plane is flying directly over the roofs of houses bordering the north side of the target. The aircraft can be seen making a turn left for home according to attack plans. Ventura I, AE692 YH-K, was flown by Pilot Officer (Pilot) D. G. J. Smith, Pilot Officer T. W. D. Cartwright, Pilot Officer D. G. Pearson, Sergeant. P. J. Pentelow and Sergeant. T. B. Rook. It dropped two 250lb GP TD half-hour and 40x30

21 Squadron Ventura drops incendiaries on Emmasingel complex. *(IWM C3268)*

21 Squadron Ventura I, AE692 YH-K, emerging from the Emmasingel smoke. *(IWM C3280)*

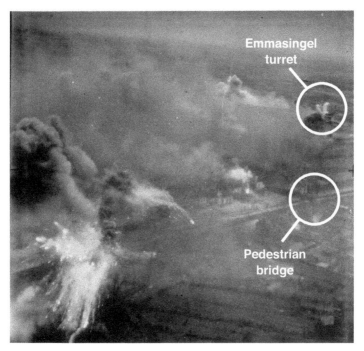

21 Squadron Ventura I, AE699 YH-J, view of Emmasingel target. *(IWM C3275)*

21 Squadron Ventura, AE692 YH-K, speeding away from Emmasingel. *(IWM C3276)*

incendiaries at 12.39 hours from a height of 130 feet. The street in the left foreground is called Hemelrijken.

The Emmasingel complex can only be recognized in IWM photo C3275with great difficulty, as it is completely enveloped in billowing clouds of smoke. To the right the Emmasingel turret, with flak-nest on top, can just be discerned. Bordering the Emmasingel the Eindhoven-Den Bosch railway line is to be seen along the Parallelweg. Just left of the Emmasingel turret a black iron structure built over the railway is visible; this was the pedestrian bridge.

The Emmasingel complex is completely hidden in huge clouds of smoke in IWM photo C3276. Note the emerging 21 Squadron Ventura to the left. The inscription on this photo reads: FEL 6.12.42 //M8" 150' H.K.21, making this Ventura I AE692 YH-K of 21 Squadron. Compared to a previous picture (C3280) from this aircraft, AE692 is making good its distance from the target escaping from the murderous flak. The houses in the foreground are standing along the Weverstraat, with the Brouwerstraat running away in the background.

Strijp Complex

Pictures from Ventura aircraft

An unrecognizable Strijp target is photographed by Ventura I, AE751 SB-M, of 464 Squadron (picture below). It attacked the Strijp target at 12.38hrs from 150 feet, dropping two 250lb GP TD one hour and 40x30 incendiaries. AE751 was crewed by Pilot Officer (Pilot) P. R. Roberts RAAF 404116, Pilot Officer (Nav) P. C. Middleton RAF 1151852, Flight Sergeant (WO/AG) W. H. Bowling RAF 922973 and Sergeant (AG) J. F. Webb RAAF 405959.

In the white triangle left-bottom a car can be recognized, this being the intersection between the Boschdijk and the Marconilaan which borders the Strijp complex on the left side. The terraced houses in the centre are along the Edisonstraat to the right and along the Marconilaan to the left. The road which originates from the white triangle and running straight up is the Johan vd Waals weg. The north side of the Strijp complex is running in parallel to this last road.

The inscription in the following photo reads: 8FEL 6.12.42 //M." 150' D.M. 464, which makes this Ventura I AE751 SB-M of 464 Squadron. AE751 is seen here tracking for home along the Frankrijkstraat. The church to the right is the St Paulus church.

464 Squadron Ventura, AE751 SB-M, picture directly after bomb-release on Strijp target. *(IWM C3278)*

In this photo other Venturas can just be seen. One is visible just above and to the right of the church and another is banking 45 degrees in the distance, in line with the first Ventura, in the upper part of the white cloud of smoke. *(IWM C3274)*

In this photo three other Venturas can be seen. One is clearly visible just above and to the right of the church, the second is just visible coming out to the left of the Frankrijkstraat above a row of hedges and the third is banking 45 degrees in the distance, in line with the first Ventura in the upper part of the white cloud of smoke.

Photo Reconnaissance (PR) Sortie

Many photographs were taken during the raid itself, including films by the RAF Film Unit, but their usefulness for assessing the results of the raid were predictably limited; some were at very low altitude, and thus oblique angles, and others were obscured by smoke. Thus it was important that a dedicated PR sortie was flown shortly after the raid to provide an accurate and immediate damage assessment, and this was performed by Squadron Leader J. E. Houlston DFC AFC (Pilot) and Warrant Officer J. L. Armitage DFC of 139 Squadron in Mosquito DZ314 XD-F, an aircraft on loan from 105 Squadron. They took off from Marham at 11.45 for Eindhoven to photograph the damage to the Philips complex – there does not seem to be an official record of their route but it seems likely they flew via Hoek den Holland and then passed between Den Bosch ('s-Hertogenbosch) and Tilburg, approaching Eindhoven from the north-west. They made two runs over the target at 800 feet between 13.00 and 13.05, half an hour after the raid. No bombs were carried and the weather was reported as 'light dull, 9/10 cloud at 800ft, visibility 5 miles'.[1] Again there is no official confirmation of the return route but a routing via Boxtel and the sea just north of Overflakkee would seem probable – they landed back at Marham at 14.05. It is sad to record that Houlston and Armitage were killed two weeks later (20 December 1942) during a raid by Mosquitos from 105 and 139 Squadrons on railway targets in the Oldenburg/Bremen area; they are buried in the Reichswald Forest War Cemetery.

The principal photo-reconnaissance run is shown in Map 7 which is based on an analysis of the photographs and (mainly) film that were shot during the sortie.

The film-material of this Mosquito has been re-worked to retrieve photographs from the original tape. To get a better idea of what parts of Eindhoven are covered, Map 7 has reference numbers relating to the ground features photographed. The map key follows the sequence of the film counter-indices.

1. Dommel brook Gestel
2. Bennekelstraat
3. Reinkenstraat
4. Willaert plein
5. Greenhouses florist 'Meulendijks'
6. Laagstraat
7. Hoogstraat
8. Botstraat
9. Kreeftstraat
10. Hagenkampweg
11. Mecklenburgstraat
12. Willem de Zwijgerstraat
13. Philips Emmasingel target
14. Gagelstraat
15. PSV stadium
16. Frederiklaan
17. Glaslaan

18. Philips Strijp target
19. Marconilaan
20. Voltastraat, Galvanistraat and Fultonhof
21. Boschdijk
22. Kattenstraat
23. Krekelstraat

This PR photo below shows extensive damage to the Strijp complex. The PR Mosquito made two passes across Eindhoven, coming in from the north-west. It arrived over the target area at 13.05 hours and at a height of 800 feet. On the first pass it overflew the Strijp target from left to right, this being one of the first photos taken. From the Strijp target it flew across the Emmasingel, both of which are in line on the route of the PR Mosquito.

PR photo of Strijp complex, Mosquito IV DZ314 XD-F, 139 Squadron. *(IWM C3281)*

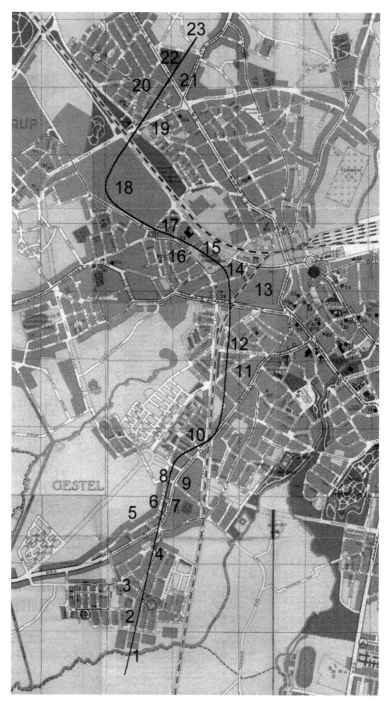

Map 7. Route of PR Mosquito DZ314 XD-F flown over Eindhoven by Squadron Leader J. E. Houlston DFC (pilot) and Warrant Officer J. L. Armitage (navigator). *(Paul Schepers)*

Further PR photo of Strijp target, Mosquito IV DZ314 XD-F, 139 Squadron. *(IWM C5756)*

The PR Mosquito has reached the eastern limit of the Strijp complex, showing the Glaslaan street which borders the complex at that side. Flying in Eastern direction it is soon to overfly the Emmasingel complex which is 500 to 600 metres away.

After flying over the Emmasingel it made a turn to the south of Eindhoven and reversed direction over the Hoogstraat for its second pass over the targets. This time it flew to the south of the Emmasingel and Strijp complexes. Unfortunately no photos could be found showing the Emmasingel complex.

DZ314 was lost on 8 December 1942, just two days after Operation OYSTER, on an operation to Den Helder while serving for 105 Squadron. Take off from Marham was at 11.58 hours; the crew, Flying Officer S. P. L. Johnson and Sergeant E. C. Draper, were taken prisoner.

The Damage to the Factories

The following pictures show bombardment damage photographed from the ground.

Radio erecting workshop on Emmasingel complex ruined. *(Philips Company Archives, ref. RZ 329-1)*

This picture shows the results from either Bostons of 107 Squadron, or Mosquitos from 105 or 139 Squadrons. Their high-explosive bombs have completely ripped two floors of this building apart. Note the sign which states 'Radio' at the workshop's entrance.

Veemgebouw building on the Strijp complex showing extensive damage from crashed Ventura AE902 EG-W of 487 Squadron. *(Philips Company Archives, ref.C19212, C30639)*

The Philips Clock tower on the Strijp complex. *(Regionaal Historisch Centrum Eindhoven, ref.0251699)*

The clock came to a standstill due to the attack, and remained indicating the time of the bombardment for the duration of the war. This photo was taken by an unknown photographer sometime in December 1942, despite the fact that this was strictly forbidden by the Germans, and photo-film material was very difficult to obtain.

The Emmasingel Lichttoren (light-tower) photographed after the bombardment. *(Regionaal Historisch Centrum Eindhoven Ref 0064410)*

This tower, part of the building known as the 'White Lady', is still a prominent feature in central Eindhoven. On 6 December 2011 a memorial to the victims of the raid was unveiled adjacent to this building.

Emmasingel photographed by B. Postema from Best in December 1942. *(Regionaal Historisch Centrum Eindhoven, Ref.0064307, reproduced by kind permission of B. Postema)*

The Operation OYSTER Evaluation Reports, which include the planning and execution of the raid, are at Appendix III and cover the intelligence interpretation (SA 176) of the effects of the raid, based on photographic evidence and de-briefing of the crews. This includes a small map showing the interpreters' assessment of obvious damage, from which it was assessed that many of the factory buildings were burning, albeit that the smoke made accurate interpretation difficult. Photographs were taken by thirty of the attacking aircraft.

Altogether forty-five tons of high-explosive (HE) bombs were dropped and eighteen tons of incendiaries. Among the buildings assessed to be burning fiercely were: workshops, components factory, glassworks, bakelite factory, lamp and valve factory, as well as important facilities such as the boiler house, compressor house and the plant's power station. Numerous other buildings were assessed as either probably or possibly burning. It was impossible to plot the many bomb bursts individually in the factory areas but a supplementary report (SA 177) indicates eleven areas in the surrounding town where HE and incendiary bombs could be seen to have fallen. Given the difficulty of concentrating some ninety aircraft over this well-defended target in just six minutes it can be said that the raid was a tactical success with relatively modest damage to other parts of Eindhoven by the standards of the time.

The Damage to civilian property

The following photographs are indicative of some of the damage in Eindhoven near the factories. This aspect of the story is expanded in the next chapter. However, these pictures are included to emphasize the difficulty of avoiding damage to property near the factories and so are intended to act as a 'lead-in' to the next chapter.

Demer shopping street. *(Stichting Eindhoven in Beeld, ref.26568)*

Harmoniestraat. *(Stichting Eindhoven in Beeld, ref.25063)*

Reporting the Raid to the Public

On arrival back at their bases the crews were met by press and movie newsreel reporters for arranged briefings so that the raid could be reported to the British people, who had had many setbacks in the war to endure in 1942 and thus were eager for positive news. It had been implied by Churchill, after the recent successes at El Alamein in North Africa, that the war had at last taken a turn for the better, with his words 'This may not be the beginning of the end, but at least it is the end of the beginning'. For three years, 'the beginning' had produced more bad news than good. So it was natural that the British authorities, and not least the leaders of the Royal Air Force, wanted to highlight any successful actions. Thus on the next day, 7 December, coincidentally the anniversary of the Japanese raid on Pearl Harbor which had brought the Americans into the war, the news of the raid on the Philips factories and the related diversionary raids were widely reported in the British press. However, no attempt was made to hide the extent of losses to the attacking force.

British Newspaper reports

In the days immediately following the raid (7 and 8 December) it was reported extensively in the British press. These reports were all essentially similar, no doubt based on the same briefings. The selection of headlines below sum up the flavour of the stories, followed by a summary of reports from several newspapers:

WAR'S BIGGEST DAYLIGHT RAID (*Daily Express*, 7 December 1942)

CREWS SAW NAZI GUNNERS ON BURNING FACTORY ROOFS – DUTCH WAVED (*News Chronicle*, 7 December 1942)

FACTORY HIT SECTION BY SECTION; NEW ACCOUNT OF EINDHOVEN RAID (*Daily Telegraph*, 8 December 1942)

The reports emphasized that the raids on 6 December were the heaviest bombing attack launched from Britain in daylight and, rightly, gave equal prominence to the diversionary force of eighty-five American heavy bombers, which were escorted by large numbers of Spitfires (see Appendix 4). American Flying Fortress aircraft pressed home heavy attacks on the Fives-Lille locomotive works at Lille while Liberators attacked the Abbeville-Drucat airfield, a major German fighter base. The reports stated that the Spitfire cover for the Flying Fortresses deterred the defending German fighters, although some stragglers were attacked. Also mentioned were smaller scale low-level raids by British fighters over a wide area of the enemy-held coast; Mustangs shot up troops, barges, shipping and railway targets in North Holland and other fighters damaged a power station at St Brieuc in Brittany.

Reporting the attack on the Philips factories at Eindhoven it was emphasized that they were German controlled and were vital targets, well defended by anti-aircraft guns and beyond the range of fighter cover. They were the chief plants in Europe for the production of radio valves – almost every weapon of modern warfare being dependent on radio valves (Radar was still secret and thus not mentioned directly). It was explained that there were two Philips sites at Eindhoven about half a mile apart, one just outside of the town (as it then was) and the other in a built up area. Together they employed 15,000 people on production for the German armed forces. The town site contained the lamp and valve assembly workshops and the rare gas plant – both important and highly vulnerable to bombing. The only way to attack without risking very heavy casualties to Dutch people had to be at low level, in daylight and good weather.

Squadron Leader Brian Wheeler DFC (pilot of Ventura EG-G, 487 Squadron) was reported thus:

It was the finest bombing I have ever seen on any target. The first thing I saw when I approached Eindhoven in the last wave of bombers was smoke towering up to 300 feet above the factory. That was only four minutes after the first bombs had dropped. Smoke and fire already covered a wide area.

One of the air gunners in the last wave was close enough to see a buckle on the uniform of a German AA gunner glinting in the sun. A Maori air gunner had his tin hat knocked off by shrapnel and two holes cut in his jacket, but he was unhurt.

Wing Commander R. H. 'Bob' Young AFC RAF (pilot of Ventura SB-H, 464 Squadron) gave a vivid account, mentioning that Dutch people were seen waving handkerchiefs and even flags as the aircraft raced low across the country. As he approached he saw two columns of smoke coming up from the targets. He said:

the Philips factory is a huge place in two parts – we took it in sections and attacked in waves – very methodical – we went in low to make sure of hitting the target properly and to avoid hitting Dutch people.

He commented that the aircraft were so close that the slipstream made it very rough for the aircraft at the rear. Bob Young continued to say that:

I pulled back on the control column and pressed the bomb release and scraped over the tops of the high buildings. My rear gunner saw our bombs enter the building we had aimed at … he told us it was on fire and he could see Germans firing from the roofs of buildings which were blazing underneath them. We kept straight ahead so that our automatic cameras would do their stuff … still very low we had to lift over electric cables and twice brushed poplar trees … there were many souvenirs of such low flight – twigs, pieces of shrapnel and lots of birds. One aircraft even brought back a duck.

Wing Commander Young, who broadcast his account, paid tribute to the skill of the navigators who had kept the attacking force on its course by identifying landmarks which flashed by in a split second only a few feet below them.

Dutch newspaper reports

Naturally the German dominated Dutch press put a different complexion on the raid, emphasizing the casualties to the Dutch people and the damage to Eindhoven generally, rather than the Philips works. For instance the *Dagblad van het Zuiden* ran this article:

British aircraft attacked Eindhoven

The Hague, 7 December 1942
In a British attempt to attack the Philips' Works in Eindhoven by a rather large formation of aircraft, the dropping of bombs of any calibre caused extensive damage to buildings in residential quarters of the town. Public buildings and traffic-plants were also damaged. Specifically the hospital in Eindhoven was badly hit, while the St Catharina church was destroyed. After the bombardment the civilian population was machine-gunned.

From reports received so far, the civilian population has suffered a loss of more than 100 casualties, among them many women and children. A great number of citizens were badly or slightly wounded. Numerous persons are reported missing. There was no damage to military objectives.

Sixteen British aircraft were shot down. It is brought especially to your attention, that the raid was executed on the festive day of Saint Nicholas (Sinterklaas), which is – as it is well known – in the Netherlands a special day for family visits in the town and from the countryside to the town. Hence the great number of victims.

OFFICIAL ANNOUNCEMENT:
1. Missing people have to be reported to the local authorities. The names of the citizens, who were killed, wounded or still missing have also to be given to the constabulary.
2. Clear the roads. People are ordered to clear the roads and pavements from glass, debris and other goods.

3. The gas supply may be interrupted because of necessary repair works.
4. The citizens are advised to drink only water from the municipal waterworks.

The following extracts are from a local Eindhoven newspaper, the *Eindhovens Dagblad*:

The following moment the city, where an electric bulb-factory is established which is marked as a strategic target, changes into hell. Bombs whistle, German flak from roofs on the Philips buildings rattles, noise of breaking glass, air-raid sirens, frightening yelling. The city burns. The whole Demer destroyed, Philips buildings, the Binnenziekenhuis, the Fellenoord, extensive damage to the Catharinakerk. Approximately 140 civilians die in the attack.

An eye-witness [then a child], living at the 'Smalle Haven' with a marvellous view to the Catharinakerk, relates: 'Because of Sinterklaas I had received an 'Amsterdams pakhuis' (toy), and was playing with it under the window. When looking out of the window I see an aircraft approaching very low, trailing smoke. The aircraft diverts so as to miss the churches' spires, and something falls from beneath it. A tremendous shock follows, the windows burst. Immediately followed by a second bomb burst. This must have been the bomb which hit the Binnenziekenhuis. More successive bomb-bursts followed.

(These reports have been translated into English by the Dutch co-authors of the book.)

It is worth recording at this point that the people of Eindhoven hold no bitterness against the British for Operation OYSTER, seeing it as a painful but necessary part of the struggle to defeat Nazi Germany and thus restore their freedom. Naturally, the raid forms a very significant memory to them, since it brought the horrors of war so close. To the British it was just one of many such actions, although a necessary step on a very long and hard road. For both nations it is a story not to be forgotten, especially given the human tragedies involved.

Note

1. NA Kew, ORB, RAF Marham.

Chapter Seven

The Cost to Philips and Eindhoven

We have already learned, in our introduction, from joint author Kees Rijken, how the raid was seen by him as a fourteen-year old living in Eindhoven. However, much closer to the object of the raid is the personal account of Frits Philips, then the director general of the Philips factories, translated and reproduced here:

The Bombardments.

The two bombardments of the allied air forces on our factories in Eindhoven were among the most shocking events I experienced during the war years. For us they came totally unexpectedly. In our opinion we produced such a tiny amount of material for the Germans that this never could justify a bombardment. The first bombardment took place on 6 December 1942, the second on 30 March 1943. The board of directors were left completely ignorant about them. The same was valid for our staff in America. Afterwards I heard from my father how offended he had felt that no consultation whatsoever had taken place with our staff who were residing in Allied territory. They had better knowledge and intelligence data regarding the actual situation and could have told exactly which parts of our plants to put out of action in order to achieve maximum effectiveness. For instance, had a pilot dropped only one bomb on our factory for broadcast equipment in Hilversum, then our people would have taken care to sabotage all vital objects. After the war it came to our knowledge, that the Allied air force had refrained from such an attack, due to the fact that this factory was situated in the middle of residential quarters.

The bombardment of 6 December was in our opinion a result of the too-good-to-be-true graphs, which we produced for the meetings with the German commission from Berlin, so that they could return home very satisfied. It was production planning which never was achieved. These graphs were seen by a number of employees, some of whom were members of the local resistance. For them it was easy enough to forward these documents to the Allies, resulting in a moment at which the other side would shout: 'Well well, look at this productivity from Philips in Eindhoven!' The effort we took *not* to be so productive at all, was not being forwarded to the Allies so readily.

That fatal Sunday morning my wife and I, along with my brother-in-law van Riemsdijk and my sister Jetty were visiting a niece whose child was being christened. After the church service we were drinking the usual cup of surrogate coffee, when suddenly we saw a formation of low-flying aircraft approaching in the distance. At the time we were near the outskirts of the town, so we could see everything very clearly and, because of the great number of aircraft involved, our suspicion was that it had to be British machines. Our first reaction was: 'Are they going to bomb the Eindhoven railway station?' At the same moment we saw the first bombs being dropped, we heard the crashing of the impact and with a feeling of deprivation the realization came that our town was being bombed! As fast as we could, my brother-in-law and myself cycled to the De Laak, where fortunately nobody was harmed. At some distance we saw the Demer, the most important shopping-street in Eindhoven, which was already ablaze.

From our house I took my bike to the city centre. Only now I realized that it had been our factories which were the target of the bombardment. Because of the momentary silence in the air I thought that the bombardment had finished; however when cycling to the Emmasingel yet another wave of bombers rushed in to the attack, so that I had to seek shelter in a cycle shop in a hurry. In the meantime I had already noticed that the office building had been directly hit several times. A fire had developed, but despite this I wanted to rescue two portraits of my father and uncle Gerard at all cost, which had been painted by Jan Veth in 1916 at the occasion of the 25th anniversary of the company. Fortunately all the other portraits and valuables had been stowed safely away long ago. The portraits were hanging in the boardroom at ground level. Through a window I climbed inside, with a helmet on my head. The fire brigade had joined me and I distributed amongst them a box of good cigars which had been left by my father. I myself was able to rescue a silver cigar set from my desk. As I went to enter the boardroom, a large piece of ceiling came crashing down. The firemen would not let me enter the room, they found it much too dangerous and so I had very sadly to offer the portraits to the fire. The building itself was burnt out completely.

The destruction in the city and our factories was enormous. The time of the bombardment, on a Sunday morning after Sinterklaas evening, was chosen because the factories were closed, but the death toll among the civilians was over one hundred, the hospital was crowded with injured people and part of Eindhoven was destroyed by fire. My wife and my sister Jetty visited all the wounded. They told us about the conversations they had had and there was one most remarkable similarity in them: not one of these Eindhoven citizens blamed the Allies! There was one man who had lost his wife and three of his seven children; no complaints could be heard from him. The morale of the Eindhoven population during that bombardment was exemplary.

My personal reaction after the bombardment is still a living memory. It was deeply emotional to see the factories, which had been erected with such devotion and offered jobs to thousands of people, go up in flames. For me this meant a terrible confrontation with the reality of war, though I realized that this war against the Germans had to be fought hard, if they were to be conquered. This thought reconciled me to this hellish scene. I could understand it. But at the same time I made myself the promise not to let it deject me, I wanted to see it as a proof of strength of the Allies, who could give a blow where they thought it was necessary. I had the feeling that now it was my duty to put a new heart into our personnel. I knew of Philips employees who were very downhearted, which I could very well understand. A piece of our life was destroyed. That was the load of war we had

Frits Philips inspecting damage to the Strijp complex. This photo was taken after the liberation of Eindhoven, September 1944. *(IWM C1250)*

to shoulder. Well, that had to be done in the proper way. Along with this thought my industrial mentality surfaced once more: it was clear that we had to grab this opportunity to rebuild our factories to be better and more effective than ever and the planning to achieve that would start the next day.

Already the following morning I had visitors from The Hague. Our commissioner Mr Woltersom, Mr Hirschfeld and Ir Ringers, the government commissioner for reconstruction, came to see the results of the bombardment themselves. Ringers and myself were on good terms and in this situation it was his help we needed the most.

He did not disappoint us. My immediate concern was to commence the repair of our factories as soon as possible, utilizing all our personnel so as to prevent the deportation of our workmen by the Germans. In the first months all the effort went into clearing away the debris. After an air bombardment the glass damage is enormous, and it took our people a long time to clear the innumerable windows. This was followed by a provisional shielding with cardboard, it was winter time, but also because there was no glass. Meanwhile, there was no way to make good the production capacity.

We circulated two different stories about the bombardment. The Germans were told that the inflicted damage was not serious. The production had suffered though, but we would be back to full capacity in a short time. This was deemed necessary to avoid the Germans from deporting our people to Germany, and we succeeded. The other story was circulated internally only, in the sure knowledge that in doing so the resistance would pick it up and brief the Allies accordingly. The content of that story was that the bombardment had been tremendously effective, and that the squadrons did not need to come back. Also in this version the truth was somewhere halfway. Towards the Germans every bombardment was utilized to the utmost to explain the arrears of all kinds of deliveries. In reality the damage owing to the bombardment was not complete. Slowly we realized that with disasters like this bombardment or fires there are three stages of recognition. The first impression is: What an enormous damage! Followed by the second stage, whereby it is established that it might have been worse. It is found for example that heavy machinery can still be repaired. This last circumstance certainly has contributed to the fact that, despite the never ending Allied bombardments, the German wartime industry has suffered less than might be expected on the basis of photographic material. Finally, in the third stage, the conclusion is reached that the inflicted damage was substantial.[1]

Naturally Frits Philips viewed the bombing of the factories with mixed emotions. Although fundamentally opposed to the German control of his nation and company he was concerned to keep his workforce as safe as possible and avoid a situation where the Germans might think there were surplus staff who could be transferred to work elsewhere, perhaps to greater danger. So there was a difficult balance to be achieved – make the Germans think that production could soon be restored while continuing with the covert policy of pretending to be more productive than was actually the case. The policy of overstating production may have caused British Intelligence to believe that Philips was a richer target than it was. The Dutch resistance undoubtedly fed the inflated production estimates to the British, thus raising the position of the company in the target assessment process.

However, such arguments are largely theoretical. Of greater value was the increasing importance of radio valves to the opposing forces – for instance, the Germans were improving their radar systems to counter British bombers and the British developed their systems for the Battle of the Atlantic, which was the theatre of war which posed the greatest threat to the survival of the United Kingdom and eventually the ability to mount the invasion of Europe. There can be little doubt that the Philips works, with their pre-eminent position in the electronic field would be attacked sooner or later: as a British newspaper, the *Daily Express*, reported the day after the raid 'Almost every weapon of modern warfare is nowadays directly dependent on the radio valve'. Frits Philips' disappointment that the Allies had not sought advice from his offices outside German control was unrealistic given the need for extreme secrecy in the planning of such raids; any slip in security on this matter would have resulted in the defences being strengthened.

Naturally, the British and German interpretation of the effect on both the Philips Factory and the citizens of Eindhoven were different. Neither side was averse to biasing their versions for propaganda reasons. For instance, *The Bomber Command War Diaries*[2] stated:

Bombing was accurate and severe damage was caused to the factory, which was situated in the middle of the town. Because the raid was deliberately carried out on a Sunday, there were few casualties in the factory but several bombs fell in nearby streets and 148 Dutch people and 7 German soldiers were killed. Full production was not reached again until six months after the raid.

It may be that the authors of the *War Diaries* had inadvertently absorbed the convenient myth (spread widely in later accounts) that the raid was on a Sunday for humanitarian reasons; however, we have seen that the raid was actually delayed by weather from a working day. The losses to Dutch civilians are, however, honestly recorded, reflecting the acceptance that attacking a target in the middle of a large town made some casualties inevitable.

The *Daily Express* made the point that 'low level attack in full daylight was the only way to smash the place without risking heavy casualties among Dutch civilians. The RAF waited for exactly the right weather for the job'. This shows that the press briefing had made the point about dependency on weather conditions. Also on the day after the raid (7 December) the *News Chronicle* reported:

> Immediate reconnaissance indicated that practically the whole of the vast factory had been wrecked by our bombers. The attack was timed to ensure maximum damage with minimum loss of life to the Dutch people.

Minimum loss of life is, of course, in this case a relative term: the 148 Dutch people killed makes a sad statistic, but is probably much lower than if the target had been attacked from high altitude by the large force of heavy bombers which would have been needed to achieve comparable damage to the factories.

As related in the previous chapter, an account by the Dutch newspaper *Dagblad van het Zuiden* on 7 December 1942 showed a different emphasis, which is understandable given the control of the country and its press by the Germans

On the fiftieth anniversary of the raid, the *Eindhovens Dagblad* of Saturday 5 December 1992 published the following account with personal recollections:

> The following moment the city, where an electric bulb factory is established which is marked as a strategic target, changes into hell. Bombs whistle, German flak from roofs on the Philips buildings rattles, noise of breaking glass, air-raid sirens, frightening yelling. The city burns. The whole Demer destroyed, Philips buildings, the Binnenziekenhuis, the Fellenoord, extensive damage to the Catharinakerk. Approximately 140 civilians die in the attack.

The Demer and Fellenoord are two civilian housing city-areas of Eindhoven situated very close to the targeted Philips complexes. Consequent damage to either was hard to avoid.

The aircraft which hit the Binnenziekenhuis, a hospital, and the Catharinakerk, a church, must have been a Boston of either 88 or 226 Squadron, since only bomb-blast damage was inflicted. This rules out the Venturas which were also carrying incendiary bombs. The Mosquito force did not attack the small target at all. When looking at the flight-paths of the Bostons, these buildings were directly in their path in front of the small target.)

Demer ruined. *(Stichting Eindhoven in Beeld, ref.25513)*

Citizens of Eindhoven cleaned out the ruins after Operation OYSTER. The Demer was, and still is, a busy shopping street in the city centre of Eindhoven. Many civilians were killed in a pub which suffered a direct hit of one of the Bostons of 88 or 226 Squadron attacking the Emmasingel complex.

Binnenziekenhuis (hospital) wrecked. *(Stichting Eindhoven in Beeld, ref.28481)*

As seen from the attacking aeroplanes, the Binnenziekenhuis (hospital) was just in front of the release point for the Emmasingel complex. Unfortunately a few bombs fell short. The hospital was demolished after the war. Currently a shopping centre occupies this location, called the Heuvelgalerie. The houses in the extreme left foreground (only roofs can be seen) are still in use today as pubs and restaurants. The street along them, the Jan van Lieshoutstraat, leads to the market.

The following is a statement about civilian casualties, issued by the Nazi-appointed Mayor of Eindhoven, and translated into English. It puts a predictably anti-British slant on the raid:

Een voorloopige doodenlijst

LIJST VAN OVERLEDENEN OP 6 DECEMBER 1942, WAARVAN OVERLIJDENSAKTEN ZIJN OPGEMAAKT.

De ramp, welke over Eindhoven gekomen is als gevolg van den laffen aanval der Britsche vliegers op leven en eigendom onzer ingezetenen, heeft naast een enorme materieele schade ook een zeer groot aantal slachtoffers onder de burgers der stad en onder vreemdelingen, in onze stad op bezoek, geëischt.

Alhoewel de op alle getroffen punten onmiddellijk ingezette opruimings- en bergingsploegen met de grootste krachtsinspanning onafgebroken hebben gewerkt, om de slachtoffers te bergen, is men daarin tot heden nog niet geheel kunnen slagen, door de volledige verwoesting op vele punten der stad aangericht en de gevaren, aan het opruimingswerk verbonden.

Naarmate de opruimingsarbeid vordert, vindt men telkens nog nieuwe slachtoffers, die onder het puin hunner woningen een droevig einde hebben gevonden.

Om tegemoet te komen aan het begrijpelijk verlangen der ingezetenen om zekerheid te krijgen ten aanzien van het lot van nabestaanden, vrienden en kennissen en aan veler ongewisheid een einde te maken, geef ik hieronder de namen bekend der gedoode inwoners van Eindhoven, zoowel als van slachtoffers, die elders woonachtig waren. Ik vestig de aandacht erop, dat deze opgave alleen betreft de slachtoffers, wier identiteit onomstootelijk is vastgesteld en dat deze opgave, zooals reeds gezegd, helaas in de komende dagen nog zal moeten worden aangevuld.

Mijn warmen dank betuigende aan de ingezetenen, die in deze dagen van zulk een waren burgerzin getuigenis hebben afgelegd en het zware werk der officieele diensten door hun spontane en belanglooze medewerking hebben helpen verlichten, beveel ik de getroffen families in aller blijvende belangstelling aan, opdat het zware leed dat hen getroffen heeft, zooveel mogelijk gelenigd zal worden. De Burgemeester van Eindhoven,

EINDHOVEN, 12 December 1942.   Dr. H. A. PULLES.

Translated content of above text:

An interim death roll, List of casualties on December 6th 1942, whose death certificates have been drawn up.

The disaster, that came over Eindhoven as a result of the cowardly assault of British airmen on life and property of our citizens has, besides an enormous material damage, resulted in a very large number of casualties of inhabitants and strangers in our town.

In spite of the salvage operations all victims could not yet be found. As the operations advance, new victims are found who had been buried under the ruins of their houses.

To meet the understandable wishes of inhabitants for certainty about the fate of relatives, friends or acquaintances, I hereby publish the names of the victims who were identified so far. Regrettably this summary will have to be updated.

I am very grateful to those inhabitants who have shown such a true testimony of civil spirit. They have lightened the heavy burden of the public services by their spontaneous and selfless co-operation. I recommend the stricken families in everybody's sympathy, so that their grief will be alleviated as much as possible.

The Mayor of Eindhoven
Dr H. A. Pulles

(Dr H. A. Pulles, a veterinary surgeon, was a Dutch Nazi who was appointed burgomaster by the German authorities.)

The funerals of the civilian victims were mostly arranged for the Thursday after the raid in various parish churches in the town, followed by burial in the cemeteries. The real cause of death (the RAF raid) was not allowed to be given in published death notices. Instead, other indeterminate phrases were used, such as: 'In His infinite Goodness God called to himself', or 'Today died by a fatal accident … , or 'Died suddenly …'.

The interim death roll and later supplements form Appendix VI.

Memorial for Eindhoven casualties of the St Antonius Fellenoord parish. *(Paul Schepers)*

Eyewitness accounts and personal interest stories

On 6 December 1942 Operation OYSTER caused the Philips factories in Eindhoven severe damage and the German war industry received a considerable blow as a result. Despite the careful Allied preparations the city of Eindhoven itself was also heavily hit. In the massive six-minute attack sixty tons of incendiary and high explosive ordnance were dropped. Not only the Philips factories but also several city districts were changed into an inferno. One hundred and thirty five civilians lost their lives and many more were wounded. Subsequently there has never been a word of reproach to the Allies from either civilians or government authorities (any resentment would have been addressed to the German occupiers). However, there are still a number of survivors for whom the raid had been a very traumatic experience. Some of them have been interviewed to recall what they observed and experienced on that day. Four people tell their story below as they remember in 2012, three of them living, during the war, in the Philipsdorp and a man who lost his mother in the centre of Eindhoven.

The reader will find a street map in Chapter 9 which will help to identify the places referred to in the eye witness accounts which follow.

Jeff Haneveer

The first of the interviewees is the now eighty-year-old Jeff Haneveer, born and raised in Philipsdorp and during the Second World War living in the Fredericklaan 26 directly opposite one of the housing blocks that were to receive a direct hit resulting in both casualties and severely injured victims. Jeff Haneveer was confronted in a very unpleasant way with the brutal methods of the German occupation force soon after the occupation. When on his free school day he was walking to the Boy Scouts' club building while wearing his Cub uniform he was grasped roughly and abruptly by a German officer and beaten about his face several times. It turned out that scouting – of origin British – had become a forbidden organization. Despite being aged only eleven he swore revenge, after having recovered from the initial shock.

Without even informing his parents he now went to a German military airfield situated near Eindhoven armed with a notepad (called his 'warbook'), pencil and binoculars. This aerodrome was originally known as Burgerluchthaven Welschap, during the German occupation as Fliegerhorst Eindhoven, and nowadays is Eindhoven Airport; it is from this airport that author Paul Schepers regularly enjoys flying General Aviation aeroplanes at the EACm (Eindhoven Aero Club motorflying). Via a sneak route Jeff managed to evade the strong German military security and approach closely to the airfield to be able to watch what was going on there. His revenge was sweet, knowing 'how upset the Germans would be if they only would know' that all their flying movements and other activities on their *Fliegerhorst* were noted down accurately (Now only the cover of this notebook remains. Finally the notebook was discovered by Jeff's father, who took the sensible precaution removing its content so as to avoid this information falling into the wrong hands – the Germans.)

On the Sunday afternoon of 6 December, the day on which the children are given presents and sweets each year by the Holy Bishop Saint Nicolas, around noon there came the totally unexpected Allied aerial bombardment on the Philips factories. Eleven at the time, Jeff and his parents and older brother were sitting in the living room of their home having a pleasant chat and he was playing with and admiring the presents he had received from Saint Nicolas the night before. The serene Sunday rest was abruptly interrupted by the sound of aircraft flying at very low level. Through his spying experience he was able to recognize, as could most of his friends,

The cover of young Jeff Haneveer's 'War Book'. *(Jeff Haneveer)*

Jeff Haneveer as a Cub Scout. *(Jeff Haneveer)*

that the noise produced by the aircraft engines was not originating from German planes. This was immediately confirmed when the German anti-aircraft guns went into action, as well as the return fire from the planes' machine guns.

Time for conversation had run out. In a hunched position Jeff was looking outside to observe a seemingly giant hand lifting the opposite housing block into the sky to smash it thunderously down to the ground again in large billowing clouds of dust. At the same time the ceiling of his own house came crashing down as a result of the enormous blast of air pressure. Windows and window frames were torn from the walls and furniture was flying about. Jeff and his parents were smashed to the ground by all this violence but miraculously escaped unharmed. Buried in dust they scrambled up again. Within only a few minutes their very neat house had been turned into an uninhabitable building. Many times worse, however, was the situation outside in the street. The housing block that he had seen lifted in the air was reduced to a large smoking ruin. As suddenly as the raid had started, an ominous silence descended after the deafening noise.

As clearly as yesterday, Jeff remembers that his mother was very upset and was crying continuously and that his eight years older brother had run outside to dig in the ruins for possible survivors. Meanwhile, several other local men and boys were digging feverishly in the rubble. The first survivor dug out from the ruins was Jeff's opposite neighbour and girlfriend, the nine-year-old Liesje Duijts. White, silent and fully in shock, she was covered in a warm woollen blanket and was taken care of in one of the lesser damaged buildings. After a while Jeff's brother returned home. His parent's questioning looks were answered with dry sobbing: 'It is really more than terrible!'

Ton van der Heijde

The second interview was with the now eighty-three-year-old Ton van der Heijde, at the time the fourteen-year-old friend and neighbour of Jeff living at Fredericklaan 22. Having a light cold, so tells Ton, he was in bed playing with a metal aeroplane he had been presented with from Saint Nicolas. Suddenly he heard a great many very low-flying aeroplanes. He also immediately and clearly realized that these were British rather than German bombers; the Allied bomber pilots always synchronized the speed of their engines but the German pilots did not, so a German plane could always be recognized by the resulting beat sound, which was both annoying and distinctive. Ton jumped out of bed immediately to catch a glimpse of them via the rear window. Apart from Ton, only his mother, his youngest sister and their neighbour's girlfriend were at home. His father and three other sisters were gone for sports as usual on a Sunday morning. From the sudden loud noise of the German anti-aircraft guns Ton realized better than anyone what was happening and he quickly went downstairs.

At the very moment he entered the downstairs hall a bomb exploded in the opposite building block. As a result of the explosion shock wave, the front door was blown off its hinges. He was only just able to evade this heavy door that came flying directly towards him to crash into a wall behind with an enormous smack. Everybody at home dived into the cellar which, though small and shallow, gave them a sure feeling of protection. When things calmed down they left their shelter after about half an hour only to be confronted with enormous chaos. All the plaster and paintings were torn off the walls and ceilings and shreds of the curtain waved in gaping holes where once the properly washed and shining windows had been. A statue of Jesus Christ with spread arms and standing on a pedestal in the master bedroom had lost both its arms as a result of the blast and looked at them seemingly very sad and very upset.

In the street the destruction and confusion were many times worse. The four houses opposite, among them Frederickslaan 117 and 119, were completely wiped away and the whole street was full of debris and the remains of rooftop tiles. An unreal panicky mood had descended whereby the inhabitants of the surrounding houses were walking past one another, seemingly without purpose. Very understandably Ton's mother, his sister, and, of course, he himself were extremely worried about the absent members of the family. Happily, however, they soon turned up one after the other, all unharmed.

Shortly after the bombardment Ton went back to the house to pick up the metal aeroplane present, a Fokker G-1, he had been given by Saint Nicolas. It was nowhere to be found – a loss he is still mourning to this day. What was found though was a dud in their very backyard. It was his neighbour Jeff's older brother Sjarel who was 'requested' by the Germans to remove this bomb and to carry it by means of a wheelbarrow to a waiting army truck for further disposal.

After the bombardment they had to evacuate their damaged house and had to live elsewhere during the time their house was being repaired. For a short while, together with his parents and four sisters, they lived in the Eindhoven area called 'het Witte Dorp' (the White Village) in the house of his mother's uncle in the 1ᵉ Wilakkersstraat. This was right next to the DAF factories, and knowing that these factories were turning out trucks for the German army it was not considered a very safe area from recent experience. Soon after they relocated to the Tongelre district of Eindhoven, where they had to stay for half a year awaiting their house to be fully renovated.

A final word from Ton was that though his story recollects the events as they happened, what they do not recall are the emotions and the suffering that went along with them. For example, one night directly after the bombardment, while staying at his uncle's house together with his four sisters, Ton was asleep in a large bed when it decided to collapse in the middle of the night with an enormous bang. Needless to stay all of the family were scared stiff as a result.

Liesje Duijts-van den Broek
From Jeff Haneveer's story the reader can recall Liesje Duijts, the now eighty-year-old Mrs Duijts-van den Broek. She was living opposite Jeff and Ton at Frederickslaan 119. Mrs Duijts explained that, surprised by the heavy roar of aircraft engines, her father, mother, brother, two sisters and herself had gone outside quickly to see with their own eyes what was going on. When the first aeroplanes opened fire though, father Duijts immediately reversed direction and ordered everyone inside yelling, 'Naar binnen jongens het is niet pluis' (Inside everybody this is not looking well). Mrs Duijts still remembers precisely how scared she was, that she was crying and that her mother was comforting her and saying to her 'Je moet niet bang zijn Liesje, we zijn fijn bij elkaar en er kan ons niets gebeuren' (You need not be afraid Liesje, we are all together and nothing can happen to us). The family had just crouched together in the kitchen when the bomb impacted. As if it was yesterday she remembers that the wall against which she was leaning suddenly was pressing in her back and immediately she was lying motionless underneath the debris. Also she remembers she had wet her pants because of the terror overcoming her, but she did not care a bit. She knew she was going to die, but also that did not concern her. What had concerned her terribly, however, was the knowledge that she was not to see her mother anymore because she never went to church and would surely not go to heaven but to hell instead.

She was lying face down and half turned, and was nearly choking due to the weight of the collapsed wall and barely able to breathe through a small opening in her mouth. How long she was lying like that she cannot recall but it felt like many hours. When the last of the heavy stones and debris that were pressing her down were removed it turned daylight again all of a sudden. Many hands had helped to excavate her from the ruins. Completely dazed she had not been able to speak, think or do anything anymore. Not even cry!

After neighbours had taken care of her for several days Liesje was transferred to a monastery in the vicinity of Eindhoven. It was only here that she heard that her mother and grandmother had perished in the bombardment. Her mother had died instantly and her grandmother was found half-charred, lying on the still burning stove underneath the debris. Her father and brother were admitted to hospital for a long time with, respectively, a broken back and a serious leg wound. It was to be many months later before she was to see them again. Both her sisters received only light wounds and had escaped with a fright. Liesje had a strongly developed tie with her grandmother who lived in their house. The way she was found under the debris is for her still a very emotional and traumatic experience. From time to time she still has, even more than seventy years later, frightening nightmares as a result. She has been assured that her grandmother was killed immediately upon bomb impact and only afterwards ended up lying across the stove. Unfortunately, this does not ease the pain she feels from her grandmother's death. The fright of the happenings of the Sinterklaas bombardment on 6 December 1942 has never vanished from Liesje. Still she cringes in panic at the sound of an unexpected low-passing aircraft.

Jan Jansen

The last interviewee was Jan Jansen, now a married man in his seventies and proud father of a son and grandfather to four grandchildren. Until the age of sixty-five Jan ran and owned a very successful butcher shop in the city centre of Eindhoven. Despite Jan being only aged one at the time of the bombardment, and clearly not able to remember anything of it, it has still haunted him all his life. The exact reason for this Jan has never known. The only thing he came to know was that his mother – Bertha Kwappenberg – was expecting but that during her pregnancy complications had developed. These were serious enough to have her admitted to the maternity ward of the Eindhoven Binnenziekenhuis. It was in this hospital that Jan's mother was lying when the 6 December bombardment started. Of the bombs that missed their target, unfortunately four came down on – of all places – that very maternity ward. As a result the ward was completely wiped away, including patients, personnel and furniture. From that time for the little Jan, who never knew his mother, she was abruptly wiped from his still young life.

Jan grew up not knowing what a normal healthy family life was supposed to be. His father drank, left half his weekly wage behind in the pub and hardly ever cared for his son. In his father's life there never was another woman who could have taken over the mother role. All this meant for Jan a very difficult and lonely youth in which he had to educate himself, so to speak. Never was there any mention of his mother and, as a result, he never knew anything about her. It was as if he had never had a mother, nor had she ever existed. What remained for Jan was a small photograph of Jan in his mother's arms. Not a day has passed that Jan has not been thinking of her. The small photograph was one of his most precious possessions for the remainder of his life.

Once retired, Jan enjoyed his own family life together with his wife, children and grandchildren. But the thought of his mother would not let go, and he told his wife: 'En nu ga ik mijn moeder zoeken' (And now I am going to find my mother). From that moment onwards a difficult but unsuccessful quest started for a possible grave of his mother. He visited all the churchyards in Eindhoven and surrounding villages (during the war the Jansen family lived near Nuenen, a village to the north-east of Eindhoven). He also studied churchyard registers and council hall archives. The only information he ever found were two formal death certificates containing, unfortunately, mismatched information.

For Jan Jansen the unveiling of the OYSTER monument was a very emotional happening (see Chapter 9). Embedded in the monument's pedestal there is a stainless tube containing a document naming all civilian and military casualties who perished as a result of the bombing. The pedestal also contains the photograph of Jan's mother. For Jan finally his mother has found a well-deserved final resting place. Weekly Jan and his wife pay a visit to the monument that for him symbolizes the grave of his mother. After all those years he can be very close to her for a while and bring her some flowers.

Notes

1. Philips, Frits (Director General of Philips factories), *45 Jaar met Philips.*
2. Middlebrook and Everitt, *The Bomber Command War Diaries*, p.329.

Chapter Eight

Aftermath and Hindsight

Wartime

When the dust had settled in Eindhoven and the euphoria of the after raid parties at the British bomber bases had died away with the headaches, all the people involved returned to the tempo of their lives as it was in wartime – 'returned to normal' is not a phrase that could be applied until well after victory and peace had been achieved. The people of Eindhoven had to look after the wounded, bury the dead and clear up the wreckage in the Philips factories and the city. They lived on stoically under the German occupation for another two years and suffered further casualties and damage from air raids and land battles until American forces liberated the city on 18 September 1944. The Philips Company repaired the factories as best they could and resumed production, albeit rather slowly as Frits Philips explained (see Chapter 7).

The bomber crews of 2 Group returned to their actions against targets at sea and in the nearer parts of Europe, albeit with smaller-scale raids. Some targets were attacked repeatedly, such as the railway viaduct at Morlaix in Brittany over which supplies to the U-boats at Brest were carried. Casualties continued to occur, both in action against the enemy and through accidents – many of these have been referred to previously in relation to individual crew members.

The Ventura aircraft were phased out of front-line service as 1943 progressed. The Bostons continued to give valuable service throughout the war, not least as part of 2nd Tactical Air Force after the invasion of Normandy. The Mosquito squadrons went from strength to strength capitalizing on the enormous versatility of the de Havilland design. Their speed and manoeuvrability made them the ideal machine for intruder raids. Indeed another, smaller, strike on the Philips factories by Mosquitos took place on 30 March 1943, aimed at hindering the recovery of production. Wing Commander Pelly-Fry's comments on the merits of the aircraft types are worth quoting:

One thing I was sure of, the Boston was just about the nicest, toughest, safest, fastest and most pleasing operational aeroplane that ever happened. Later on, let it be whispered ever so softly, I kind of got to have a passion for the aeroplane to beat all aeroplanes; its name, that magic word Mosquito.

Perhaps Pelly-Fry's admiration for the Boston was enhanced by the fact that his badly damaged aircraft got him back from Eindhoven, aided by his considerable skill – and it was no doubt a more comfortable aeroplane for the pilot.

It is not possible to assess accurately the effects of the raid on loss and delay to production by Philips. The company was keen to mislead the Germans, not least to avoid their staff being taken to an uncertain future working elsewhere. Indeed the threat of such redeployment led to strikes, at which time Frits Philips was imprisoned for several months. However, one estimate that the raid cost six months' lost production might be taken as reasonable, since history has shown, both in Britain and Germany, that manufacturing processes recovered faster after aerial bombardment than pictures of the damage would suggest at first sight. In particular, the heavier machine tools in factories proved to be resistant to serious damage.

If, indeed, the equivalent of six months' interruption is accepted then the raid may be said to have been worthwhile, even allowing for the loss of fourteen aircraft and many of their crew members. The raid took place at a critical time in the war. The Axis forces in North Africa, which threatened the Middle East oil supplies of the Allies, had suffered a setback but had yet to be defeated. The Battle of the Atlantic was approaching a climax and continued heavy shipping losses would have been disastrous. The German army at Stalingrad was in a perilous position but was still fighting. The great Allied air offensive against Germany by the British and American air forces had yet to develop to its full force – eventually it grew to represent the 'second front' that Stalin wanted, absorbing large numbers of troops and armaments in the defence of the 'Fatherland'. But all this was in the future at the time of Operation OYSTER – victory was apparently distant and uncertain.

Even as the major air offensive built up many tactical diversions occurred, not least the need to attack the French railway system before the invasion of Normandy and strikes against the German Vengeance weapons (V-1 and V-2). The air strikes against the V-1 and V-2 weapons started with the 600-bomber raid in August 1943 on the Peenemünde complex, followed by many attacks on the launching sites. Even with these strenuous countermeasures the V-weapons cost the British 8,958 dead and 24,504 injured.[1] Much of the intelligence which enabled countermeasures against the V-weapons was gained through the interception and decoding of German radio traffic – this required the development of primitive computing systems. The skills of British telecommunications' engineers and their familiarity with radio technology was of the utmost importance, and by inference the value to the Germans of similar skills at Philips was appreciated.

Thus, coming when it did and aimed at a vital technological industry, Operation OYSTER, by a relatively modest force of available aircraft types, can fairly be judged a valuable blow at a perilous time.

Post-war

Wing Commander J. E. 'Johnny' Pelly-Fry continued his career in the Royal Air Force and in 1953 his duties took him to the Royal Netherlands Air Force at Eindhoven aerodrome. Learning of his part in the raid on the Philips factory in 1942, his hosts arranged a visit to the company. On arrival he was escorted to the Chairman's office where Mr Otten, then boss of over 30,000 employees at Eindhoven alone, made him very welcome. Johnny Pelly-Fry started by apologizing for knocking the factory down, but Mr Otten smiled and said, 'As you can see, we have a much better one now!'

A copy of this picture given to Wing Commander Pelly-Fry carried the inscription 'To our valiant Allied "intruder" Wing Commander J. Pelly-Fry at the occasion of his first post-war reconnaissance to Eindhoven, after his wartime bombing mission. No hard feelings!', 6.12.'42-24.9.'53, signed 'Otten'.

In the decades after the war the Philips Company did indeed expand their research activities and improve their facilities – 'The sky was the limit'.[2] For instance, television, built on research from the 1930s, became a mass-produced consumer phenomenon. The invention of the transistor by Bell Labs changed the world of electronics forever. Philips built up a strong patent position in magnetic materials, and contributed many breakthroughs such as the LOCOS process (LOCal Oxidation of Silicon), used in every modern Metal-Oxide-Semiconductor Integrated Circuit. The company produced the ubiquitous rotary head Philishave electric shaver (1950s) and the compact audio cassette (1963), a landmark in audio recording technology. Research laboratories were founded in England, France, Germany and the USA.

Wing Commander J. E. 'Johnny' Pelly-Fry DSO, and Mr Otten. *(Philips Company Archives, ref. RZ 4021-1)*

The company has continued in the forefront of technological developments, including the introduction of the CD and DVD. In the medical field, Philips have made great strides forward in Magnetic Resonance Imaging (MRI) and ultrasound. The year 2006 saw the first commercial launch of a 3D scanner. As a consequence of the international nature of its business the company headquarters have now moved to Amsterdam. However, the iconic De Witte Dame (White Lady) building with its prominent tower, De Lichttoren (Light House), remains a major feature in the centre of Eindhoven.

The reader attempting to relate the photographs taken from the Operation OYSTER aircraft to the present-day centre of Eindhoven would have some difficulty. There has been much re-development resulting in a clean, modern, vibrant city. However, some older buildings, such as the restored Catharinakerk with its notable twin spires, stand as a guide to help the visitor looking for the earlier street layout. The White Lady remains; it was the most prominent aiming point for the bombers attacking the Emmasingel site. And for the historian studying Operation OYSTER this building is the best starting point, since on 6 December 2011, sixty-nine years on from the raid, a very imaginative memorial, in the form of an Oyster enclosing a ruined factory, was unveiled in the presence of many citizens of Eindhoven and representatives of the nations involved in the raid. Encased within the memorial are the names of those, of all nationalities, who lost their lives as a consequence of Operation OYSTER.

Notes

1. Bates and Ogley, *Flying Bombs over England.*
2. www.research.philips.com

Chapter Nine

Monument: Memorial in Eindhoven

This chapter, written by Paul Schepers, describes the processes by which the monument to Operation OYSTER and its victims, mentioned at the end of a previous chapter (Chapter 8), was commissioned and installed.

It was eyewitness Ton van der Heijde who set the ball rolling to raise a permanent monument in memory of the many casualties, both military and civilian, of the Allied bombing of the Philips factories in Eindhoven on 6 December 1942. At the time of the raid Ton was living in the 'Philips dorp', an Eindhoven district built at the time by the Philips company for its employees and right next to the Philips Strijp plant's southern border (it was from this direction that the raid took place). How close by he was living can be derived from a stray bomb hitting the houses opposite his parents' house, completely demolishing them. The bomb blast badly damaged Ton's parental house, making them homeless for half a year. No wonder Ton has a life-long association with this particular bombing attack.

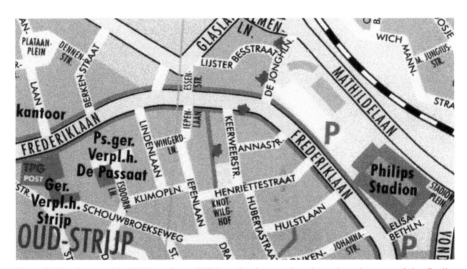

Map 8. Bombs outside Philips. Stray HE bombs dropped early and to the east of the Strijp target (second bomb – Frederiklaan – caused above described damage); the 'Glaslaan' can just be seen; this marks the most eastern entrance to the Strijp plant. *(Jeff Haneveer)*

On 5 May 2009, on behalf of Ton, a carefully prepared and documented proposal was sent to the Art and Culture department of the Eindhoven town hall. Three weeks later he was invited to provide further details in person at the council meeting, an opportunity enthusiastically welcomed. Big was the disappointment when, two months later, on 21 July 2009, he received the reply that the Eindhoven policy was to commemorate the Second World War and its victims as centrally as possible with already existing monuments and not to have monuments erected for dedicated groups of people or events. Initially, this answer was not only a bitter blow but also doom for the initiative.

Only much later, about one and a half years, Ton van der Heijde was notified of a possibility to have the Eindhoven city council reconsider their reply by means of a citizens' initiative. Such an initiative, valid by law, must be accompanied by at least 250 signatures of Eindhoven citizens who are in favour of the proposed idea. Collecting the signatures proved to be very easy, so after only two weeks the initiative was handed over to the council in January 2011.

The next round was to present the initiative to the weekly council meeting in the council chamber. At this point Ton decided to call in reinforcements; it should be noted that he was already eighty-four years of age at the time.

So it was that I became involved a second time with an Operation OYSTER related subject (the first one being the thorough investigation of the raid in various archives). Since I was, of course, one of those who had put a signature under the initiative, and Ton knowing I was quite knowledgeable on the topic, he asked me to join him at the council meeting to answer any detailed questions that might be raised. Of course, I also attended in a supportive role, since having to deal with politics and politicians alone is very different compared to normal daily life.

Thus it was that the initiative was presented during the council meeting of 8 February 2011. The presentation went well and several questions (mostly financially related) were answered and we had the feeling we were on our way to becoming amateur politicians. From this council meeting it was decided to transfer the initiative to one of the dedicated council committees in order to prepare it for final voting in a future council meeting. Finally the big day arrived: 4 April 2011. Voting day for the initiative! Ton and myself were asked to join, temporarily of course, the ranks of politicians prior to the voting. Then all the political parties were offered time to present their views on the initiative and, where necessary, to ask us questions. The main issue here was again related to possible financial consequences for the council of

Eindhoven. After we explained that the idea was to start fund-raising without any financial obligation required from their side it took the parties no time at all to come to a unanimous vote: green light for the OYSTER monument. The Eindhoven council also offered assistance in finding a proper location for the statue.

There we were, political endorsement but no money yet. It was decided to form a foundation having three members: Ton van der Heijde (the initiator), Jeff Haneveer and myself. The third member, Jeff Haneveer, was a former neighbour of Ton whose parental house was damaged as a result of the aforementioned stray bomb. The foundation was named 'Stichting Bombardement Eindhoven 6 December 1942' (Foundation Bombardment Eindhoven 6 December 1942).

We were lucky in having the cooperation of a well-known Eindhoven artist and sculptor, Peter Nagelkerke, who offered to design the monument for free. The design was to be in the form of an oyster shell, very aptly, of course, considering the codename given to the raid. But it went further than that. The artist envisioned an opened oyster shell in which part of the buildings that were bombed and are still existing today was to be visible. Furthermore, stories as told by eyewitnesses were to be part of the monument. For example, there was the story of a young child still sitting on a wooden chair in the middle of the living room of his bombed house, visible from the street since the walls of the house had collapsed. Also the story of a mother with child escaping from the damaged Binnenziekenhuis (hospital). A gaping hole in the top part of the shell was to symbolize bomb impacts on the Philips factories, shops and civilian property. The base of the monument would be a concrete base on which the bronze oyster shell was to be mounted.

But first the foundation had to be formed and registered at the Chamber of Commerce. This was all arranged in June 2011. To have ease of communication and decision making, it was decided on the first foundation meeting to limit the number of members to three (this proved to be a very good decision). Each member was assigned a specific task: Ton was made responsible for all technically related aspects, to Jeff went the important task of actually raising the money and contact with the media, and my task was the financial administration, planning and secretariat. The goal of the foundation was the very ambitious wish, to have the monument manufactured, erected and unveiled in the calendar year 2011. As the target for the monument unveiling, aptly, 6 December 2011 was chosen. A rough cost estimation indicated that around Euro 30,000 would be required to realize the whole plan.

The first fundraising letters, focused on Eindhoven trade and industry, were sent in the first week of July. The local media were used to raise money from private contributions.

Though the many reactions received to this proposed bombardment monument were very positive, the fundraising initially raised concerns about whether we could keep to our intended schedule. To balance the fundraising concerns we received the offer of 'Wooncooperatie TRUDO' (translated real-estate cooperation TRUDO) to have the monument placed right in front of the Emmasingel complex (then the small target, nowadays converted to apartments, sport hall, shops and restaurants). A second offer was received from building company Stam + de Koning (rebuilders of the Philips Emmasingel complex) to manufacture the concrete base for the monument free of charge. For the reader who intends to have a look at the monument, pay particular attention to this concrete base. In design it looks like the same concrete material as used for the Philips factory building.

At the end of August 2011 the foundation members were forced to consider postponement of the whole project due to the financial situation, only a quarter of the required sum having been raised. This was not enough to commission the oyster shell part of the monument from the bronze foundry. However, a famous Dutch saying came true: 'Als de nood het hoogst is, is de redding nabij' ('the darkest hour is before the dawn'). Shortly after having told the press of our low financial tide, rescue came from the Eindhoven-based funeral insurance company DELA. This company's name stands for 'Deelt Elkanders LAsten' (Share Each Other's Burdens), and in line with that motto the company has a charity fund for good causes (Goede Doelen Fonds). It was this fund that offered the full sum to cover the bronze casting. The joy of the foundation members was enormous, and a small celebration was called for. Completely in style of the monument to be erected, by being treated to the eating of oysters (thanks to Annette, Jeff's wife, for preparing them deliciously)! So all of a sudden it was possible again to meet the originally planned deadline of 6 December of the same year for the monument to be unveiled. Also the reaction of the media was very positive, with the added advantage that fundraising got a welcome injection. Along came DNC Vastgoedontwikkeling (a subsidiary of Stam + de Koning) who took care of not only the actual manufacturing of the concrete base, but also acted as project leader for erection of the monument. Along came Mansveld Company taking care of the electric lighting side of the monument. Along came Boelhouwers Company, specialists in organising festivals who offered to sponsor and organize the unveiling ceremony requirements and catering,

Memorial organisers: from left to right Ton van der Heijde (initiator), author Paul Schepers and Jeff Haneveer. *(Annette Haneveer)*

as well as the ART hotel who sponsored the catering. Without them the monument would never have been realized. So a big thank you to all our sponsors.

With only three months left and only the artistic design of the monument completed, a lot was still to be done, so planning was continued in full earnest. The artist Peter Nagelkerke put the final touches to the design and the bronze foundry was formally given the go-ahead to start the bronze casting. The concrete base dimensions were discussed and manufacturing started. Behind the scenes, due to the ever increasing number of bronze thefts, negotiations were ongoing in relation to measures to be taken against theft as required by our main sponsor. The invitations could now be sent out for the unveiling ceremony. Having put all this in motion, the foundation was ready to announce the date for the formal unveiling of the 'Sinterklaasmonument' (named after the Holy Bishop Saint Nicolas, celebrated in The Netherlands on 6 December). The date was set to 6 December 2011, exactly sixty-nine years to the day after the drama of the Allied bombing of Eindhoven.

On 9 November, as a prelude to the formal unveiling, a short ceremony took place in the Eindhovens Regionaal Historisch Centrum (Eindhoven

Author Paul Schepers lays wreaths at Oude Toren and Ysselsteyn cemeteries. *(Annette Haneveer)*

Regional Historical Centre). In the presence of the Municipal Councillor for Culture, Mrs Mary-Ann Schreurs, a scroll listing all those killed in the raid was placed in a stainless steel protective casing by two ladies (themselves victims of the bombing). The scroll was also officially sealed with the wax seal of the city of Eindhoven. After that the protective casing was welded closed, to be put finally in its designated place, inside the monument, a few days later by the bronze foundry.

On Sunday 4 December, two days before the unveiling ceremony, the foundation members accompanied by their wives laid wreaths on the graves of the Allied crew members on the Eindhoven cemetery, De Oude Toren, as well as on the German military cemetery in Ysselsteyn on the graves of the German soldiers who were killed.

Then on Tuesday afternoon, 6 December 2011 on the Eindhovense Lichtplein at three o'clock, with the overwhelming interest of many hundreds of invitees and Eindhoven citizens, the ceremony to unveil the monument started. After a short introduction speech on behalf of the foundation by spokesman Jeff Haneveer, Mr Edzo Doeve director of DELA,

Operation Oyster monument
adjacent to the Emmasingel site.
(Annette Haneveer)

as main sponsor, gave an impressive speech. Then the long awaited moment had arrived and the monument was unveiled by ten-year-old Bob van der Heijde, grandson of Ton, assisted by his grandfather. The unveiling was followed by the laying of flowers by official representatives of the British and French embassies on behalf of the United Kingdom and the République Française. Flowers were also laid by the Council of Eindhoven, DELA and TRUDO companies, the foundation and various individual persons. After the floral tributes were laid, artist Peter Nagelkerke gave a short explanation about the 'how and why' of his design of the monument. The ceremony was ended by a speech from the Municipal Councillor of Culture.

During the ceremony it became obvious that this magnificent remembrance monument will be seen as a well-respected and long overdue present to many Eindhoven citizens – those concerned, eyewitnesses and next of kin.

Chapter Ten

Postscript: Comments on Appendices

The authors of this book have spent many hours collecting, transcribing and analyzing the official records, both British and Dutch, which form a solid basis of this story. The narrative in preceding chapters has attempted to convey this heroic and yet painful episode in words that can be appreciated by a general readership. However, for the keen student of aviation history, the principal source documents are copied in the following appendices to assist those readers wishing to delve deeper. These documents are, however, less than appealing to the eye on first glance. Therefore the authors have attempted to draw attention to the principal points in this introduction to the appendices.

Authors' note: The transcribed archive material has been reproduced as found with the same page layout and no editing (for example references to Phillips rather than Philips have been left unchanged and place name spellings have been left as in the original material).

No. 2 Group Operation Order 82

The first point to note is that there were two versions, the first dated 17 November 1942, followed by a revised order on the 23rd. There are some significant differences.

The Mitchell bombers were included in the first order but were dropped from the second 'due to technical and training difficulties'.

In the first order the Venturas were to bomb first at low level with time delay bombs and incendiaries, but it was realized that the smoke from such an attack would make the bombing by the Bostons and Mosquitos less accurate. The second version of the order put the Bostons to attack first (at Zero hour, 12.30), then the Mosquitos (Zero plus two minutes) followed by the Venturas (Zero plus six minutes), and this was the order for the raid.

The revised order anticipated a force of eighty-four aircraft (thirty-six Venturas, thirty-six Bostons and twelve Mosquitos). In the event thirty-six Bostons set out, ten Mosquitos plus one photo-reconnaisance aircraft, and forty-seven Venturas – ninety-three bombing sorties and one reconnaissance.

The first two Bostons on each of the two targets were to attack at low level with delayed action bombs. The rest of the Bostons and the Mosquitos were to bomb from 1,000 to 1,500 feet, spending as little time as possible at that height.

In the first order all aircraft were to leave the English coast at Orfordness, but this was revised so that the Bostons and Mosquitos were to coast out at Southwold. All routes were to cross the Dutch coast at Colijnsplaat.

Radio silence was to be maintained except in emergency and all aircraft were to keep below fifty feet crossing the North Sea to escape detection by enemy radar.

Weather conditions for the attack were specified by 2 Group HQ at 'Good visibility and cloud base not lower than 1500ft'.

As many aircraft as possible were to be fitted with cameras to record bombing results.

Airspeeds were specified to achieve concentration at the target and at Colijnsplaat on the return flight, where fighter cover was to be provided by 12 Group, Fighter Command. This cover would extend ten to fifteen miles inside the Dutch coast. No. 11 Group fighters would provide a diversion over Ostend. The return route for the Mosquitos was to be decided by the station commander at Marham – these aircraft would rely on their high speed to evade the enemy.

Introduction to Appendix II

Low level navigation to Eindhoven

This account of the navigation to the target was written by Flight Lieutenant E. F. Hart, who was the navigator in the leading Ventura, commanded by Wing Commander R. H. 'Bob' Young AFC, the leader of the Ventura force in aircraft AJ466, SB-H of 464 Squadron. Young was awarded the DSO and Hart the DFC for the Eindhoven raid.

Flight Lieutenant Hart's report on the navigation of the raid speaks for itself. It is comprehensive and well written but quite long so the principal points are highlighted below.

A big daylight raid at low level requiring as much preparation as possible.

Four exercises previous to the raid provided valuable experience in low-level map reading.

The navigational briefing was particularly good; strip maps of the route with photographs of landmarks, pinpoints, ground speeds and ETAs; it provided a 'complete picture in my mind's eye'; a silhouette of the projected landfall enabled it to be recognized six to eight miles out to sea.

Careful preparation bore fruit from the time of take off which, despite the large number of Venturas, was carried out with precision.

Because the Bostons and Mosquitos were attacking before the Venturas it was essential to arrive exactly on time.

The advantage of ten-mile marks and 10-degree lines marked along the track became apparent as it was found that the wind was lighter than forecast, and the speed had to be increased in order to reach the target on ETA and to meet the fighter escort for withdrawal. The formation of forty-eight Venturas (forty-seven attacked, one turned back with technical trouble) looked 'a very impressive armada'. One alteration of course was made for drift.

The enemy coast was 'a dark smudge on the horizon', easily recognized. Landfall was slightly south of intended. Intense light flak was encountered from gunpits in the sand dunes. Visibility was good at eight to twelve miles. The course was altered towards our first turning point inland.

The coast to target track was maintained without difficulty, just clearing hedges, trees, roads, railways and the roofs of clean little Dutch hamlets and towns.

Only one enemy fighter was seen, in pursuit of a Mosquito flying on a reciprocal course.

Near the target two sections split to attack designated targets, one section (including Hart's leading aircraft) towards the northern (Strijp) works which was immediately visible although covered by a pall of smoke from the Boston and Mosquito attacks. The other section aimed at the southern works (Emmasingel). The timing was so good that after bombing the two sections once again joined company in fairly good formation after a gradual turn onto course for the coast.

Enemy fire was intense over the target – gunners were seen firing from the tops of buildings.

The route to the coast started from a point north of the correct track. This was rectified to avoid a large, heavily defended town (probably Tilburg). The enemy coast was reached 'just over the treetops' with evasive actions as necessary. Some fierce but inaccurate fire was experienced along the sides of a river estuary (Oosterschelde).

The return journey over the sea was uneventful, with track maintained by checking drift and the landfall was on track within half a minute of ETA.

Flight Lieutenant Hart summed the operation up as an 'exciting trip … job gone according to plan … with good results'.

Details of the navigation landmarks are taken from Amendment List No. 2 to Operation Order No. 82 (23 November 1942):[1]

Landmarks were taken from 1/50,000 scale maps. Churches, railway lines, woods and canals noted.

Kolijnplaat (cf. spelling on Michelin roadmaps Colijnsplaat) taken as Mile 0 (Zero)

Turnhout (turning point for Bostons and Mosquitos) noted for convergence of roads, canal and tramway. Oostmalle was the turning point for Venturas.

Zeelst (Eindhoven) aerodrome 1 mile on port beam when Eindhoven town two and a half miles ahead.

Cross canal when target 1 mile ahead – bomb doors open. (In fact Boston aircraft remained on an easterly heading until the Belslyne (Bels lijntje) railway was seen, then turned for the target which was by then visible.)

Similar landmarks were chosen for the return flight, via Boxtel, passing close to Tilburg and Breda via Oudenbosch to Kolijnsplaat for the Bostons, and via Oirschot for the Venturas. In reality the track keeping was not so precise on the return after the battle over the targets.

Both Boston and Venturas aimed to make landfall in England at Orfordness.

Note

1. NA Kew, AIR25/35.

Introduction to Appendix III

Operation Oyster Evaluation

This appendix starts with the original operation order (17 November 1942) which included Mitchell aircraft. It analyzes the practice flights (17-20 November), noting a steady improvement in performance.

The ordering of the aircraft types for the attack is discussed and the removal of the Mitchells from the programme.

Tracks and timings are explained to enable Bostons and Venturas to arrive at the Dutch coast on return close together to benefit from fighter cover. (Z+19 Bostons, Z+26 Venturas).

A four-minute gap was allowed between the Boston/Mosquito attacks and the Ventura attack, to allow some dispersal of smoke and dust.

The latest plans were tested by the final exercise which was rated a 'great improvement'.

Unfavourable weather necessitated the postponement of the raid from Thursday 3 December to Sunday 6 December, thus undermining the convenient myth that Sunday had been chosen to reduce risk to the workers at Philips. During the period of postponement all crews were confined to their stations.

In the event ninety-four aircraft were detailed to attack, plus one Mosquito for photo reconnaissance. Only one aircraft turned back early due to technical trouble. Thirteen aircraft were missing after the raid, including one in the sea on the flight out. Five of the missing aircraft were known to have bombed the target.

Forty-six aircraft were damaged and these are listed in the appendix, which also gives the causes of losses to flak and fighters.

The level of effort involved in Operation OYSTER is highlighted by comparing the ninety-four sorties on 6 December with the 2 Group total of 191 for the whole of December.

The appendix includes a detailed analysis of damage to the Philips works, civic and residential properties from photographic evidence, taken from attacking aircraft and the photo-recce Mosquito. A map is included with a key to damage on individual buildings.

Later photo-recce sorties were carried out by 541 Squadron on 14 and 16 December and these were analyzed by the photographic assessment unit at RAF Medmenham. They confirmed that the Philips works had been seriously damaged but at the cost of collateral damage in the town.

Introduction to Appendix IV

American Diversionary Raid

In order to divert enemy fighter forces from Operation OYSTER a raid was made by American bombers over Northeast France. Sixty-six B-17s attacked Lille and nineteen B-24s the aerodrome at Abbeville; they were given extensive support by Spitfires flown by RAF and USAAF pilots.

The time over target was 12.08 to 12.10, bombing from 20,000 to 23,000 feet.

One B-17 and one B-24 were lost. About twenty enemy fighters were encountered, mostly Fw190s. One Fw190 and one Spitfire were destroyed, although more were claimed.

The enemy fighters refrained from attacking while the Spitfires were covering the bombers from 'up sun'.

Introduction to Appendix V

RAF Casualties

For aircrew with known graves the names, locations and pictures of their graves are shown. One member each of two crews have known graves, but their crew mates without known graves are commemorated at The Air Forces Memorial at Runnymede.

Also commemorated at Runnymede are the crews of one Ventura, four Boston and one Mosquito.

Introduction to Appendix VI

Civilians Killed

This is a contemporary list showing 133 names, each with date of birth, next of kin and address. The total number killed eventually reached 148.

Introduction to Appendix VII

German Soldiers Killed

This appendix lists the seven German soldiers killed in the raid, giving their names, date of birth, rank and pictures of their graves. Their age range was nineteen to twenty-eight – very similar to the ages of the attacking RAF crews.

Introduction to Appendix VIII

Philips Fire Service Report

This appendix is the narrative report by the professional engineer responsible for the Philips Fire Service, Ir A. P. T. Advocaat. It is dated 17 December 1942 and has been translated by co-author Paul Schepers. A picture is included showing the three fire engines of the Philips fire brigade.

The raid came as a surprise – there was no air raid warning and the firemen were at lunch.

As often in such raids the water supply was affected making firefighting difficult. The damage is described.

One fireman was killed by a delayed-action bomb. A small number of Philips' employees were killed and many were injured. Improvised casualty treatment posts were set up.

The Philips Brigade helped with firefighting outside the factories as required. Help was also called on from fire brigades outside Eindhoven.

The efforts of the firefighting actions are described in some detail; heroic attempts were made to save people and buildings.

The efforts of the air raid wardens to help people are described – their command post became untenable and was moved to the undamaged fire station.

Appendix I: Operation Order No. 82

(*source: Operation Record Book 2 Group RAF; Public Record Office AIR-25/35*)

MOST SECRET

NO. 2 GROUP OPERATION ORDER NO. 82

Copy No. <u>20</u>
17th November, 1942

OPERATION "OYSTER".
INFORMATION.

1. The PHILLIPS Wireless, Valve, and Radio Works, situated close to the town of EINDHOVEN, is the largest factory producing radio valves in EUROPE. Although, in 1929 decentralisation took place, by the establishment of subsidiary manufacturing plants abroad, the EINDHOVEN works still remain the largest plant of its kind in EUROPE.

    Since the occupation of HOLLAND, this Factory has been under GERMAN management, and the whole output is for the GERMAN Fighting Forces.

INTENTION.

2. To cause maximum damage to the PHILLIPS Wireless, Valve, and Radio Works.

FORCES AVAILABLE.

Bombers.
3. Thirty-six – Venturas.
   Twelve   – Mitchells.
   Thirty-six – Bostons.
   Twelve   – Mosquitos.

Fighters.
4. No. 12 Fighter Group will provide main cover at the DUTCH Coast for the returning Bombers, this cover will penetrate approximately ten to fifteen miles inside the DUTCH Coast-line.

    No. 11 Fighter Group will arrange suitable Fighter diversions in the OSTEND area to confuse enemy defences.

EXECUTION.

5. The target consists of two parts, the Main Factory and Workshops to the West of EINDHOVEN, and the Valve and Lamp Factory situated about half-a-mile South West of the Main Plant.

/Page 2.

-2-

6. All aircraft are to attack the target as follows:-

   (i)   Main Factory and Workshops.
         24 Venturas   at ZERO hour.
         12 Mitchells   at ZERO plus two minutes.
         12 Mosquitos   at ZERO plus six minutes.

   (ii) Valve and Lamp Factory.
         12 Venturas   at ZERO hour.
         36 Bostons   at ZERO plus four minutes.

   ZERO hour will be detailed on the day of the operation.

Bomb load.
7. The bomb load for each type of aircraft is to be as follows:-

   (i)   Ventura   – maximum 30 lb. Incendiary bombs, plus two x 250 lb. GP
                     fused L.D.
   (ii) Mitchell – maximum H.E. fused T.D. 0.025.
   (iii) Boston   – maximum H.E. fused T.D. 0.025.
   (iv) Mosquito – maximum H.E. fused T.D. 0.025.

METHOD OF ATTACK.

8. All aircraft are to fly in pairs and in company echelon to starboard. No formation is to exceed six aircraft. The route from Base to the Target is to be flown at low level, and, with exception of the Venturas, all aircraft are to climb to between 1,000 and 1,500 feet to release bombs. The Venturas are to bomb from low level.
9. The aircraft which climb to bombing height over the target are to reduce the time spent at bombing height to a minimum and are to dive to low level as soon as their bombs have been released.
10. In order to escape detection by Enemy R.D.F. Stations for as long as possible, it is most important that all aircraft do not exceed a height of 50 feet when crossing the NORTH SEA.

Route.
11. The route for all aircraft is to be as follows:-

   Base – ORFORDNESS – COLIJNSPLAAT – TURNHOUT
   Target Base – OIRSCHOT – COLIJNSPLAAT – ORFORDNESS

Timing.
12. All watches are to be synchronised with

/Page 3.

-3-

B.B.C. time signal prior to the operation.

The success of this operation depends almost entirely on strict adherence to the Route, Indicated Air Speeds, and Timings.

Navigation.

13. All Navigators are to use the distance between the railway line running S.S.W. from NORWICH to STOWMARKET and ORFORDNESS as a check on the accuracy of their ground speeds.

Time/distance scales with prominent features marked are to be prepared by every Navigator in accordance with A.P. 1234, Chapter III, paragraph 28.

Photography.

14. As many aircraft as possible are to be fitted with cameras, and every endeavour must be made to photograph bombing results.

Weather.

15. Suitable weather for this operation will be conditions of good visibility with cloud base not lower than 1,500 feet.

COMMUNICATIONS.

16. A listening watch is to be kept on the Station H.F. D/F frequency for the first fifteen minutes of the flight. After fifteen minutes, continuous listening watch is to be kept on the Group Operational frequency.
17. This continuous watch is to be kept until the Captain of the aircraft subsequently requires to call Base for homing purposes.
18. The watch on the Group frequency may only be varied to make a specific call for navigational assistance.
19. Strict W/T and R/T silence is to be maintained on the ground and in the air throughout the operation and must only be broken in emergency.
20. ACKNOWLEDGE by teleprinter.

{signature}
Group Captain,
Officer Commanding,
No. 2 Group

DISTRIBUTION.	Copy No.
R.A.F. Station, Feltwell.	1–4.
R.A.F. Station, Foulsham.	5–7.
R.A.F. Station, Marham.	8–9.
R.A.F. Station, West Raynham.	10–11.

R.A.F. Station, Swanton Morley.	12–14.
Headquarters, Bomber Command.	15–16.
Headquarters, No. 11 Group.	17.
Headquarters, No. 12 Group.	18.
Ops. Dossier.	19.
Ops. Record Book.	20–22.
Intelligence.	23.
Signals.	24.
Spares.	25–27.

Headquarters, No. 2 Group,

Royal Air Force,
Huntingdon.

2G/S. 479/19/Ops.   19th November, 1942.

Amendment List No. 1 to No. 2 Group
Operation Order No. 82, dated 17th
November, 1942.

1. Under paragraph 15, headed "Weather" ADD the following new paragraph 15A:-

"15A. The weather conditions for this operation will be decided at this Headquarters and a Route Forecast issued to all No. 2 Group Stations concerned. It is most important that the winds given in this forecast are used by all Squadrons when planning the operation."

2. Under paragraph 11, headed "Route" ADD the following new paragraph 11A:-

"11A. The route from the Target to Base for the unarmed Mosquito aircraft will be decided by the Station Commander, MARHAM."

{signature}
Group Captain,
Officer Commanding,
No. 2 Group

DISTRIBUTION.	Copy No.
R.A.F. Station, Feltwell.	1–4.
R.A.F. Station, Foulsham.	5–7.
R.A.F. Station, Marham.	8–9.
R.A.F. Station, West Raynham.	10–11.
R.A.F. Station, Swanton Morley.	12–14.

Headquarters, Bomber Command.	15–16.
Headquarters, No. 11 Group.	17.
Headquarters, No. 12 Group.	18.
Ops. Dossier.	19.
Ops. Record Book.	20–22.
Intelligence.	23.
Signals.	24.
Spares.	25–27.

Operation Order No. 82, 23 November 1942[1]

MOST SECRET

NO. 2 GROUP OPERATION ORDER NO. 82

(This Order cancels No. 2 Group
Operation Order, No. 82, dated
the 17th November, 1942, all copies
of which are to be destroyed by fire.)

Copy No. 22
23rd November, 1942

OPERATION "OYSTER".
INFORMATION.

1. The PHILLIPS Wireless, Valve, and Radio Works, situated close to the town of EINDHOVEN, is the largest factory producing radio valves in EUROPE. Although, in 1929 decentralisation took place, by the establishment of subsidiary manufacturing plants abroad, the EINDHOVEN works still remain the largest plant of its kind in EUROPE.

Since the occupation of HOLLAND, this factory has been under GERMAN management, and the whole output is for the GERMAN Fighting Forces.

INTENTION.

2. To cause maximum damage to the PHILLIPS Wireless, Valve, and Radio Works.

FORCES AVAILABLE.

Bombers.
3. Thirty-six   – Venturas.
    Thirty-six   – Bostons.
    Twelve   – Mosquitos.

Fighters.
4. No. 12 Fighter Group will provide main cover at the DUTCH Coast for the returning Bombers, this cover will penetrate approximately ten to fifteen miles inside the DUTCH Coast-line.

No. 11 Fighter Group will arrange suitable Fighter diversions in the OSTEND area to confuse enemy defences.

EXECUTION.

5. The target consists of two parts, the Main Factory and Workshops to the West of EINDHOVEN, and the Valve and Lamp Factory situated about half-a-mile South West of the Main Plant.
6. All aircraft are to attack the target as follows:-

   (i)   Main Factory and Workshops.
      12 Bostons   at ZERO hour.
      12 Mosquitos   at ZERO plus two minutes.
      24 Venturas   at ZERO plus six minutes.
  (ii) Valve and Lamp Factory.
      24 Bostons   at ZERO hour.
      12 Venturas   at ZERO plus six minutes.

     ZERO hour will be detailed on the day of the operation.

Bomb load.
7. The bomb load for each type of aircraft is to be as follows   :-

   (i)   Ventura - maximum 30 lb. Incendiary bombs, plus two x 250 lb. GP fused L.D.
  (ii) Boston - maximum H.E. fused T.D. 0.025.
 (iii) Mosquito - maximum H.E. fused T.D. 0.025.

METHOD OF ATTACK.

8. All aircraft are to fly in pairs and in company echelon to starboard. No formation is to exceed six aircraft. The route from Base to the Target is to be flown at low level, and, with exception of the Venturas, all aircraft are to climb to between 1,000 and 1,500 feet to release bombs. The Venturas are to bomb from low level.
9. The aircraft which climb to bombing height over the target are to reduce the time spent at bombing height to a minimum and are to dive to low level as soon as their bombs have been released.
10. In order to escape detection by Enemy R.D.F. Stations for as long as possible, it is most important that all aircraft do not exceed a height of 50 feet when crossing the NORTH SEA.

Route.

11. The following are the routes for the various types of aircraft   :-

    (i)   Bostons:-   Base – ORFORDNESS – COLIJNSPLAAT –
                       TURNHOUT – Target – BOXTEL – COLIJNSPLAAT
                       – ORFORDNESS – Base.

    (ii) Venturas:- Base – SOUTHWOLD – COLIJNSPLAAT
                       – OOSTMALLE – Target – OIRSCHOT –
                       COLIJNSPLAAT – SOUTHWOLD - Base.

    (iii) Mosquitos:- Base – ORFORDNESS – COLIJNSPLAAT –
                       TURNHOUT – Target.

12. The route from the target to Base for the unarmed Mosquito aircraft will be decided by the Station Commander, MARHAM.

13. In order to obtain concentration over the target and COLIJNSPLAAT on the homeward route, aircraft must conform to the following indicated air speeds:-

			I.A.S.
(i)	Bostons:-	Base – ORFORDNESS – COLIJNSPLAAT.	200.
		COLIJNSPLAAT – TURNHOUT – Target – BOXTEL – COLIJNSPLAAT.	240.
		COLIJNSPLAAT – ORFORDNESS – Base.	200.
(ii)	Mosquitos:-	Base – ORFORDNESS – COLIJNSPLAAT.	210.
		COLIJNSPLAAT – TURNHOUT – Target.	260.

      Return I.A.S. from target at Station Commander, MARHAM's, discretion.

(iii)	Venturas:-	Base – SOUTHWOLD – COLIJNSPLAAT.	180.
		COLIJNSPLAAT – OOSTMALLE – Target.	210.
		Target – OIRSCHOT – COLIJNSPLAAT.	220.
		COLIJNSPLAAT – SOUTHWOLD – Base.	180.

      All aircraft are to approach, attack, and leave the target area at the maximum speed consistent with good formation flying.

Timing.

14. All watches are to be synchronised with B.B.C. time signal prior to the operation.

The success of this operation depends almost entirely on strict adherence to the Route, Indicated Air Speeds, and Timings.

Navigation.

15. All Navigators are to use the distance between the railway line running S.S.W. from NORWICH to STOWMARKET and ORFORDNESS as a check on the accuracy of their ground speeds.

Time/distance scales with prominent features marked are to be prepared by every Navigator in accordance with A.P. 1234, Chapter III, paragraph 28.

Photography.
16. As many aircraft as possible are to be fitted with cameras, and every endeavour must be made to photograph bombing results.

Weather.
17. The weather conditions for this operation will be decided at this Headquarters and a Route Forecast issued to all No. 2 Group Stations concerned. It is most important that the winds given in this forecast are used by all Squadrons when planning the operation. Suitable weather will be conditions of good visibility with cloud base not lower than 1,500 feet.

COMMUNICATIONS.

18. A listening watch is to be kept on the Station H.F./D.F. frequency for the first fifteen minutes of the flight. After fifteen minutes, continuous listening watch is to be kept on the Group operational frequency.
19. This continuous watch is to be kept until the Captain of the aircraft subsequently requires to call Base for homing purposes.
20. The watch on the Group frequency may only be varied to make a specific call for navigational assistance.
21. Strict W/T and R/T silence is to be maintained on the ground and in the air throughout the operation and must only be broken in emergency.

Additional Information.
22. Due to technical and training difficulties, Mitchell aircraft will not be available for this operation. If it is found, however, that a number of Mitchells can be made available, they will be included in the Boston phase of the operation.

23. ACKNOWLEDGE by teleprinter.

{signature}
Group Captain,
Officer Commanding,
No. 2 Group

DISTRIBUTION.	Copy No.
R.A.F. Station, Feltwell.	1–4.
R.A.F. Station, Foulsham.	5–7.
R.A.F. Station, Marham.	8–9.
R.A.F. Station, West Raynham.	10–11.
R.A.F. Station, Swanton Morley.	12–14.
Headquarters, Bomber Command.	15–16.

Headquarters, No. 11 Group.	17.
Headquarters, No. 12 Group.	18.
Ops. Dossier.	19.
Ops. Record Book.	20–22.
Intelligence.	23.
Signals.	24.
Spares.	25–27.

MOST SECRET

Headquarters, No. 2 Group,
Royal Air Force,
Huntingdon.

28th November, 1942.

Amendment List No. 1 to No. 2 Group
Operation Order No. 82, dated the
23rd November, 1942.

Paragraph 13,   sub-paragraph (i)   Bostons:-
Under I.A.S. column DELETE 200 and
SUBSTITUTE 210 in both cases.

Sub-paragraph (ii)   Mosquitos:-
Under I.A.S. column DELETE 210 and
SUBSTITUTE 230.

{signature}
Group Captain,
Officer Commanding,
No. 2 Group

DISTRIBUTION.   Copy No.

R.A.F. Station, Feltwell.	1 – 4.
R.A.F. Station, Foulsham.	5–7.
R.A.F. Station, Marham.	8–9.
R.A.F. Station, West Raynham.	10–11.
R.A.F. Station, Swanton Morley.	12–14.
Headquarters, Bomber Command.	15–16.
Headquarters, No. 11 Group.	17.
Headquarters, No. 12 Group.	18.
Ops. Dossier.	19.
Ops. Record Book.	20–22.
Intelligence.	23.

Signals.	24.
Spares.	25–27.

<u>MOST SECRET</u>

Headquarters, No. 2 Group,
Royal Air Force,
Huntingdon.

1st December, 1942.

Amendment List No. 2 to No. 2 Group
Operation Order No. 82, dated the
23rd November, 1942.

Paragraph 11,   sub-paragraphs (i) (ii) and (iii).

Amend detailed routes as follows:-

    (i)   <u>Bostons</u>:-   Base – Southwold – Colijnsplaat etc.
    (ii) <u>Venturas</u>:- Base – Orfordness – Colijnsplaat etc.
    (iii) <u>Mosquitos</u>:- Base – Southwold – Colijnsplaat etc.

{signature}
Group Captain,
Officer Commanding,
No. 2 Group

<u>DISTRIBUTION.</u>   <u>Copy No.</u>

R.A.F. Station, Feltwell.	1–4.
R.A.F. Station, Foulsham.	5–7.
R.A.F. Station, Marham.	8–9.
R.A.F. Station, West Raynham.	10–11.
R.A.F. Station, Swanton Morley.	12–14.
Headquarters, Bomber Command.	15–16.
Headquarters, No. 11 Group.	17.
Headquarters, No. 12 Group.	18.
Ops. Dossier.	19.
Ops. Record Book.	20–22.
Intelligence.	23.
Signals.	24.
Spares.	25–27.

Note

1. NA Kew, AIR25/35, op. cit.

Appendix II: Low level navigation to Eindhoven[1]

LOW LEVEL NAVIGATION TO EINDHOVEN.

F/Lt. E.F. Hart D.F.C.

No. 2 Group

1. It was with a feeling of pleasant anticipation and some excitement that I heard that I was to be the Leading Navigator in a big daylight low level raid. I was anxious to make as much preparation as possible and all crews were fortunate in having four exercises previous to the raid. These approximated very closely to the actual thing. I, personally, gained valuable experience in low level map reading and timing.

2. In the interests of security the identity of the target was kept a close secret but I had a little prior warning. This was utilized by a series of regular Epidiascope sessions, during which a strip map of the route together with photographs of landmarks was projected. I had a complete picture in my mind's eye of the whole trip.

3. The Briefing was particularly good. All crews were given a thorough description of the job both from the Intelligence and Navigation standpoint. A strip map, to one side of which was attached the Navigational Observations Column of the Log Sheet was prepared by the Station Navigation Officer. This was found most useful in saving time so essential in low level navigation for pinpoints, ground speeds, E.T.A.'s etc., were jotted actually opposite the landmark. A silhouette of the projected landfall was drawn from the data contained in the North Sea Pilot. This was shown through the Epidiascope and carried in the air and recognized 6 to 8 miles out to sea.

4. It was after all this careful preparation that the big day dawned. The exercises which we had carried out beforehand bore fruit right from the time of take-off, which, in spite of the considerable number of Venturas, was carried out with precision. The factor which concerned me most was that of timing. Bostons and Mosquitos were attacking the target before us and it was essential that we arrived there right on time. Course was set precisely and I busied myself with the first leg to the coast. It should be mentioned that I carried the Continental style British ¼″ and found it very helpful, as I did not have to change my ideas when reaching the other side.

5. The advantage of 10 miles marks and 10 degree lines marked along my track became readily apparent and I found that the wind was much lighter than forecasted. Consequently, speed had to be increased in order to reach the target on E.T.A. and to meet our fighter escort, which was covering our withdrawal.

6. The whole formation of forty-eight Venturas left the British coast and it looked a very impressive armada as we flew just over the surface of the sea. I altered course once on drift and the Navigation was quite uneventful until the enemy coastline appeared as a dark smudge on the horizon. The coast was easily

recognized, landfall being slightly south of that intended. The evasive action taken, which consisted of a porpoising motion due to the size of the formation, had little effect on the Navigation. As soon as the Dutch coast was crossed, to the accompaniment of some fairly intense light flak from gun pits on the sand dunes, course was altered to our first turning point inland. Visibility was good: 8 to 12 miles, and from the coast to the target, track was maintained without difficulty, just clearing hedges and tress, over roads and railways, and the roofs of the clean little Dutch hamlets and towns. Part of the formation crossed over a landing ground and met with some opposition from the ground defences.

7. The first turning point was reached on track. Immediately after this I saw the only German fighter of the day and this was in pursuit of one of our Mosquitos flying on a reciprocal course. I mentally wished the Mosquito luck as we flew on.

8. Soon the point came in sight at which the two sections split up momentarily to attack their individual targets. My section turned to port and attacked the Northern Works which were immediately visible overcome by a pall of smoke testifying to the accuracy of the Bostons and Mosquitos. The other section carried on to the Southern Works and the timing worked out so well that after bombing, the two sections once again joined company still in fairly good formation, and after completing a gradual turn, settled down to the homeward run to the coast.

9. Enemy fire over the Phillips Works was naturally intense and gunners could be seen firing from the tops of buildings enveloped in smoke and flame.

10. The route out to the coast started from a point north of the correct track. This was rectified as it was necessary to avoid a large heavily defended town. The enemy coast was reached on track in Grand National style just over the tree tops, doing similar evasive action as before, amidst a spot of fierce but inaccurate fire from the coastal defences situated along the sides of a river estuary.

11. The journey over the sea was uneventful, track being maintained by checking drift, and our landfall at the British coast was on track and within half a minute of E.T.A. So it was that base was reached after a somewhat exciting trip and everyone had a grand feeling of satisfaction and elation after a job which had gone according to plan and with such good results.

Low level navigation landmarks[2]

SECRET

From: Headquarters, No. 2 Group.

To: R.A.F. Station, Feltwell,	No. 21, 464, and 487 Squadrons.
R.A.F. Station, Marham,	No. 105 and 139 Squadrons.
R.A.F. Station, Swanton Morley,	No. 88 and 226 Squadrons.
R.A.F. Station, West Raynham,	No. 107 Squadron.

Date: 25th November, 1942.

Ref: 2G/S. 479/19/Ops.

Operation "OYSTER".

1. The landmarks enumerated below have been obtained from 1: 50,000 maps of the route area.
2. It is suggested that all Navigators, especially those in leading aircraft, be given an opportunity of studying the route carefully on maps of the above scale, using the following landmarks, and any others which may be considered useful, to assist in navigation.
3. Maps required:-
   Folio No.13, Sheets   42, 43, 44, 45, 48, 49, 50 and 51.
   Folio No.12, Sheet   25.
   Folio No.11, Sheet   24.
4. Miles   Landmarks, Mosquito and Boston Routes.

Miles	Landmark
–	Approach from ORFORDNESS over NOORDLAND sand bank. (This is incorrectly marked as an Island on 1: 1,000,000 map). It will only be visible at low tide.
–	KOLIJNPLAAT ahead ten miles.
0	Position KOLIJNPLAAT - alter course, if necessary, for TURNHOUT.
–	Cross over OOSTER SCHELDE waterway, look for ST MAARTENSDYK ahead.
11	Cross over the Church at ST MAARTENSDYK.
17¼	Position 1¼ miles South of THOLEN, crossing waterway between THOLEN Island and mainland. Look for BERGEN OP ZOOM 3¼ miles ahead.
20½	Pass North of BERGEN OP ZOOM, Railway line appears on port beam running North/South.
22¼	Begin to pass over thickly wooded country.
23¾	End of woods.
26½	Cross over railway line running due North/South.
31	Low lying marsh land. Lake 1¼ miles ahead on track and to starboard.
34	Cross over road running through wood N.N.E/S.S.W.
37½	Lake ¼ mile long in a wood parallel to track 300 yards to starboard.
39¾	Church in wood with roads radiating from it, ¾ of a mile to starboard.
40½	Cross main road running due North/South.
46½	Cross over tramway, which runs due North/South. Look for TURNHOUT 3¾ miles ahead. Main road to this town converges on track to port. Canal and tramway converges on track to starboard.
50¼	Position TURNHOUT, alter course for EINDHOVEN.

53¼	Pass over marsh land situated between woods North and South.
55¾	Cross over intersection of canal and main road, then over large lake in woods.
65	Pass over village of HOOGELOON (1 mile long, running North/South).
70	Position ¼ mile South of OERLE (The single track railway running S.W. from EINDHOVEN shown on 1: 500,000 map is of no use as a guide. It is a disused overgrown tramway).
71¾	Position ¼ mile North of ZEELST Aerodrome 1 mile on port beam. (EINDHOVEN 2¼ miles ahead).
73	Cross over canal, bomb doors should be open, targets one mile ahead.
74	TARGETS, turn left after bombing.
76	Main road into EINDHOVEN from N.W. is ¼ mile on port beam, parallel to track.
78¼	Cross canal, main road 300 yards on port beam, parallel to track, woods on starboard beam.
82½	Cross main road. Railway line ½ mile on port beam, BOXTEL 3¼ miles ahead.
84½	Cross railway line – a branch line off the main line, which is ¼ mile on port beam.
85¾	BOXTEL, alter course for KOLIJNSPLAAT.
91¼	Cross main road running N.E/S.W.
93	Cross railway line, ODENHOUT 1¼ miles on starboard beam.
95¾	Cross over main road running N/S wooded area ½ mile on port bow.
98¼	Cross over road running N.W/S.E., canal 1½ miles ahead.
99¾	Cross canal.
101	Town of DONGEN 1½ miles on starboard beam.
103	Cross main road running N.W/S.E. in wooded area.
105½	Railway line ¼ mile on port beam. BREDA 2½ miles on port bow.
108	Cross over main road, canal ½ mile ahead.
108½	Canal.
110¼	Cross railway line running N.W/S.E. at BEEK.
117½	Cross railway line running N.E/S.W. to OUDENBOSCH.
119¼	Cross road from STANDDAARBUITEN to OUDENBOSCH, river ¼ mile on starboard beam.
125½	Lakes and river ½ mile on port beam. STEENBERGEN 2½ miles on port beam.
128½	FORT HENDRIK on track.
133	Leave mainland at HEEREN and cross waterway to THOLEN Island, ST ANNALAND 4¼ miles ahead on track.
137½	ST ANNALAND.
140½	Leave THOLEN Island at KYKEDUART.
147¼	KOLIJNSPLAAT.

LANDMARKS – <u>Ventura route.</u>

0	KOLIJNPLAAT.
11	Position GORISHOCK a promontory on the Island of THOLEN.
18	Look for BERGEN-OP-ZOOM, three miles E.N.E.
22	Landfall 3 miles South of BERGEN-OP-ZOOM, a railway line runs due N/S parallel with coast line turning off West on Starboard beam.
24	Position ZANDVOORT. Town of HOOGERHEIDE one mile on starboard beam.
26	Large lake one mile on starboard bow surrounded by trees.
30¼	Crossing main railway line running due N/S, railway station 300 yards to starboard.
32¼	Cross over road running N/S from ACHTERBROEK. Power cable runs parallel to road 200 yards East of it.
34¾	Main road running N.E/S.W., marsh land ahead.
37¾	Cross over village of STERNHOVEN, look for canal 1¼ miles ahead. Town of BRECHT 1 mile on port beam.
39	Cross over canal running N.E/S.W., look for brick works on port beam and power cable running parallel to canal.
41	Cross over road which converges from starboard. OOSTMALLE 2¼ miles ahead.
43¼	OOSTMALLE, alter course for target.
44½	Flying parallel to woods on starboard beam.
45¾	Crossing large wooded area, look for chimneys, proceed with canal on port beam.
48¾	Power cables diverge from central point at HEILAAR.
50	Cross over canal and brick works on either side of it. TURNHOUT 2¼ on starboard bow.
51	Cross over main road running N.W/S.E. into TURNHOUT.
52½	Pass over railway line and road. TURNHOUT 1 mile on starboard beam, look for canal ½ mile ahead.
53	Cross over canal and over woods ¼ mile wide running parallel with it. Brick works and lakes ¾ mile on port bow.
54¾	Cross over main road running N.E/S.W. into TURNHOUT.
56¼	Cross over Canal which converges on track on port side. Large wooded areas on port and starboard bow.
58	Pass over road running N.N.W/S.S.E in woods. Large lake in woods 1¼ miles on Starboard beam.
63¾	Village of HULSEL 300 yards on port beam.
66¼	Cross over Church in village of CASTEREN.
67½	Cross village of HOOGELOON.
74¼	Town of ZEELST ¼ mile on starboard beam, Aerodrome 1 mile on port beam.
76	Cross over canal, bomb doors should be open, Targets one mile ahead.
77	TARGETS, turn left after bombing.
81	Cross over canal running North/South.
85	Cross canal running East/West. OIRSCHOT ¼ mile ahead.

85½	Position OIRSCHOT, alter course for KOLIJNSPLAAT.
87¼	Pass to North of woods through which canal runs 1½ miles to port.
88¾	Cross over Southern tip of small wood.
93	Pass over road running N.N.E/S.S.W. through wood. Look for town of GOULE 2½ miles ahead on track.
95½	GOULE.
98	Cross over railway line running N.E/S.W. at RIEL.
100¾	Pass over road at edge of wood. Large wooded area begins 2 miles ahead with road running N.E/S.W. through it.
103½	Cross over this road in wood.
106½	Main road comes from S.S.E. at RAKENS, runs parallel to track for ½ mile then veers off N.W.
108	Cross over first of two roads running South at NOTSEL.
108¾	Cross over second road running South and proceed South of large wooded area ¼ mile to starboard of track.
111	Cross over main road running N.N.E/S.S.W. from PRENSENHAGE to RIISBERGEN.
112½	Cross over main road running N.W/S.E. from ETTEN to RISSBERGEN.
115¾	Town of SPRUNDEL ½ mile ahead on port beam.
118¼	Cross roads in wood ¼ mile on starboard beam.
120½	Cross over railway line converging on track from E.N.E. Look on port bow for town of ROOSENDAAL.
121¾	Cross over railway line converging on track from N.E. Marshalling yards on port beam.
122¾	Canal runs into ROSSENDAAL from North.
124½	Cross over main road running S.E. from KRUSLAND which is ¾ mile on starboard beam.
128¼	Cross over road running S.E. from STEENBERGEN, which is 1¾ miles on starboard beam. Look for elongated lake ¾ mile ahead on port bow.
129	Lake, N.W/S.E.
132	Cross water between mainland and Island of THOLEN.
133¾	Town of OUD VOSSEMEER on track.
143	Leave island of THOLEN. STAVENISSEN ¼ mile to starboard.
149	KOLIJNSPLAAT, alter course for ORFORDNESS.

(signed)
Group Captain,
Officer Commanding,
No. 2 Group.

Notes

1. NA Kew, AIR14/523, Flight Lieutenant E. F. Hart, navigator in Ventura II AJ466 SB-H of 464 Squadron.
2. NA Kew, AIR25/35 (D27), ORB, 2 Group RAF.

Appendix III: Operation Oyster Evaluation[1]

SECRET

From: Headquarters, No. 2 Group.
To: Air Ministry   (D.A.T.) (2)
    Headquarters,   Bomber Command,
    Headquarters,   U.S.A.A.C.,
    Headquarters,   R.C.A.F.,
    Headquarters,   No. 5 Group,
    Headquarters,   No. 92 Group.

Date: 8th December, 1942.
Ref: 2G/S.479/19/Ops.

ATTACK ON PHILLIPS RADIO & VALVE FACTORY, EINDHOVEN, BY NO. 2 GROUP AIRCRAFT ON SUNDAY 6th DECEMBER, 1942

1. It is proposed to lay out in this paper the detail of the planning and the various difficulties which were overcome prior to the above Operation.
2. On November 9th authority was given by Headquarters, Bomber Command to commence planning an attack by a large number of aircraft in concentration of time on both sections of the target.
3. Forces available consisted of Mosquitos, Venturas, Bostons and Mitchells. How to consolidate this motley collection of aircraft constituted difficulty number one. The range of speed and manoeuvrability was at a maximum in the Mosquito, and at a minimum in the Ventura, with the Boston and Mitchell completing the scale as numbers two and three respectively.
4. The comparative short range of the Ventura dictated to a considerable extent the routes to and from the target. To obtain the concentration required, and to curtail the difficulties of timing which would occur through the use of too many routes, with the possible additional increase of navigational errors, all aircraft became subject to the limitations imposed by the characteristics peculiar to the Ventura.
5. A rough operational plan was decided upon, and timings considered. In this connection, it may be stated that each Ventura was to carry a 30 lb. incendiary load, plus two 250 lb. G.P. long delay bombs, while all other aircraft were bombed up with 500 lb. M.C. bombs. The next problem in order of rotation was bomb fusing for the H.E. loads. Previous experience in daylight operations had proved conclusively that due to bomb skid, the wastage of bombs when they had definitely been aimed at targets from low level with eleven second delay fuses, reduced considerably the effective results of the attack. In addition, the complicated timings, with no margin of error which would be required using delay bombs in a low level attack by numbers of aircraft would have spread the time on target over too long a period, with a consequent risk of effective fighter interception on aircraft bombing late in the attack.

The final decision and one which offered the greatest prospect of success from all angles, except perhaps flak at the target, was that all aircraft with H.E. loads would have their bombs fused T.D. 0.025 sec. And that bombing would be carried out from between heights of 1,000 to 1,599 feet. The Venturas with their incendiaries and long delay bombs were to remain at low level.

6. The order of bombing was to be as follows:-

Venturas	– ZERO
Mitchells	– ZERO plus two minutes.
Bostons	– ZERO plus four minutes.
Mosquitos	– ZERO plus six minutes.

ZERO being time on target.

The target being in two sections half a mile apart they were classified and allocated as follows:-

	Large Target	Small Target
Venturas	24	12
Mitchells	12	–
Bostons	–	12
Mosquitos	– 12	

7. Representatives of this Headquarters then visited Headquarters, No. 12 Group, on the 9th November, and Headquarters No. 11 Group on the 13th November, 1942, and the plans for the operation were explained with a request concerning the degree of fighter cover that would be granted to cover our withdrawal and the diversions which could be arranged to contain the enemy fighter defences. The substantial assistance which was promised by these Headquarters did much to allay the fears concerning the probable result of having to route our aircraft through so dangerous an area.

8. The Operation Order was produced and forwarded to Stations on the 17th November, 1942.

9. Since an operation of such magnitude had not been undertaken by the Group before, and bearing in mind the high degree of inexperience of many of our crews (for four Squadrons it would be their first operation) and the various types of aircraft, it was contemplated that many practices would be necessary, the main essentials being good low level navigation, accurate timing and methods of approaching, delivering the attack and getting away afterwards.

10. The first practice was held on November the 17th. The route simulated in many ways the actual operation. This route with its simulations is given below:-

Bases to Spalding	Overland run to
Spalding to Goole	our Coast.
Goole to Flamborough Head	
Flamborough Head to Cromer	Sea crossing

Cromer to Newmarket	Run in over enemy territory.
Newmarket to St. Neots Power Station St Neots Town	Large and small Target.
Targets to Kimbolton Kimbolton to Digby Digby to Bases	Withdrawal from Target area.

11. It was unfortunate that this Exercise had to be organized at short notice. This coupled with unfavourable weather and convoys necessitating alterations of course on the sea crossing, prevented the exercise from being as successful as had been hoped. However, many lessons were learnt and the following conclusions arrived at by witnesses of the attack, were passed to Stations immediately:-

(a) Stations require more notice of an Exercise of this nature. (This will be ensured in future).

(b) Accurate timing is essential, only in this way can the concentration of aircraft necessary be obtained.

(c) Formation flying must also be improved, there is no room for the straggler when a large number of aircraft are involved.

(d) Bombing practices involving a rapid climb from low level to 1,000 or 1,500 feet will be necessary to obtain accuracy.

(e) The target area be crossed only once.

(f) Evasive action until well clear of the target area must be as violent as formation flying permits.

(g) The climb to bombing height must not be commenced too soon, the dive away after crossing the target must be as steep as possible.

(h) Flocks of birds are always a potential source of danger while low level flying. It has been noticed in practice that birds invariably tend to dive when aircraft approach. During practice flights it is permissible to climb to avoid flocks of birds if these are seen in time, since damage to aircraft and injuries to crews must be kept to a minimum.

(i) It is advisable to take off well before the time of setting course.

(j) Aircraft must attack the allotted target. The number of aircraft involved makes it necessary that this point is borne in mind. Even one aircraft on the wrong target may upset the attack by the formation detailed to bomb it.

(k) The target must be approached and bombed at maximum speed, this applies particularly to the Ventura aircraft.

(l) The requirements of the Mitchell aircraft, viz., Sutton Harness and clear vision panels, will be brought to the attention of the Group Engineer Officer.

(m) At least one more large scale Exercise will be arranged in the near future during which it is intended to include interception by Fighter aircraft of No. 12 Group.

(n) To exercise Fighting Control, imaginary attacks by Fighters should be presumed at odd intervals during the practices.

12. The planned formation pattern was to be as follows. All aircraft in pairs, three pairs in company (six aircraft). In this way the slipstream effect and other difficulties usually attendant upon mass formations of aircraft were obviated. As was to be expected on the first exercise this ideal was not realized, hence conclusion (c) in Paragraph 11.

13. On November 18th, the Venturas carried out the Exercise detailed in paragraph ten alone, since theirs were the major errors in the previous Exercise. A vast improvement was noticed and the following observations were passed to the Squadrons concerned:-

(a) Thirty Ventura aircraft only were employed. The route and targets were similar to those used on the previous Exercise. Zero hour was 1515 hours.

(b) A marked improvement was noticed on this occasion, and the attack was delivered according to plan.

(c) Approximately fourteen aircraft bombed the Power Station from low level at 1513½ (1½ minutes early) and the remainder attacked the Town at 1515 hours.

(d) The approach, attack, and getaway were excellent. The time during which aircraft would have been open to attack from flak defences was reduced to a minimum.

(e) Two aircraft were seen to pass between the two targets, and it is considered that these aircraft would have attacked no useful objective.

(f) All Venturas were off the target by 1516 hours, with the exception of two, which, due to a late take off, arrived seventeen minutes late. These aircraft had been allowed to proceed to gain experience.

14. A further Exercise employing all aircraft took place on November 20th, routes and the order of attack were similar to those flown on the previous Exercises. Zero was 1430 hours. The observations made by witnesses of the attack were teleprinted to Stations immediately afterwards and are reproduced below:-

(a) Ventura. Attack on Power Station was excellent. Concentration achieved. First aircraft arrived at 1429 hours, attack completed in one minute. Attack on town more scattered. Three aircraft on town at 1436, one at 1440. Two aircraft attacked Power Station singly, letters 'R' and 'M', attack should have been abandoned. Low approach good, evasive action after bombing good.

(b) Boston. Approach, attack and evasive action after bombing excellent. Timing good. Low approach good. Period of attack too long, required concentration not obtained.

(c) Mitchell. Four aircraft crossed Power Station at 1432 hours. Commencement of climb improvement on previous Exercise. Aircraft did not appear to cross target and make getaway at maximum speed.

Five aircraft bombed at 1437. Two aircraft <u>recrossed</u> target at 1441 hours heading N.N.E.

(d) <u>Mosquito.</u>   First aircraft arrived at 1445, nine minutes late. Approached from S.E. Five aircraft attacked in scattered manner, did not appear to be at maximum speed. Only one aircraft got down quickly to low level after crossing target.

(e) <u>General.</u>   Timing a big improvement on last Exercise. Number of stragglers reduced. Group Flak Officer present at target is of opinion that the aircraft which passed over targets in concentration would have been less vulnerable than stragglers who presented a perfect target to flak defences.

During this Exercise Royal Observer Corps reports were passed to Headquarters, No. 12 Group, and forwarded to this Group on the completion of the practice. These comments on the formation flying and errors in timing at turning points were also passed to Stations.

15. While forwarding these conclusions and observations to Squadrons, extracts from papers received from Headquarters, No. 5 Group, were also included for information. It was realized, however, that although many points in these extracts were useful, in the main there was little comparison between the problems solved by No. 5 Group during the training for their major operations and the current difficulties being encountered by this Headquarters. This was due primarily to the different types of aircraft employed.

16. At this stage occurred a development which altered completely the arranged plans.

17. Referring to paragraph 6 it will be seen that the Venturas with their incendiary load were to bomb their target first. Due to the fires and smoke which would envelope the target it was realized that precision bombing by the following H.E. loaded aircraft would suffer considerably. It was decided, therefore, to alter the order of events and to employ the fire raisers last.

18. This alteration constituted a major problem since, before, the slower and less manoeuvrable aircraft had been granted the privilege of a more or less straight run to the target with the added advantage of achieving the surprise necessary to compensate for their limitations. The faster and more manoeuvrable aircraft were considered to be more capable of dealing with the "hornets nest" stirred up by the leading formations. Now, with the situation reversed, it appeared difficult to co-ordinate all phases of the attack. Two alternatives presented themselves, and are given below with their advantages and disadvantages:-

(i) Employ the Venturas first, but give them the H.E. load, plus 4 lb. incendiary bombs which give less smoke.

Advantage: Achieve surprise with slowest aircraft as heretofore.
Disadvantage: It would be necessary for the Venturas to climb to 1,000/1,500 feet to bomb. The slow rate of climb of this

type would necessitate the point of commencement of the climb being too far from the target with the resultant danger from flak defences.

(ii)   Employ the Venturas last with the original incendiary load.

Advantage: The S.B.C. capacity and consequent substantial incendiary load would be put to a good purpose. The attack could be delivered at low level.

Disadvantage: Difficulty of timing these aircraft to afford them the maximum safety conditions possible, considering their disadvantageous position.

19. Representatives from this Headquarters visited the Ventura Station and in conjunction with the Station and Squadron Commanders debated the above alternatives. It was decided to adopt alternative (ii) and as result the problems of routing, timing, and order of attack had to be reconsidered.

20. At this stage the Mitchell aircraft were removed from the program since it was apparent that it would not be possible to make these aircraft operationally serviceable in time.

21. Left then with only three types of aircraft to consider, the following order of attack was decided upon:-

Large Target.	Small Target.
12 Bostons	24 Bostons
12 Mosquitos	12 Venturas
24 Venturas	

22. The timing difficulty was overcome in the following manner. Originally all aircraft were to use the same route to and from the target, the faster aircraft gaining on the slower aircraft until only a small time margin ensued at the enemy coast during the withdrawal. This provided a concentration of aircraft that would be a formidable target for enemy fighters which, it was anticipated, would be active at this later stage of the operation.

Plan number two achieved the same object in a different manner. From the point of entry on the enemy coast to the target, the Bostons and Mosquitos were to fly the route originally planned for them. The Venturas, however, although making their landfall at the same place and approximately the same time as the Boston and Mosquitos, would be detailed to make good a longer track calculated to bring them the required time interval on the target behind the H.E. aircraft. After bombing the situation would be reversed. If the original route from the target was left unaltered, the faster aircraft, having bombed first, would arrive at the enemy coast long before the Venturas to the detriment of the latter type.

To decrease the time interval between aircraft types during the withdrawal, the Venturas made good the original and more direct route out, while the Bostons flew a longer route calculated to bring them at the coast only seven minutes ahead of the Venturas. It was then decided that the Mosquitos after bombing should find their own way out to the northwards. The advantages here were twofold. Firstly, it was most difficult to fit into one time-table, over a given distance, two types of aircraft, one flying at 260 I.A.S. (Mosquito) and the other 220 I.A.S. (Ventura) and obtain a small time margin at the point of exit. Secondly, the effect of the Mosquitos veering North would serve as an additional diversion to the main effort, besides increasing the difficulties of the probably overwhelmed ground reporting system.

23. This being the final plan, and there having been numerous amendments to the Operation Order, it was decided to re-write it and destroy all copies of the original. In the revised Order, detailed indicated air speeds were laid down. This was necessary since the accuracy of the required time intervals depended on the aircraft flying at the speeds which had been used during the calculations and planning. In the original Operation Order, it was only necessary to give a Zero time on target, the slower aircraft being in front until the later phase of the operation when they were overhauled by the remainder.

24. The allocations of times on targets were as follows:-

Large Target.	Small Target.
Bostons – Zero hour	Bostons – Zero hour
Mosquitos – Zero hour plus two mins	Venturas – Zero plus six minutes
Venturas – Zero plus six minutes.	

It was considered that the four minute gap between the H.E. and incendiary attacks would allow sufficient time for all debris to have settled and most of the dust to have drifted from the target area before the low flying aircraft arrived.

25. The planned routes and speeds were as follows:-

(a) Boston: Base to Orfordness   200 I.A.S.
              Orfordness to Kolijnsplaat

              Kolijnsplaat to Turnhout   240 I.A.S.
              Turnhout to Targets
              Targets to Boxtel

              Kolijnsplaat to Orfordness   200 I.A.S.

(b) Mosquito: Base to Orfordness
               Orfordness to Kolijnsplaat   210 I.A.S.

               Kolijnsplaat to Turnhout   260 I.A.S.
               Turnhout to Targets

               Targets to Base (Own routes and speeds)

(c) Venturas: Base to Southwold   180 I.A.S.
                Southwold to Kolijnsplaat

                Kolijnsplaat to Oostmalle   210 I.A.S.
                Oostmalle to Target

                Target to Oirschot   220 I.A.S.
                Oirschot to Kolijnsplaat

                Kolijnsplaat to Southwold   180 I.A.S.

It will be noticed that to further reduce the time interval at the enemy coast on the way out, the Venturas flew their shorter route at an increased airspeed (220 m.p.h.) after bombing, while the Bostons maintained their 240 M.P.H. over the longer route.

26. Minor alterations were made to these routes and speeds eventually, they were as follows. To avoid a cross over of aircraft near the enemy coast the Venturas were to leave at Orfordness and the Bostons and Mosquitos from Southwold. (The Venturas had to fly a more southerly track to the target than the other two types.) With regard to speeds, the Bostons were stepped up to 210, instead of 200 I.A.S., during the sea crossings, and the Mosquitos to 230, instead of 210 I.A.S. The only effect of these speed adjustments was to alter the time of leaving the departure points on our coast.

27. The following times at turning points were calculated for all types using the above speeds and no wind:-

	Boston.	Mosquito.	Ventura.
Kolijnsplaat	Z–19	Z–15½	Z–16
Turnhout	Z–6	Z–3½	—
Oostmalle	—	—	Z–3½
Targets	Zero	Zero + 2	Zero + 6
Boxtel	Z + 3	Own	—
Oirschot	—	Routing	Z + 8½
Kolijnsplaat	Z + 19	—	Z + 26

From the above it will be seen that all aircraft were to cross the coast in between Z–19 and Z–16 (three minutes), and that Bostons and Venturas were to cross the coast out between Z + 19 and Z + 26 (seven minutes). These details were passed to the Fighter Groups to assist them in the organization of their diversions and cover for the bombers.

28. To put these new arrangements to the test an Exercise with new routing and targets was arranged. Simulation of the actual operation was again the aim and the speeds decided upon for the operation were to be employed. The Exercise detail is given below, and the targets were Huntingdon and Godmanchester.

(a) <u>Boston and Mosquito</u>

		I.A.S.	
From.	To.	Boston.	Mosquito
Base	Sheringham	210	230
Sheringham	Flamborough	210	230
Flamborough	Goole	210	230
Goole	Kettering	240	260
Kettering	Targets	240	260
Targets	Chatteris	240	260
Chatteris	Spalding	240	260
Spalding	Wragby	210	230
Wragby	53°10'N 01°00'E	210	230
53°10'N 01°00'E	Sheringham	210	230
Sheringham	Base	210	230

(b) <u>Ventura</u>

From.	To.	I.A.S.
Base	Cromer	180
Cromer	Flamborough	180
Flamborough	Goole	210
Goole	Market Harborough	210
Market Harborough	Targets	210
Targets	Ramsey	220
Ramsey	Spalding	220
Spalding	Wragby	180
Wragby	Holbeach	180
Holbeach	Base	180

In the main essentials, viz., length of sea crossing and deviations before and after the target, affecting the timing, this Exercise simulated the operation accurately.

29. <u>All</u> Navigators were detailed to employ the winds contained in a route forecast to be issued by this Headquarters before the operation. This was also ordered prior to the Exercise described above.

30. This final practice was a great improvement on the previous ones, and the timing was most accurate. The few minor comments such as isolated cases of straggling and insufficient evasive action were passed to Stations by teleprinter. Interception was effected by Fighter Squadrons of No. 12 Group and the following observations made:-

"Formations reported to be good. Pilots state that beam, three quarter, or astern attacks would have subjected them to intense cross fire. Head on attacks would probably have been effective."

31. A discussion on all aspects of the operation was then arranged at R.A.F. Station, Swanton Morley on November the 30th. All Squadron and Station Commanders concerned, representatives of Headquarters, Nos. 11 and 12 Groups and of this Headquarters attended. The phases of all the Fighter assistance were decided upon and the adverse comments which had been made after the Exercises were again emphasized. At this discussion it was also decided that to divert the attention of the target defences, the first three Bostons on each target would carry a bomb load fused 11 seconds delay, and would attack at low level, the remainder would climb and bomb with their original bomb load from 1,000 to 1,500 feet.

32. Using 1: 50,000 maps of the route area, a detailed list of landmarks to be looked for by Navigators was prepared at this Headquarters and dispatched to Stations. Landmarks were picked out for all routes to and from the target every two or three miles. The object here was to ensure that Navigators would study the route well on maps of the above scale, using the list of landmarks as a check during their study. Photographs of landmarks that would be observed on the run in from the sea were also obtained. It was emphasized that a good landfall was essential to the success of the operation. In an attempt to obtain even better photographs, a Mosquito with a cine camera flew the first few miles of the run in on November the 20th. The photographs obtained were unfortunately of no value. It is interesting to note that this aircraft received no attention from the flak defences.

33. Leading Navigators had been given the route to study in good time. Not until confirmation of the Fighter plan was received were all Navigators given the route and target.

34. In the time between the combined Exercises, Squadrons had been practising not only low level bombing and bombing from 1,000 and 1,500 feet, but also formation flying in pairs, and combinations of three pairs.

35. With the stage finally set, unfavourable weather intervened. This necessitated day to day postponement of the operation from the 3rd to the 6th December, 1942. For security reasons during this period all air crews and ground personnel connected with the operation were confined to their Station.

36. Favourable weather conditions arrived on December 6th, and the operation was ordered with a Zero hour at 1230 hours. The Fighter Groups were informed and the many diversions took place at their appointed times.

37. The total number of Bomber aircraft employed by this Group was ninety-four, a total made up as follows:-

```
Bostons    – 36 (Squadrons Nos. 107, 226 and 88)
Mosquitos  – 10 (Squadrons Nos. 105 and 139)
Venturas   – 47 (Squadrons Nos. 21, 464 and 487)
```

One Mosquito of No. 139 Squadron arrived in the target area soon after the attack for photographic reconnaissance with a vertical camera, while many aircraft engaged in the attack carried mirror cameras. The pictorial evidence obtained confirmed visual reports of the damage observed in the target area.

38. Of the ninety-three aircraft detailed to attack, only one returned due to technical trouble (one engine cutting). This was a commendable effort on the part of ground crews. One other aircraft returned due to a faulty hatch. Ninety-one aircraft set course from their departure points on our coast. A total of thirteen aircraft are missing, one of these a Ventura flew into the sea soon after leaving our coast on the way out. Five of the missing aircraft are known to have bombed.

39. (a) The total effort is analysed below:-

A/C Type	Effort	Primary	Abortive	Abandoned	Missing
Ventura	47	36	2	1	8
Boston	36	34	–	2	4 (All bombed)
Mosquito	10	8	–	2	1 (Bombed)
Mosquito Recce	1	–	–	–	–
Totals	94	78	2	5	13

(b) Damage: The following number of aircraft returned damaged:-

Minor damage from light flak & M.G.	– 18 A/C (3 Bostons, 15 Venturas)
Major damage from light flak & M.G.	– 2 A/C (1 Boston, 1 Ventura)
Minor damage from enemy aircraft.	– 2 A/C (1 Mosquito, 1 Boston)
Damaged by birds.	– 23 A/C (6 Bostons, 16 Venturas, 1 Mosquito)
Hit trees	– 1 A/C (Boston)

TOTAL 46

(c) Losses are listed below:-

A/C Type	Missing	Flak	E/A	Unknown
Venturas	9 (1 crew rescued from sea)	1	–	7
Boston	4	–	3 (2?)	1
Mosquito	1	–	1 (?)	–

The above assumptions are made after analysing reports by crews. It is possible that at least one Ventura loss was due to phosphorous splash from bursting bombs. One pilot reports seeing an incendiary bomb burst on a flat roof near an aircraft the tail of which was seen to be on fire. This observation was made at a distance of 1200 yards however.

40. Few enemy fighters were seen. Two Fw190s and two Bf109Fs were active on the route in to the target and were observed by many crews to be following the formations. Many crews report having been fired at by coastal defences after leaving the enemy coast until two or three miles out to sea.

In one Ventura the observer was hit in the face by a large duck which came though the windscreen, nevertheless, this observer held a tin hat against the damaged perspex throughout the return journey.

In another Ventura a hit by flak ignited three Very cartridges. These were put out by the use of the fire extinguisher.

A Boston aircraft received damage by birds to the navigators compartment early in the operation. Despite the loss of all his maps the observer continued to navigate by memory – an excellent argument in favour of careful study of the route before an operation.

Although photographs taken by the Venturas show dense volumes of smoke in the target area during their attack, in no instance have pilots complained that this prevented them from pressing home their attack.

A Mosquito, while in formation, was attacked by a Fw190 which approached from the starboard quarter both aircraft being at feet. Drawing the E/A away from the main unarmed formation this pilot carried out his own evasive action which consisted of turns into the attack, skilful evading the fire of the enemy fighter.

An appreciation by the Group Flak Liaison Officer on the losses sustained is appended to this report.

The operation appears to have been successful in every way. A large percentage of the aircraft dispatched bombed their targets with a very high degree of accuracy and concentration. Low level navigation was exceptional. Undoubtedly the diversions by fighter aircraft of Nos. 11and 12 Groups and Bombers of U.S.A.A.C. were responsible for the almost negligible enemy fighter opposition encountered.

(signed)
Group Captain,
Officer Commanding,
No. 2 Group.

Flak Liaison Officer's report: AIR25/35 [D28]-FLO[2]

Appendix "A"

SECRET

No. 2 Group Flak Liaison Officer's Report

ATTACK ON EINDHOVEN

Effective Sorties: 34 Bostons
10 Mosquitos
                    44 Venturas
Casualties: 4 Bostons   – 3 hit by LFF and 1 by
                    1 Mosquito   Missing – none hit by flak. / M.G.F
                    8 Venturas   – 15 hit by L.F.F. and 3 by M.G.F

Appreciation: Of the missing aircraft, definite information exists for only two. One Boston was seen to be shot down by fighters and one Ventura was seen to crash (as a result of L.F.F.) after passing over Woensdrecht A/D. Of the remainder, two other Bostons were seen to crash after the bunch of aircraft, in whose company they were flying, had been attacked by fighters. The fourth one just disappeared with no indication of cause. The missing Mosquito was seen flying with one engine smoking, possibly as a result of being hit by L.F.F. when crossing the coast coming home. This aircraft was seen to stall and dive into the sea.

Of the other seven Venturas, one was seen to crash just before the target, possibly as a result of L.F.F. from Eindhoven A/D, one and possibly two were seen to crash in the target, either as a result of L.F.F. from the A/D or from inability to see where they were going for the smoke, and two others crashed just past the target, one for similar reasons, the other being observed to have been set on fire as a result of the incendiaries from the previous aircraft bouncing into it. One other was observed to put down in the sea before crossing the enemy coast with bombs still aboard, presumably due to engine failure, leaving one outstanding.

The Bostons undoubtedly suffered their losses because they were not bunched together enough. After leaving the target they did not keep together, with the result that fighters were able to pick up odd aircraft without receiving the concentration of return fire that they should have. In fact, on the way to the target when they were closer together, though still not particularly well bunched, fighters were seen to follow but not attack.

The Mosquito is an unknown quantity, but if indeed it was hit by L.F.F. when crossing the coast it could only have been avoided by being in cloud. Most of the Venturas are also doubtful but the indications are that the majority of losses were NOT a result of flak or fighter. It seems quite possible that the terrific pall of smoke over the target, the bouncing incendiaries, etc., accounted for at least three of them and quite possibly four, especially as photographs show that they were flying really low, though flak is a possible cause. Two more might be credited to flak, one definitely. Both of these could have been avoided by not flying over or near A/Ds.

N.B. This was a point particularly stressed before the operation.

In fact, the Ventura's track was unfortunate from the start. Landfall was made over Walcheren, not a healthy spot at the best of times, and it was here that the great majority of aircraft that suffered damage from flak were hit. From there the track passed straight over Woensdrecht A/D where one aircraft was shot down and a few more hit. No further trouble was experienced until the target area, which was approached from north of official track, bringing them well within range of the A/D defences. The casualties at the target are doubtful and it is impossible to say that they were caused by flying too near the A/D, but at any rate a number of aircraft were hit by flak there. A few further aircraft were damaged when coming out of the Schelde estuary on the way home.

Of the Bostons hit by flak two were over the target – one was the leader – and one at Woensdrecht again. Birds accounted for a very large number of aircraft damaged, far more than fighters and flak.

As far as the defences go, it was not visualized that aircraft would make a landfall at Walcheren and the avoiding of A/Ds I attempted to stress before the operation took place. At the target flak fire was exactly as I visualized it. A H.F. fixed barrage of very low intensity over the target after the first aircraft attacked and at the height from which they had bombed. The first low level Bostons took the L.F. gunners completely by surprise at the small target - they were presumably watching what was happening at the other targets. The gunners at the big target gave a better display and the leading aircraft was hit, obviously as a direct approacher probably as a result of being a bit high in attempting to find the target. They also continued to fire even though the buildings on top of which they were sited, were tottering. There was also a considerable amount of M.G. fire from both sides of the target area. The conglomeration of aircraft apparently bewildered the gunners and the very haphazard formation of Bostons appeared to be more effective than the tightly packed bunch of Venturas, though it must be borne in mind that other factors played a big part in the distribution of casualties, e.g. previous warning, track, etc.

The ability of the coastal gunners to engage aircraft flying at 0 feet out from the coast was again brought home, several crews reporting accurate H. and L.F.F. up to five miles out to sea.

No. 2 Group Tactical Report[3]

SECRET

From: Headquarters, No. 2 Group.
To: Headquarters, Bomber Command,
Date: 4th January, 1943.
Ref: 2G/S. 419/Tactics.

No. 2 Group Tactical Report, December, 1942.

OPERATIONS.

1. Daylight operations were carried out on only twelve days during the month of December. On these days a total of 191 sorties were flown. This total includes 94 sorties which were carried out to attack the Phillips Valve and Radio Factory at Eindhoven on the 6th December, 1942. No night operations were carried out.

   Detail of the sorties are tabulated under aircraft types below:-

2. BOSTON III.

	Sorties.	Missing.	Primary.	Alternative.	Abandoned.
Medium Level	18	–	18	–	–
Low Level	36	4	34 +	–	2
Cloud Cover	10	–	–	–	10
TOTALS	64	4	52	–	12

+ Includes four missing aircraft, which were seen to attack.

(a) <u>Medium Level.</u> Only one "Circus" operation took place during the month when eighteen Bostons in three boxes of six attacked the Lock Gates at St Malo. The usual tactics were employed, the approach being made at low level, until close to the target, when a rapid climb was made to 11,000 feet, and bombing was carried out from 10,000 feet. Very little flak was experienced, and that was inaccurate, and a good bombing run was made. Unfortunately, the forecast wind was very inaccurate and, as this was used for bombing, the results were poor in spite of slight opposition. No enemy aircraft were encountered, and none of the Bostons were damaged.

(b) <u>Low Level.</u> The only low level attacks during the month were those on the Phillips Valve and Radio Factory at Eindhoven, and this was the subject of a separate tactical report.

(c) <u>Cloud Cover.</u> Attempts were made on the 13th December, 1942, to attack railway marshalling yards at Courtrai and Ghent using cloud cover. Two aircraft were detailed for each target, but owing to complete lack of cloud cover when approaching the enemy coast all sorties were abandoned.

<u>Interpretation Report dd. 7-12-1942</u>:[3] AIR29/259 [K1446]
[Operations Record Book No. 2 Group RAF, AIR29/259 [K1446]]

SECRET.
7.12.42

<u>IMMEDIATE INTERPRETATION REPORT NO.K.1446.</u>
(Subject to correction and amplification from a more detailed assessment).

Photographs taken by 139 Squadron on 6.12.42.

Actual time of photography: 1233 hours

SORTIE F.L.139.

Scale: Variable (obliques only).
Flying Height: 1,000 feet.

LOCALITY: EINDHOVEN (Phillips Radio Works).

<u>COVER.</u>
The works are divided into two groups, The EINDHOVEN GROUP and The STRIJP GROUP.
    Only the S.W. corner of The EINDHOVEN GROUP is covered.
The S.W. corner of the STRIJP GROUP is covered, though obscured by smoke in places.

<u>QUALITY.</u> Generally hazy.

PERIOD UNDER REVIEW.
No previous report on damage to the works has been issued.

PROVISIONAL STATEMENT ON DAMAGE.
Owing to the fact that the photographs are obliques and clouds of smoke are drifting across the target area, it is only possible to give an approximate estimate of damage. It must also be borne in mind that no part of the E. half of the STRIJP GROUP can be seen.

STRIJP GROUP (Main Plant).
The following buildings are seen to be on fire:

The ELECTRO TECHNICAL FACTORY (print 29).
A new store house (built this year) (print 29).
The centre block of the MACHINE SHOP BUILDINGS. (print 29).
An unidentified building. (prints 14 and 28)
RADIO ASSEMBLY SHOP S.E. building (Prints 14 and 28).
PAPER and CARDBOARD store (Prints 14 and 27).
PAPER MILL (Print 27).
INDUSTRIAL SCHOOL (Print 27).
GLASS WORKS. (Print 27).

Damaged by H.E.
COMPONENT BUILDINGS centre block   (Print 29)
COMPONENT BUILDINGS centre block   (Print 14)
The ELECTRO TECHNICAL FACTORY is not only damaged by blast from a nearby H.E. incident, but smoke is issuing from both sides of it.
The RADIO ASSEMBLY SHOP is also burning fiercely at several places along its whole length.
   The most complete damage seen on this Sortie is to the INDUSTRIAL SCHOOL which is nearly gutted.

EINDHOVEN GROUP (VALVE AND LAMP FACTORY).
The S. wing of the VALVE and LAMP FACTORY is seriously damaged both by H.E. and fire. Several small sheds and buildings surrounding it have been damaged by H.E.
   This is the only part of the works which appears on the sortie, and owing to the direction of the wind it is not possible to estimate the possibility of fires in the remainder of the works from smoke.

OTHER INDUSTRIAL DAMAGE.

STOOM LINNEN (TEXTILE FACTORY) .
A direct hit on the main building with a large area of blast surrounding it.

RESIDENTIAL DAMAGE.

Six separate incidents involving many houses can be seen, but owing to fires no estimate of the number can be given.

2 prints distributed, Nos. 27 and 28. (Negs. Nos. 12161 and 12162).

SECRET.	DISTRIBUTION.
R.A.F. STATION,	Standard K. No. 1
MEDMENHAM.	Plus

		Reports.	Prints.
WVC/PW/A.			
	H.Q.B.C.		
	Groups	9	9
	No. 2 Group Stations.	11	11
	R.A.F. Station, Wyton.	6	6
	C. Arm. O.	1	3
	G/C Nav.	1	–
	Air Ministry.		
	P.A. to C.A.S.	1	1

Interpretation Report dd. 8–12–1942[4]
(see Appendix 4 for aircraft reference letters)

SECRET
8.12.42.

INTERPRETATION REPORT NO. S.A.176.
Photographs taken on 6.12.42.
LOCALITY: EINDHOVEN.

EINDHOVEN (G.S.G.S.4083 Sheet 51).
6.12.42. 1230 – 1239 hrs 100 – 1500 ft.

Camera and Aircraft Reference Letters.
21 Squad	FU, HK, LJ, PZ, RO.
88 Squad	CS, DF, EK, JG, NP.
105 Squad	AV, CG, CO, EC, FP, NX.
107 Squad	DG.
226 Squad	AF, CL, DW, FZ, HV, JA, LX, LH.
464 Squad	DM.
487 Squad	AY, BV, CS, OG.

(i) GENERAL.
    (a) These photographs were taken during a daylight attack on the Philips Radio Works at EINDHOVEN by 93 aircraft of No. 2 Group, Bomber Command. The attacking force which consisted of 47 Venturas, 36 Bostons and 10 Mosquitos had withdrawal Fighter Support.
    (b) 45 tons of H.E. and 18 tons of incendiaries were dropped.
    (c) Photographs were taken by 30 aircraft.

(ii) BOMB BURSTS OBSERVED.
    (a) This report refers only to incidents seen within the limits of the two sites comprising the PHILIPS RADIO WORKS, and the nearby STOOMLINNEN FABRIEK Textile Factory. A supplementary report on outlying incidents will be issued later.
    (b) As these photographs are mostly low obliques no accurate statement can be made on the number of bomb bursts. Large clouds of smoke caused by many bombs bursting close together further hinder interpretation.
    (c) It is quite obvious that a great many more incidents have occurred than it has been possible to plot on the accompanying plan.

(iii) DETAILS OF ATTACK.
In order to clarify the plan the incidents have been classified in the following categories. The numbers following the names of the buildings refer to the attached plan:-

A. <u>BUILDINGS BURNING FIERCELY</u>.
Industrial School (1)
Workshops (7)
Components Factory - East half of East block (14)
Boiler house - East half (19)
Mechanical Glassworks (20)
An unidentified building - West half (21)
Power Station - East half (25)
Bakelite Factory (26)
Lamp and Valve Factory - South end (29)
Compressor House (32)

B. <u>BUILDINGS PROBABLY BURNING</u>.
Component Factory - West end of central block (14)
An unidentified building (21)
Metal works (23)
Power Station (25)
Lamp and Valve factory - North wing (29)

C. <u>BUILDINGS POSSIBLY BURNING</u>.
Glass works - East end (6)
Electro-Technical factory - West end (17)
Store House - East half (18)

D. <u>BOMB BURSTS</u>.
S.E. of Power Station (25)
On East block of Machine Shops (24)
On West and South-east sides of Lamp and Valve factory (29)
N. of the railway at the East end of the Strijp Group.

(iv) ACCOMPANYING PRINTS.
Prints I, II and III accompanying this report give a general view of the
EINDHOVEN GROUP of buildings during the attack.

(Photo Nos. HK.21, 14–16)

<u>DISTRIBUTION</u>.

<u>Bomber Command</u>.

C. in C.	1	C.A.S.	1
G/C Ops. (S.A.S.O.)	1	Admiralty	3
Ops. I.B.	1	A.M. War Room.	2
Intelligence (B.C.)	5	A.I.3 (c).	1
O.R.S.	1	D.D.A.T.	1
W/Cdr. Photos.	1	H.Q.F.C.	41
Narrative Officer.	2	M.I.14 (h)	1
P.R.O.	1	D.B. Ops.	1
U.S.A.S. High Wycombe		Int. C.C.	2
(F/Lt. Boggis).	2	P.R.U. Benson.	1
R.A.F. Station, Upwood		P.I.S. Benson.	1
(S.I.O.)	1	D.P.R.	2
R.A.F. Station, Bicester		A.I.3 (U.S.A.)	4
(S.I.O.)	1	M.E.W. (Mr Lawrence).	1
H.Q. 1 Group	1		
H.Q. 2 Group	11		
H.Q. 3 Group	1		
H.Q. 4 Group	1		
H.Q. 5 Group	1		
H.Q. 91 Group	1		
H.Q. 91 Group	1		
H.Q. 93 Group	1		

<u>SECRET</u>.

R.A.F. STATION,
<u>MEDMENHAM.</u>

TDW/C/MLF/B.

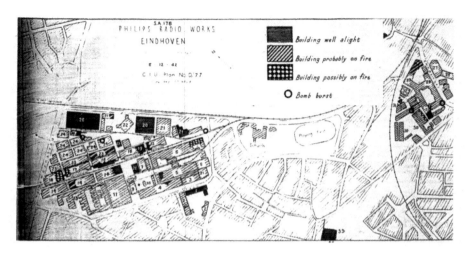

Philips plant maps to interpretation report no. S.A. 176

KEY TO NUMBERED BUILDINGS

STRIJP GROUP.

1. INDUSTRIAL SCHOOL.
2. BUILDINGS ASSOCIATED WITH INDUSTRIAL SCHOOL.
3. CARDBOARD WORKS.
4. PAPER MILL.
5. STORE ROOMS FOR PAPER AND CARDBOARD.
6. GLASS WORKS.
7. WORKSHOPS.
8. TRANSFORMER HOUSE.
9. COMPRESSOR HOUSE.
10. WATER TOWER. (J.ELIAS)
11. TESTING SHOP.
12. PHYSICAL LABORATORY.
13. I-RAY LABORATORY.

14. COMPONENT FACTORY.
15. GLASS STOREROOMS.
16. RADIO ASSEMBLY SHOP.
17. ELECTRO TECHNICAL FACTORY.
18. STOREHOUSE.
19. BOILER HOUSE.
20. MECHANICAL GLASS WORKS.
21. UNIDENTIFIED BUILDINGS.
22. GARAGE.
23. METAL WORKS.
24. MACHINE SHOPS.
25. POWER STATION.
26. BAKELITE FACTORY.

EINDHOVEN GROUP.

27. HEAD OFFICES.
28. COMMERCIAL OFFICES.
29. LAMP AND VALVE FACTORY.
30. VALVE STORAGE BUILDINGS.
31. AIR LIQUEFACTION PLANT.
32. COMPRESSOR HOUSE.

33. STOOMLINNEN FABRIEK TEXTILE FACTORY

Interpretation Report dd. 8–12–1942[5]

INTERPRETATION REPORT NO. S.A.177.
Photographs taken on 6.12.42.
LOCALITY: EINDHOVEN.

EINDHOVEN (G.S.G.S.4083 Sheet 51).

6.12.42. 1230–1239 hrs 100–1500 ft.

(i) GENERAL.

The present report supplements Report S.A.176 and is concerned with details of the attack other than those in the target areas already dealt with. The camera and aircraft reference letters are the same as in Report S.A.176.

For a preliminary assessment of damage based on photographs taken approx. half an hour after the attack (F.L.139), reference should be made to Report No. K.1446.

(ii) DETAILS OF ATTACK.

(a) One possible H.E. burst, and incendiaries, with much smoke are seen on the railway line and at the N.E. corner of the Station where a bridge crosses a small stream
(CL.226, Photo 21; HV.226, Photo 236).

(b) The remaining incidents have occurred in residential areas and in open country nearby. They are listed below.

    1. Incendiaries burning on town area and
       railway N. of Eindhoven Group.   LJ. 21.   Ph.195.

    2. Small houses, S. of main entrance to Strijp
       Group, hit by H.E. and incendiary bombs.
       Bombs (4) falling towards main target.   CE.105.   Ph.197.

    3. Fires burning on small houses outside S.E.
       corner of main Strijp target, near Sports
       Field and in Frederik Laan.   CE.105.   Ph.198.

    4. Incendiaries falling in open ground and
       among houses N.E. of the Strijp group.   DM.464.   Ph.197.

    5. Incendiaries falling on shops and houses
       N., E., and S. of the Church at the corner
       of KERK STR. AND STRATUMS
       EIND. S.E. of Eindhoven group; probably
       a direct hit on N.E. chapels of Apse   AF.226.   Ph.209.
       of Church.   AF.226.   Ph.210.

    6. H.E. burst and incendiaries N. of
       Eindhoven Group, near Church.   AF.226.   Ph.211.

    7. H.E. burst in open ground S.S.E. of
       Eindhoven target.   DF. 88.   Ph.318.

    8. Incendiary burst in open country in
       WOENSEL district N. of Eindhoven town. AU.487.   Ph.61.

9. H.E. and incendiaries on space N. of
Eindhoven target between factory and
church.   FU. 21.   Ph.113.

10. H.E. and incendiaries bursting on new   HK. 21.   Ph.149.
housing estate and houses and shops   Ph.150.
W.S.W. of Eindhoven target, near Railway
line and Wilhelmina Plein up to target.

11. H.E. burst in open ground immediately
N.E. of Railway line bordering N.E.
side of Strijp target.   OC.105.   Ph.62.

DISTRIBUTION.

Bomber Command.

C. in C.	1	U.S.A.S.* High Wycombe	
G/C Ops. (S.A.S.O.)	1	(F/Lt. Boggiss)	2
Ops. I.B.	1	Admiralty	3
Intelligence B.C.	5	A.M. War Room	2
O.R.S.	1	A.I.3. (c)	1
W/Cdr Photos.	1	D.D.A.T.	1
Narrative Officer.	2	H.Q.F.C.	41
P.R.O.	1	M.I.14 h	1
R.A.F. Upwood	1	D.B. Ops	1
R.A.F. Bicester	1	Int. C.C.	2
H.Q. 1 Group	1	P.R.U. Benson	1
H.Q. 2 Group	11	P.I.S. Benson	1
H.Q. 3 Group	1	D.P.R.	1
H.Q. 4 Group	1	A.I.3. U.S.A.	4
H.Q. 5 Group	1		
H.Q. 91 Group	1		
H.Q. 92 Group	1		
H.Q. 93 Group	1		

SECRET.

R.A.F. STATION,
MEDMENHAM.

DKP/B/PIW/A

---

* United States Air Station.

Interpretation Report dd. 21–12–1942[6]

INTERPRETATION REPORT NO.K.1450.

Photographs taken by No.541 squadron on 14 and 16.12.42.
Mean times of photography: 1500 & 1135 hrs.

SORTIES C/699, C/711.
Scales: C/699 – 1/16,200 approx. (F.L.20")
C/711 – 1/9,000 approx. (F.L.36")

LOCALITY: EINDHOVEN.

DAMAGE ASSESSMENT.
On C/699 the whole town is covered by prints of poor scale and quality.
On C/711 the north and south of the town are covered by prints of good scale and
very fair quality; but of the PHILIPS WORKS only the extreme S.W. edge of the
STRIJP GROUP and the southern half of the EINDHOVEN GROUP.

PERIOD UNDER REVIEW.
Immediate interpretation report No. K.1446 (Sortie F.L./139) was issued on
7.12.42., but no report on damage to EINDHOVEN was issued before the date of
the recent daylight raid, 6.12.42.

GENERAL STATEMENT.
Owing to the poor scale and quality of C/699 and the lack of cover on C/711 this
statement is made with some reserve, though it can be seen that both groups of the
PHILIPS WORKS have been very heavily damaged. There is also serious damage
at the STOOMLINNEN TEXTILE FACTORY; one, possibly two or more, hits
on the railway; possibly some damage to the station; and many houses have been
partly or wholly destroyed.

DETAILS OF DAMAGE.
With the exception of 6 minor points, 2 of which are in outlying districts, all the
damage is seen on the annotated photograph accompanying this report, and is listed
in the appendix.

1 print distributed: portion of enlargement of 2010 C/699
(Neg. No. 15234).
Maps used: EINDHOVEN town plan 1/10,000
C.I.U. plan No. D/77, of PHILIPS RADIO WORKS.

SECRET   DISTRIBUTION NO.23.
R.A.F.STATION,
MEDMENHAM.   E. 202
IG/FW/B.   I.   24
                                          226 copies.

                                                        SECRET
                                                        21.12.42

                          APPENDIX
              to Interpretation Report No. K 1450.

     (Portion of enlargement of print 2010 of C/699 Neg.No.15234).

INDUSTRIAL DAMAGE.
PHILIPS RADIO WORKS, STRIJP GROUP.
  1a CARDBOARD: possible damage to lower storey.
  1b INDUSTRIAL SCHOOL: severely damaged by H.E. and fire; large hole in
      roof; crater nr. S.E. end, where there is blast damage.
  1c PAPER MILL: large hole on S.W. side of roof.
  1d STORE ROOMS FOR PAPER AND CARDBOARD: area of about 40 x 15
      yd. is gutted.
  1e GLASSWORKS: single-storey building at N.W. end very severely damaged;
      single-storey building near above, very severely damaged; low building on
      S.E. side, possibly damaged.
  1f WORKSHOPS: single-storey building completely destroyed; 2-bay single-
      storey building roofless, severely damaged by fire; single-storey flat-roofed
      building destroyed by fire.
  1g X-RAY LABORATORY: portion of N. end damaged by fire.
  1h COMPONENT FACTORY BUILDINGS: centre block damaged by H.E.;
      S.E. block: about 1/3 of roof severely damaged by H.E. and fire; rest of
      building possibly damaged.
  1i ELECTRO TECHNICAL FACTORY: damaged by H.E.
  1j STOREHOUSE: upper part very badly damaged by H.E.
  1k RADIO ASSEMBLY SHOPS: S.W. portion of buildings damaged.
  1l MACHINE SHOPS: 1 building completely destroyed; hole in roof of 2-bay
      shed; irregular 2-bay shed damaged; long shed has bay added in centre since
      18.8.42.
  1m BAKELITE FACTORY: low portion of building on N.E. side probably
      damaged.
  1n UNIDENTIFIED SINGLE-STOREY BUILDING: completely destroyed
      by fire.
  1o GARAGE: W. end and adjoining sheds destroyed.
  1p UNIDENTIFIED SQUARE BUILDING: severely damaged.

1q MECHANICAL GLASS WORKS: long building on S.W. side has almost half the roof destroyed; large adjoining shed has possible damage to roof.

1r LARGE UNIDENTIFIED MULTI-BAY BUILDING: hole in roof and S. corner destroyed.

PHILIPS RADIO WORKS, EINDHOVEN GROUP.

2a HEAD OFFICES: building of at least 7 storeys, whole roof discoloured by fire and large skylight damaged.

2b COMMERCIAL OFFICES: multi-storey building has half the roof gutted over the whole of its length.

2c UNIDENTIFIED BUILDING: roof damaged.

2d LAMP & VALVE FACTORY: S.W. side has direct hit on edge of roof.

2e LAMP & VALVE FACTORY: S.W. wing severely damaged, probably from a direct hit.

2f LAMP & VALVE FACTORY: S.W. wing has 2 large holes in roof, probably from direct hit.

2g LAMP & VALVE FACTORY: N.W. side has much fire damage on the roof.

2h LAMP & VALVE FACTORY: block connecting N. wing to main block has 4 bays of its 6-bay roof gutted, and damage to roof on N.E. corner.

2i LAMP & VALVE FACTORY: N. wing has a hole in the roof from a direct hit; a long low shed adjoining is completely gutted.

2j TWO UNIDENTIFIED BUILDINGS: appear to be destroyed, probably by fire.

2k TWO UNIDENTIFIED BUILDINGS: 1 gutted; 1 damaged.

STOOMLINNEN FABRIEK. (J. ELIAS: TEXTILES).

3a MAIN BUILDING: very large hole in roof, and surrounding area.

3b MAIN BUILDING: blast damage at S. corner; 1 crater near and 2 more, probably from a stick of 4, in allotments nearby.

RESIDENTIAL DAMAGE.

4 WAATSTRAAT: row of houses; 2 or 3 destroyed by H.E.

5 NR. WAATSTRAAT: row of houses; 2 or 3 gutted.

6 NR. N.E. SIDE OF PHILIPS' (STRIJP GROUP): 7, possibly more, craters in open ground.

7 HETHEIN STRAAT: row of houses; 2 or 3 destroyed by H.E.

8 HARMONIE STRAAT: several houses destroyed and damaged.

9 JUNCTION OF BOSCH DIJK & KRUIS STRAAT: at least 9 houses destroyed by H.E.

10 NR. OUDE BOGERT: 3, possibly more craters; the railway-track may have been hit.

11. NR. N.E. SIDE OF PHILIPS' (EINDHOVEN GROUP), EITHER SIDE OF HET EINDJE, FELLENOORD & DEMER: about 11 acres of houses, mostly destroyed.

12 VEST DIJK: 1 house demolished.

13   WILLEM STRAAT: 4 houses gutted.
14   PRINS HENDRIK STRAAT: 4 houses gutted.
15   JULIANA STRAAT: row of houses; 5 or 6 gutted, and 1 crater in open ground nearby.
16   JULIANA STRAAT: row of houses; 3 or 4 gutted.
17   FREDERIK LAAN: block of about 4 houses completely destroyed.
18   DE JONG LAAN: block of about 4 houses mostly destroyed.
19   NR. EAST CORNER OF PHILIPS' (STRIJP GROUP): group of many houses; many very badly damaged by H.E., some by blast; 1 crater on railway-track.

SECRET.
R.A.F. STATION,
MEDMENHAM.
IG/MLF/B.

Notes
1. NA Kew, AIR25/35 (D28), op. cit.
2. Ibid.
3. NA Kew, AIR25/35 (D29)
4. NA Kew, AIR29/260 (SA176), ORB, No. 2 Group RAF.
5. NA Kew, AIR29/260 (SA177), ORB, No. 2 Group RAF.
6. NA Kew, AIR29/259 (K1450), ORB, No. 2 Group RAF.

Appendix IV: American Diversionary Raid[1]

HEADQUARTERS
EIGHT AIR FORCE
WIDEWING
Office of the Assistant Chief of Staff A-2

(D-62-35)
9 December, 1942.

COMPOSITE INTELLIGENCE NARRATIVE NO. 10

of

OPERATIONS UNDERTAKEN 6 DECEMBER 1942

by

U.S.A.A.F and R.A.F.

In this offensive 66 B.17s of VIII U.S.A.A.F. Bomber Command were dispatched to attack the Ateliers d'Hellemes at Lille and 19 B.24s of 44th Group were dispatched to attack the Abbeville/Drucat Airdrome.

Six B.17s of 11th C.C.R.G. were to make a diversionary flight in connection with this operation and 16 B.17s of 306th Group were detailed on a mock diversion.

Twenty-two squadrons of R.A.F. Spitfires and three squadrons of U.S.A.A.F. Spitfires (36 Spitfires VB of 334th, 335th and 336th Squadrons) were detailed to provide cover and support for the attacks against Lille and the Abbeville/Drucat Airdrome.

Of 85 bombers dispatched, 43 attacked the primary targets.

The chronology of the U.S.A.A.F. groups in these operations is:

GROUPS	DISPATCHED	ATTACKING	TARGET	RETURNED
44	19 B-24s	6	Abbeville-Drucat A/D	18

Part II

91	22 B-17s	18	Lille-Ateliers d'Hellemes	22
303	20 B-17s	15	Lille-Ateliers d'Hellemes	20
305	24 B-17s	4	Lille-Ateliers d'Hellemes	23
	66	37	65	

Part III

11 CCRC	6 B-17s	0	Diversion	6	
306	16 B-17s	0	Mock Diversion		16
	22	0	22		

CONFIDENTIAL

77½ tons of H.E bombs were dropped on Lille and six tons on the Abbeville/ Drucat Airdrome.

Many hits are reported in the target area of Lille but results at Abbeville were unobserved due to the overcast.

Numerous encounters took place, our crews claiming 11 E/A destroyed, five probably destroyed and seven damaged. One of our B.17s and one B.24 were lost.

PART I
LILLE

66 B.17s took off and of these 37 dropped 20 x 1000 lb. H.E. and 320 x 500 lb. H.E. bombs.

Take-off was between 1016-1040 hours, with rendezvous over Felixstowe at 20,000–23,000 feet at 1140 hours. The target was reached at 1208-1210 hours, and the A/C landed back at base at 1210–1358 hours.

From bases to the French Coast there were 8/10ths – 10/10ths clouds, decreasing inland to 2/10ths at the target area with clear visibility over the target.

Slight inaccurate heavy flak was met north of Dunkirk; red bursts of heavy flak were seen at Gravelines, and heavy black flak at Tournai. Over Lille, intense heavy flak, inaccurate for height and deflection, was fired in barrages of six bursts. No flak was observed at the coast on return.

Bombing was from 20,000–23,000 ft. Numerous hits are reported in the target area, especially on the railroad yard and tracks. Fires were seen in factory buildings. Bombs dropped totalled 180,000 lb. H.E.

Most encounters took place after bombing, approximately 20 enemy fighter mostly Fw-190s – attacking. One B.17 was seen to go down in flames near Tournai and between one and four crew members baled out. Claims on enemy aircraft total nine destroyed, one probably destroyed and seven damaged.

Two men were injured seriously and two slightly in addition to ten crew members missing from the A/C shot down.

Thirteen planes returned early because of mechanical failures, 17 bombers of one group failed to find the target, and on two others the bomb bay failed to function.

To provide escort cover for the first box of B.17s 23 R.A.F. Spitfires IX of the Hornchurch Wing (64th and 122nd Squadrons) took off from Manston at 1140 hours. The wing flew across the channel to the St Omer area, where 12 to 15 Fw-190s were seen flying at 35,000 feet. Shortly afterwards the bombers were picked up returning over the Cassel area and as the Spitfires remained up sun the E/A refrained from attacking. While orbiting to cover the withdrawal of the bombers north-west of Calais one section of the 122nd Squadron which was slightly behind was jumped by Fw-190s. As a result of combats one Fw-190 is claimed as destroyed and one Spitfire and pilot is missing.

At 1125 hours 24 R.A.F. Spitfires IX of the North Weald Wing (331st and 332nd Squadrons) took off to provide escort cover for the second box of B.17s. The formation flew to the target area where slight flak was experienced well below. Shortly after leaving Lille, two Fw-190s dived through the wing and unsuccessfully attacked one of the bombers. A further eight E/A were seen but were too far below to be engaged.

To provide escort cover for the third box of B.17s, 25 R.A.F. Spitfires IX of the Northolt Wing (306th and 315th Squadrons) took off from Northolt at 1110 hours, crossed the French Coast five miles east of Dunkerque and when about 10 miles inland one of the bombers was seen to catch fire and explode. A few Fw-190s were seen after leaving the target, only one of which attacked the bombers before diving away.

Target support was provided by 22 R.A.F. Spitfires IX of 401st and 402nd Squadrons[2] which left Kenley at 1130 hours and made rendezvous over Biggin Hill with 24 Spitfires IX of 340th and 611th Squadrons, also R.A.F. The wing crossed the French Coast at 24,000 feet and flew direct to Lille where boxes of bombers were seen to attack accurately before their withdrawal over Gravelines was covered by the fighters. At this stage ten E/A were seen above the Kenley Wing, coming up from the south. These E/A would not engage and did not approach the bombers. In the same area two Fw-190s approached the Biggin Hill formation from the starboard beam and were attacked by a section of 611th Squadron. One Fw-190 was probably destroyed.

First rear support was provided by 24 Spitfires VB of 131st and 165th Squadrons and 12 Spitfires VIB of 616th Squadron, all R.A.F., which took off from Tangmere at 1150 hours and reached the Gravelines area stepped up from 23,500 feet to 25,000 feet. Two boxes of bombers, seen coming out at 22,000 feet were escorted back. Between 30 and 50 E/A were seen by the wing pilots operating singly, in pairs and in fours, making diving attacks on the bombers from 3/4000 feet above and then refusing combat with the fighters by diving away. A group of 12 E/A followed 131st Squadron back to the Channel, breaking into pairs to make separate attacks. As a result of combats one Fw-190 was destroyed and another damaged by pilots of 131st Squadron, one of whose pilots was slightly wounded.

To provide second rear support, 36 Spitfires VB of 334th, 335th, and 336th (U.S.A.A.F.) Squadrons left Debden at 1152 hours and climbed over the Channel to reach Gris Nez at 20,000/23,000 feet. Height was increased another 1000 feet for a sweep over Audruicq, Gravelines and Gris Nez. The B.17s were seen coming out over Gravelines-Dunkerque shadowed by about 12 E/A at about 28,000 feet. When approaching mid-Channel six Fw-190s were sighted in pairs at 15/25,000 feet north of Calais and as the wing orbited two more Fw-190s were seen. One was attacked and damaged by a pilot of 335th Squadron.

Part II
(Abbeville - Drucat Airdrome)

Of the 19 B.24s dispatched only one squadron attacked the airdrome, the others having returned on a recall signal from the fighter escort which turned back.

The remaining squadron did not hear the recall order and continued without fighter cover to the target where an overcast obscured it from view.

On the run-up, however, the target area was seen and the squadron dropped 111 x 100 lb. H.W. bombs.

Take-off was at 0920–0930 hours with rendezvous at Beachy Head. Time over the target was 1124 hours.

Over the Channel 3/10ths clouds were encountered while at the target there were 6/10ths - 7/10ths alto-stratus with tops apparently at 14,000 feet.

Fairly intense heavy flak was thrown up immediately north of the target and some heavy flak in the vicinity of Pte Haut Banc which was accurate for height but burst behind the formation. Slight heavy flak was encountered near Crecy.

Due to cloud over target, no results were observed following release of 111 x 100 lb. H.E. at 1124 hours. Others totalling 9 x 100 lb. H.E. were hung up and brought back to base

Approximately 30 E/A, mostly Fw-190s with a few Bf-109s, attacked at 1130 hours, just after the formation bombed. The Fw-190s lay to the starboard in the sun, then came around to the front, attacking directly through. The E/A stayed below the arc of the top turret.

One B.24 had No. 3 and No. 4 engines knocked out; whereupon, as it became separated from the formation, it was attacked by 11 - 14 Fw-190s in javelin formation. Three of these came in directly from behind and below against the tail turret, which was put out of action, and are believed to have shot our plane down. One Bf-109 attacked abeam out of the sun. Our crews claim two destroyed, four probables and one damaged.

Three men of one crew were slightly wounded by a 20 mm shell bursting in the plane, and one crew of ten is missing from one plane which was seen to crash and burst in flames in the Channel.

Five planes returned early because of mechanical failures. Eight making sorties returned when they received the recall signal and one of these jettisoned 20 x 100 lb. H.E. bombs because of the loss of a bomb pin; all other planes brought back their bombs except those dropped at target.

To provide escort cover 36 R.A.F. Spitfires VB and VC of the Middle Wallop Wing (66th, 118th and 504th Squadrons) took off at 1052 hours and made rendezvous with the B.24s off Beachy Head at 20,000 feet. As the formation was leaving Beachy Head a Fw-190 was seen flying at 25,000 feet; the E/A passed over and behind the wing and disappeared. The formation flew over the French Coast between Le Treport and Dieppe at 20,000 feet where the bombers split into two boxes. One box which returned was escorted to the English Coast.

Top cover was provided by 24 R.A.F. Spitfires VB and VC of the Exeter Wing (312th and 312th Squadrons) up from Exeter at 1015 hours.

PART III

18 B.17s of 306th Group took off at 1028 hours on a mock diversion, returning to base at 1157–1221 hours.

6 11th C.C.R.C. planes were to make a diversionary flight, but when two B.17s failed to take-off, the remainder which were circling the field were recalled.

At 1050 hours 24 Spitfires VB of the Northolt Wing (302nd and 308th Squadrons) and 23 Spitfires VB of the Kenley Wing (412th and 416th Squadrons)[2] all R.A.F., made rendezvous over Felixstowe at 15,000 feet to carry out a diversionary sweep over the Ypres - Cassel - Gravelines area. The French Coast was crossed north-east of Furnes with the bottom

CONFIDENTIAL

squadrons flying at 23,000 feet and the area was swept without incident apart from two sections of two E/A which were seen by 416th Squadron at 26,000 feet five miles south-west of Gravelines.

R.D.F. plotted a reaction of 40 E/A but only four were seen.

PART IV
(Casualties and Statistics)

As a result of these operations casualties and statistics are as follows:

U.S.A.A.F.	1 B.17 and 1 B.24 missing, (including crews of ten each) Seven crew members injured.
R.A.F.	1 Spitfire and pilot missing. 1 pilot slightly wounded.

Enemy casualties claimed to have been inflicted by U.S.A.A.F. bombers were: 11 destroyed, 5 probably destroyed, and 7 damaged.

By U.S.A.A.F. fighters: 1 Fw-190 damaged.
By R.A.F. fighters: 2 Fw-190s destroyed, 1 Fw-190 probably destroyed, and 1 Fw-190 damaged.

JULIAN B. ALLEN,
Major, A.C.,
Assistant A-2.

United States 8th Air Force B-17s of 305th Bomb Group. Displaying recently applied squadron code letters and flying the stagger formation which it was developing, the 305BG returns from Lille, 6 December 1942. *(Authors' Collection)*

Operational Diary United States 8th Air Force: 6 December 1942

VIII BC 24 (ed. Mission number)

	Dispatched	Effective	Target	Bombs Tonnage	E/A	Losses MIA	E	Dam	Casualties KIA	WIA	MIA
2BW											
B-24	19	6	Abbeville/Drucat A/F 1124 hrs	111 x 100GP	0-3-1	1		1	0	3	10
1BW											
B-17			Lille I/A 1208–1210 hrs								
91BG	22	18		20 x 1000GP	2-3-1	0		6	1	2	0
303BG	20	15		320 x 500GP	1-1-1	0		3	0	0	0
305BG	24	4			1-1-3	1		0	0	0	10
TOTALS:	85	43		95.55	5-8-6	2	0	10	1	5	20
1BW											
11CCRC	6	–	Diversion								
B-17 306BG	22	–	Mock Diversion								
TOTALS:	22	–									

REMARKS: B-24s recalled by fighters; one sqn did not hear the recall and carried on. 11CCRC recalled whilst over their base.

VIII FC

Dispatched		Groups	Losses				Casualties		
			E/A	MLA	E	Dam	KIA	WIA	MIA
Spitfire	36	4FG	0-0-1	0	0	0	0	0	0
REMARKS: As support to RAF Bostons.									
Spitfire	8	4FG	0			0	0	0	0
REMARKS: Dispatched on convoy patrols.									

Notes
1. NA Kew, AIR40/372.
2. These two squadrons were from one of the Commonwealth air forces. The squadron designations 400 to 499 were allocated to Royal Canadian, Royal Australian and Royal New Zealand Air Force units under what was known as Article VX of the British Commonwealth Air Training Agreement of 1939, also known as the Empire Air Training Scheme.
3. *Mighty Eighth War Diary*, p.28

Appendix V: RAF Casualties

All photographs in Appendix V by Paul Schepers

Aircrew with a known grave
Ventura II, AJ196 EG-C, was hit by German flak from Woensdrecht fighter base, and crashed at Schaapskooi on the airfield at 12.25hrs. All crew perished, and are buried at Bergen op Zoom Allied War Cemetery and Bergen op Zoom Canadian War Cemetery:

W/Cdr (Pilot) F. C. Seavill,	RAF, 29216	(grave 3.C.9, Allied section)
F/O (Nav.) J. A. W. Withers,	RCAF, J/10182	(grave 3.B.12, Allied section)
F/Sgt (WO/AG) F. E. King,	RCAF, R/106627	(grave 1.A.6, Canadian section)
Sgt (WO/AG) T. M. Richings,	RAF(VR), 1066223	(grave 1.A.1, Canadian section)

Crew of Lockheed Ventura II, AJ196 EG-C, 487 Squadron.

Ventura I, AE707 YH-N, was attacked by Uffz. Rudolph Rauhaus, one of the pilots in II./JG1 returning from combat with the American attacks in France. It was shot-down and crashed near Rilland-Bath at 12.29hrs.

Three crew-members were taken prisoner of war:

P/O (Pilot) H.T. Bichard   RAF(VR), 1269422
Sgt. A.L. Saunders   RAF(VR), 121544
Sgt. D.E. Clift   RAF(VR), 931083

Their navigator died and is buried at Bergen op Zoom Allied War Cemetery:

Sgt. (Nav.) R.C. Lamerton   RAF(VR), 1376980 (grave 3.B.11)

Crew of Lockheed Ventura I YH-N, 21
Squadron.

Ventura II, AE940 YH-T, was hit by flak from the Emmasingel complex, and crashed in the Nieuwe Dijk street just North of the target 12.39hrs. All crew are buried at the local Woensel General Cemetery:

F/Lt (Pilot) K. S. Smith,	82499	(plot JJ, grave 140)
F/Lt (Nav.) W. Martin DFC, RAAF, 402450		(plot JJ, grave 137)
Sgt (WO/AG) W. P. Gregory, RAF(VR) 961670		(plot JJ, collective grave 141-146)
Sgt (WO/AG) A. T. Milton, RAF(VR) 1378025		(plot JJ, collective grave 141-146)

Crew of Lockheed Ventura II, AE940 YH-T, 21 Squadron.

Ventura II, AE945 SB-E, was hit by flak from the Strijp target, and crashed on the complex into the 'FITTERIJ' at 12.39hrs. All crew are buried at the local Woensel General Cemetery:

F/Sgt (Pilot) B. M. Harvey,	RCAF, R.88469	(plot JJ, collective grave 141–146)
W/O (Ob) B. Marrows,	RAF(VR), 905358	(plot JJ, collective grave 141–146)
Sgt (WO/AG) J. B. A. MacPherson,	RAF(VR), 1194240	(plot JJ, collective grave 141–146)
Sgt F. Proctor,	RAAF, 8063	(plot JJ, collective grave 134)

Crew of Lockheed Ventura II, AE945 SB-E, 464 Squadron.

Ventura I, AE702 SB-Q, was hit by flak when attacking the Strijp target. It was seen to pull up sharply, right wing enveloped with fire, stall and dive into the ground. It crashed in an open area near the Schoolstraat at 12.39hrs. All crew died, and are buried at the local Woensel General Cemetery: .

F/O (Pilot) M. G. Moor,	RCAF, J/10139	(plot JJ, collective grave 141–146)
F/O (Nav.) N. Cohen,	120429	(plot JJ, grave 136)
P/O (WO/AG) S. A. Venneear,	RAF(VR), 123683	(plot JJ, grave 138)
Sgt M. L.V. Hass,	RAAF, 414026	(plot JJ, grave 139)

Crew of Lockheed Ventura I, AE702 SB-Q, 464 Squadron.

Ventura II, AE902 EG-W, was probably hit by flak from the Strijp target, and flew straight into the VEEMGEBOUW on the complex at 12.39hrs. All crew perished and are buried at Woensel General Cemetery:

F/Sgt (Pilot) J. L. Greening,	RAF, 533208	(plot JJ, collective grave 131)
Sgt (Nav) E. C. Mowforth,	RAF(VR), 1038399	(plot JJ, collective grave 132)
Sgt (WO/AG) D. H. Harries,	RAF(VR), 1377756	(plot JJ, collective grave 135)
Sgt (AG) B. H. Thomas,	RAF(VR), 1318061	(plot JJ, grave 133)

Crew of Lockheed Ventura II, AE902 EG-W, 487 Squadron.

Boston III, AL737 OM-U, was shot down by fighters (Fw-190s of 5./JG1 from Schiphol) and crashed into the sea off the coast of Holland at 12.50hrs. All crew perished. Two crew-members have no known graves and are commemorated at the Runnymede Memorial:

Sgt (Pilot) C. A. Maw,	RAF(VR), 1215930	(panel 89)
F/Sgt (Nav) H. E. Wilson,	RCAF, R/71741	(panel 101)

Their WO/AG is buried at Bergen op Zoom Allied War Cemetery:

Sgt (WO/AG) R. A. Barnes,   RAF(VR), 1377006   (grave 13.C.11)

Boston III, Z2252 OM-M, was shot down by fighters and crashed into the sea off the coast of Holland at 12.52hrs. All crew perished. Three crew-members have no known graves and are commemorated at the Runnymede Memorial:

W/O (Pilot) A. J. Reid,	RAF(VR), 906270	(panel 73)
F/Sgt (WO/AG) W. J. A. Spriggs,	RAF(VR), 751129	(panel 76)
P/O (AG) J. W. Beck,	RCAF, J/16163	(panel 99)

Their navigator is buried at Vlissingen Northern Cemetery:

F/O (Nav) D. R. Redbourn,   RAF(VR), 117644   (grave 27, row D)

Crew of Douglas Boston III, AL737 OM-U, 107 Squadron.

Crew of Douglas Boston III, Z2252 OM-M, 107 Squadron.

Aircrew with no known grave

Commemorated at the Air Forces Memorial, Runnymede.

Time lost	Squadron	Aircraft	Crew	
12.17	487	Ventura I EG–F	F/Sgt A. G Paterson	Pilot
			Sgt E. J. F. Vick	Nav
			Sgt S. J. Isaac	WO/AG
			Sgt P. J. Stokes	AG
12.50	107	Boston III OM–U	Sgt C. A. Maw	Pilot
			F/Sgt H. E. Wilson	Nav
12.52	107	Boston III OM–M	W/O A. J. Reid	Pilot
			F/Sgt W. J.A. Spriggs	WO/AG
			P/O J. W. Beck	AG
12.55	226	Boston III MQ–S	F/O N. J. A. Paton	Pilot
			F/Lt J. G. A. Maguire	Nav
			P/O J. L. Fletcher	WO/AG
12.59	107	Boston III OM–A	W/Cdr P. H. Dutton	Pilot
			F/Lt N. H. Shepherd	Nav
			F/Lt R. W. McCarthy	WO/AG
			P/O M. L. Delanchy	WO/AG
13.15	139	Mosquito IV	F/O J. E. O'Grady	Pilot
			Sgt G. W. Lewis	Nav

Appendix VI: Civilians Killed in the Bombardment

Following is the interim death roll and up to six supplements forming together the complete death roll of Eindhoven casualties.

1 Maria J. J. Andriessen, born in Utrecht, 7 September 1920, daughter of P. Andriessen-Putman, living Jan van Lieshoutstraat 5

2 Cornelis M. M. Bakers, born in Eindhoven, 4 March 1938, son of C. Bakers-Mandigers, living van Kinsbergenstraat 27

3 Elisabeth W. M. Bakers, born in Eindhoven, 25-12-1936, daughter of C. Bakers-Mandigers, living van Kinsbergenstraat 27

4 Johanna M. Bakers, born in Eindhoven, 23 July 1934, daughter of C. Bakers-Mandigers, living van Kinsbergenstraat 27

5 Johannes Chr. M. Bakers, born in Eindhoven, 21 June 1941, son of C. Bakers-Mandigers, living van Kinsbergenstraat 27

6 Petrus W. M. Bakers, born in Eindhoven, 4 August 1930, son of C. Bakers-Mandigers, living van Kinsbergenstraat 27

7 Martinus F. Bakers, born in Woensel, 31 October 1901, husband of La. van Grimbergen, living Kruisstraat 67

8 Petrus H. J. Th. Bergstein, born in Eindhoven, 26 April 1934, son of A. Bergstein-Hulshof, living Wal 13

9 Geertruida A. de Bie, born in Venlo, 27 May 1920, daughter of G.D. de Bie-Priest, living Hendrik de Keijzerlaan 77

10 Willem Boer, born in Hazerswoude, 22 November 1933, son of W. Boer-vd Heiden, living Lijmbeekstraat 230

11 Margaretha Bremmers, born in Valkenswaard, 2 June 1919, daughter of Chr. Bremmers-Meeuwissen, living Jan van Lieshoutstraat 5

12 Edithe Cett, born in Weenen, 3 January 1921, daughter of Wenzel Cett-Oeh, living 2nd Akkermunt Straat 6

13 Adrianus van Dommelen, born in Nuenen, 22 August 1876, husband of J.C. Jansen, living Smalle Haven 22

14 P. J. M. E. Eikenaar, born in Nuland, 1 April 1919, daughter of T. Eikenaar-van Hommelen, living Rechtestraat 34

15 Maria Sibyila Elbers, born in Sankt Tönis, 13 April 1897, wife of L.A. Raaijmakers, living Harmoniestraat 30

16 Wilhelmina A. van Emden, born in Kessel, 22 February 1921, daughter of A. van Emden-Scheres, living Ten Hagestraat 2

17 Elisabeth Free, born in Bergen op Zoom, 17 June 1901, wife of G.W. Govaarts, living De Jonglaan 10

18 M. F. Gruijthuijsen, born in Woensel, 22 July 1890, married to P. Vermulst, living Willem Barentsstraat 61

19 Johannes L. van Hal, born in Eindhoven, 3 November 1903, husband of Hubertina Snel, living Kamillestraat 58

20 Adrianus P. van Ham,   husband of P. de Jong,
    born in 's–Bosch, 11 June 1891,   living Mathildelaan 103
21 Hubertus P. van Ham,   son of A.P. van Ham-de Jong,
    born in Venlo, 13 January 1926,   living Mathildelaan 103
22 Simon P. A. van Hapert,   husband of C. Spanninks,
    born in Stratum, 27 July 1911,   living Laurierstraat 48
23 Albertus J. van Helvoirt,   son of H. van Helvoirt-Schijndel,
    born in Oss, 16 September 1913,   living M. Stuartstraat 30
24 Catharina P. M. Hendrikx,   daughter of G. Hendrikx-
    born in Eindhoven, 28 May 1924,   Rooijakkers, living Harmoniestraat 17
25 Francisca J. M. Hezemans,   wife of A. J. P. Stuitiens,
    born in Eindhoven, 31 May 1891,   living Demer 49
26 Carolina H. Heijkoop,   wife of Arie Peilekaan,
    born in Vlagtwedde, 27 August 1913,   living Edisonstraat 165
27 Gerardus L. M. van Hirsel,   son of J. van Hirsel-van Helden,
    born in Eindhoven, 29 July 1924,   living Groote Berg 9
28 A.C. Hoppenbrouwers,   wife of F. vd Broek,
    born in 's–Bosch, 27 July 1891,   living Harmoniestraat 17
29 Rosalia Horsten,   wife of J. A. Nijsten,
    born in Stratum, 11 November 1918,   living Pioenroosstraat 60
30 Cornelia C. Janssen,   Religionist,
    born in Hontenisse, 24 September 1874, living Jan van Lieshoutstraat 5
31 Petronella de Jong,   wife of A. P. van Ham,
    born in Rucphen, 21 February 1894,   living Mathildelaan 103
32 Helena P. C. Jonkergouw,   daughter of G. Jonkergouw-van Beek,
    born in Eindhoven, 29 November 1921, living Strijpschestraat 116
33 Johanna M. A. Joosten,   daughter of P. J. Joosten-Giessen,
    born in Helden, 11 January 1919,   living Jan van Lieshoutstraat 5
34 Cornelis Kant,   son of H. Kant-Ippel,
    born in De Werken en Sleewijk,   living Ampèrestraat 98
    16 February 1922,
35 Helena G. C. van Kemenade,   daughter of A. van Kemenade-
    born in Eindhoven, 17 May 1925,   Verbeek, living Kronehoefstraat 8
36 Hendrik A. Kemper,   husband of W. E. vd Broek,
    born in Weststellingwerf, 22 September 1860, living Lijmbeekstraat 404
37 Antonetta Ketelaars,   wife of J. Pruimboom,
    born in Weert, 5 March 1870,   living Frederiklaan 119
38 Adrianus Kivits,   son of G. Kivits-Meyer,
    born in 's–Gravenhage, 23 December 1914,   living Schootschestraat 78
39 Hendrik Kromdijk,   husband of Anna Sprankenis,
    born in Gorssel, 28- -1908,   living Jan van Eindh.straat 15
40 Anna M. M. C. Kuipers,   wife of J. C. Wernaart,
    born in Strijp, 24 July 1912,   living Piet Heinstraat 15
41 Jan Derk Oderkerk,   husband of Maria F. H. Litjes,
    born in Arnhem, 12 February 1906,   living Fellenoord 2

42 Johanna A. T. Le Pair,   daughter of J. Le Pair-ten Dam,
    born in Eindhoven, 30 September 1934,   living Frederiklaan 117
43 Jan Le Pair,   husband of J. ten Dam,
    born in Schiedam, 5 February 1884,   living Frederiklaan 117
44 Wilhelmina A. Mandigers,   wife of Corn Bakers,
    born in Stratum, 26 November 1904,   living van Kinsbergenstraat 27
45 Elisabeth J. Matheij,   wife of W. J. Brok,
    born in 's-Bosch, 17 October 1891,   living Schootschestraat 82
46 Hendrikus H. van Melis,   husband of Paulina Mortier,
    born in Gestel, 30 January 1915,   living Broekscheweg 4
47 Hendrikus vd Meulen,   husband of Paula Mechovsky,
    born in Maastricht, 7 February 1899,   living Kabelstraat 28
48 Christina S. Meurs,   wife of A. T. vd Voort,
    born in Kesteren, 15 March 1913,   living Harmoniestraat 32
49 Josephina Moerkens,   daughter of C. Moerkens-
    born in Uden, 2 December 1915,   Mermans, living Melkweg 35
50 Lena J. de Mul,   daughter of N. de Mul-Lotens,
    born in Eindhoven, 6 January 1941,   living Wattstraat 66
51 Catharina H. Mulder,   wife of J. Naumann,
    born in Rotterdam, 26 March 1893,   living De Jonghlaan 12
52 John C. H. B. Naumann,   husband of Catharina H. Mulder,
    born in London, 25 September 1891,   living De Jonghlaan 12
53 Jack Douglas Naumann,   son of J. Naumann-Mulder,
    born in Eindhoven, 8 December 1931,   living De Jonghlaan 12
54 Kitty M. Naumann,   daughter of J. Naumann-Mulder,
    born in Eindhoven, 15 August 1927,   living De Jonghlaan 12
55 Jacobus H. Niessen,   husband of Hendrika Joosten,
    born in Beesel, 15 September 1890,   living Heezerweg 114
56 Bernardina A. Peffer,   daughter of J.H. Peffer-Gerrits,
    born in Driel, 10 January 1924,   living Hoogstraat 204
57 Ida Christina Pruijmboom,   wife of W. R. Duijts,
    born in Weert, 7 April 1896,   living Frederiklaan 119
58 Albertina A. Raaijmakers,   daughter of L. Raaijmakers-Elbers,
    born in Eindhoven, 5 January 1927,   living Harmoniestraat 30
59 Elisabeth S. Raaijmakers,   daughter of L. Raaijmakers-Elbers,
    born in Eindhoven, 8 August 1924,   living Harmoniestraat 30
60 Gerardina C. Raaijmakers,   daughter of L. Raaijmaker-Elbers,
    born in Eindhoven, 21 November 1925, living Harmoniestraat 30
61 Joanna H. Raaijmakers,   daughter of L. Raaijmakers-Elbers,
    born in Woensel, 23 September 1918,   living Harmoniestraat 30
62 Lamert A. Raaijmakers,   husband of M. S. Elbers,
    born in Schijndel, 6 April 1895,   living Harmoniestraat 30
63 Sibylla H. Raaijmakers,   son of L. Raaijmakers-Elbers,
    born in Eindhoven, 24 August 1939,   living Harmoniestraat 30
64 Johannes T. Reijntjes,   living Kabeljauwstraat 2
    born in Boxtel, 25 November 1884,

65 Elisabeth M. van Schaijk,
born in Tongelre, 10 May 1909,
daughter of F. van Schaijk-
Soerland, living Koudenhovense
weg 115

66 Mathea G. C. Senders,
born in Stratum, 31 August 1913,
daughter of J. Senders-Oomen,
living Jan van Lieshoutstraat 5

67 Cornelia T. Smeets,
born in Eindhoven, 17 August 1926,
daughter of J. M. Smeets-Driessen,
living Harmoniestraat 36

68 Johanna M. Smulders,
born in Woensel, 21 February 1883,
wife of Luigi Zanetti,
living Broekscheweg 111

69 Alphonsus M. J. Stultiëns,
born in Eindhoven, 25 April 1893,
husband of F. J. M. Hezemans,
living Demer 49

70 Anna P. Termeer,
born in St. Oedenrode, 20 July 1912,
Roman Catholic Nun,
living Jan van Lieshoutstraat 5

71 Christina D. M. Thier,
born in Breda, 4 August 1915,
daughter of Thier-Kramer,
living Maria Stuartstraat 27

72 Johanna M. H. Thijs,
born in Woensel, 23 December 1903,
wife of Wilhelminus Heldens,
living Demer 78

73 Jacob den Tuinder,
born in Eindhoven, 18 March 1921,
son of J. den Tuinder-Olden,
living Zeelsterstraat 163

74 C. J. M. van der Velden,
born in Eindhoven, 21 January 1924,
son of A. van der Velden-van Rijn,
living Hoogstraat 31

75 Hendricus C. Vilé,
born in Veghel, 29 September 1889,
husband of Anna Hezemans,
living Boschdijk 28

76 Joannes W. M. Vilé,
born in Eindhoven, 23 August 1921,
son of H. Vilé-Hezemans,
living Boschdijk 28

77 A. T. van de Voort,
born in Woensel, 17 September 1910,
husband of C.S. Meurs,
living Harmoniestraat 32

78 Dirk P. van de Voort,
born in Eindhoven, 19 July 1941,
son of A. van de Voort-Meurs,
living Harmoniestraat 32

79 Hubertus J. Vorstenbosch,
born in Eindhoven, 19 July 1936,
son of Vorstenbosch-Hermans,
living van Kinsbergenstraat 25

80 Annette van Wel,
born in 's-Gravenhage, 11 February 1921,
wife of W. van Vliet,
living Merellaan 5

81 Johannes H. C. Wernaart,
born in Eindhoven, 4 February 1935,
son of J. Wernaart-Kuipers,
living Piet Heinstraat 15

82 Gijsberta G. van Zijl,
born in Delft, 30 October 1896,
Roman Catholic Nun,
living Jan van Lieshoutstraat 5

83 Isabella Bel,
born 7 March 1894,
wife of C. Huijbregts,
living in Reusel

84 Frans F. Bouman,
born 26 June 1922,
living in Oosterhout

85 Johanna L. M. Elshout,
born 22 May 1926,
daughter of A. Elshout-Swinnen,
living in Valkenswaard

86 Marinus van Kasteren,
born 1901,
husband of G. van Gerwen,
living in Son c.a.

87 Maria C. Lucas,   wife of J. Vos,
    born 20 September 1888,   living in Best
88 Maria E. Merkelbach,   daughter of Merkelbach-de Vroom
    born 9 April 1905,   living in Valkenswaard
89 Catharina Mickers,   wife of A. van Berlo,
    born 9 February 1877,   living in Gemert
90 Johanna M. Plompen,   daughter of J. Plompen-Rijkers,
    born 28 February 1921,   living in Valkenswaard
91 Adrianus Rooijmans,   son of F. Rooijmans-Wanrooij,
    born 12 November 1918,   living in Lieshout
92 Roza Velleman,   wife of Karel Bobbe,
    born 11 August 1916,   living in Rotterdam
93 Johannes Zijdenbosch,   son of H. Zijdenbosch-Bonesch,
    born 16 December 1924,   living in Delft
94 Joanna C. van den Broek,   wife of H. Bongaarts,
    born in Duizel c.a., 21 November 1901,   living Lijmbeekstraat 404
95 Catharina Bongaarts,   daughter of H. Bongaarts-van den
    born in Amsterdam, 20 August 1926,   Broek living Lijmbeekstraat 404
96 Hendrik A. Bongaarts,   son of H. Bongaarts-van den Broek
    born in Eindhoven, 15 February 1929,   living Lijmbeekstraat 404
97 Margaretha Bongaarts,   daughter of H. Bongaarts-van den
    born in Eindhoven, 17 May 1932,   Broek living Lijmbeekstraat 404
98 Wilhelmina E. Bongaarts,   daughter of H. Bongaarts-van den
    born in Eindhoven, 6 June 1937,   Broek living Lijmbeekstraat 404
99 Clara C. Hendrikx,   daughter of C. Hendrikx-vd
    born in Stratum, 18 July 1909,   Heijden living Vlokhovense weg 22
100 Cornelia H. de Zeeuw,   daughter of A. de Zeeuw-
    born in Eindhoven, 2 September 1921,   Duitsman, living Lijmbeekstraat 402
101 Bertha Kwappenberg,   wife of G. Jansen,
    born 4 November 1918,   living in Nuenen c.a.
102 Maria H. C. T. Kliebisch,   daughter of T. Kliebisch-
    born in Eindhoven, 18 July 1925,   Lommelaars, living Demer 47
103 Theodorus Kliebisch,   son of T. Kliebisch-Lommelaars,
    born in Eindhoven, 17 September 1921,   living Demer 47
104 Theodorus C. M. Kliebisch,   son of L. F. Kliebisch-Reiniers,
    born in Eindhoven, 24 November 1939,   living Parallelweg 17
105 Hendrica A. Lommelaars,   wife of T. Kliebisch,
    born in Woensel, 26 October 1884,   living Demer 47
106 Maria C. de Zeeuw,   wife of J. Verschueren,
    born in Woensel, 29 October 1915,   living Lijmbeekstraat 447
107 Elisabeth Duitsman,   widow of A. de Zeeuw,
    born in Geldrop, 30 December 1877,   living Lijmbeekstraat 402

1st supplement, 12 December 1942
108 Sytske van der Werf,   living Demer 76
    born in Baarderadeel 16 February 1890,

109 Theodora A. de Kruijff,   wife of A. C. A. van Meerhoff,
     born in Amsterdam, 3 August 1913,   living Demer 56a
110 Pieter Jan Hoppenbrouwers,   living Demer 58
     born in Wageningen, 16 December 1907,
111 Anna J. M. Segers,   wife of P. J. Hoppenbrouwers,
     born in Breda, 23 June 1913,   living Demer 58
112 Adriana P. M. Hoppenbrouwers,   daughter of P. J. Hoppenbrouwers
     born in Eindhoven, 1 November 1938,   and A. J. M. Segers, living Demer 58
113 Paulina M. Hoppenbrouwers,   daughter of P. J. Hoppenbrouwers
     born in Eindhoven, 25 October 1940,   and A. J. M. Segers, living Demer 58
114 Dorothea F. H. Meerhoff,   daughter of Andreas C. A.
     born in Eindhoven, 3 October 1937,   Meerhoff and T. A. de Kruijff
                                                living Demer 56a

2nd supplement, 13 December 1942
115 Wilhelminus P. H. Heldens,   living Demer 78
     born in Tilburg, 2 February 1902,
116 Antonetta Johanna van Hoof,   daughter of Anthonius van Hoof
     born in Eindhoven, 18 July 1923,   and Philomena de Cock,
                                                living Demer 58 (servant)
117 Anna M. H. Holtackers,   wife of Petrus Kuijpers,
     born in Tegelen, 22 October 1885,   living Demer 35
118 Philomena C. R. Kuijpers,   daughter of Petrus Kuijpers and
     born in Eindhoven, 14 November 1919, Anna M.H. Holtackers, living
                                                Demer 35

3rd supplement, 14 December 1942
119 Wilhelminus H. J. van de Mortel,   son of Hendrikus C. van de Mortel
     born in Eindhoven, 21 May 1926,   and Johanna E. Zeeuwe
                                                living Sint Annahof 3
120 Sophia R. van der Zwaluw,   wife of Ludovicus A. M. J. B. van
     born in Gouda, 7 January 1905,   Dun, living Demer 2

4th supplement, 15 December 1942
121 Jacobus Ph. Bongaarts,   son of Hendrik Bongaarts- vd
     born in Eindhoven 28 Maart 1934,   Broek, living Lijmbeekstraat 404
122 Wilhelmus v Luijk,   husband of Cornelia v Cuijten,
     born in Heeze, 25 December 1887,   living Oude Bogert 12
123 Pieter Hubergsen,   husband of Johanna M. Vermeulen
     born in Aardenburg, 28 Maart 1891,   living Tramstraat 5

5th supplement, 16 December 1942
124 Roelof W. Abbes,   husband of Cornelia ten Boer,
     born in Leeuwarden, 3 September 1906, living Demer 44
125 Cornelia ten Boer,   wife of Roelof W. Abbes, living
     born in Groningen, 16 February 1911,   Demer 44

6th supplement, 17 December 1942

126 Catharina van den Heuvel,   wife of Jacobus P. A. Wiggers,
     born in 's-Bosch, 7 February 1902,   living Oude Bogert 28
127 Clara M. G. Wiggers,   daughter of J. P. A. Wiggers and C.
     born in Eindhoven, 15 November 1936, G. van den Heuvel, living Oude
                                       Bogert 28
128 Maria Ph. J. Wiggers,   daughter of J. P. A. Wiggers and C.
     born in Eindhoven, 28 April 1938,   G. van den Heuvel, living Oude
                                       Bogert 28
129 Ludovicus A. M. J. B. van Dun,   husband of Sophia R. van der
     born in Vught, 29 August 1901,   Zwaluw, living Demer 2
130 Laurens L. Slootjes,   widower of Anna M. van der
     born in Gouda, 19 August 1892,   Zwaluw, living Bergstraat 28
131 Anna M. J. Hezemans,   wife of Henricus Ch. Vilé,
     born in Woensel, 22 March 1890,   living Boschdijk 28
132 Johanna M. E. Vilé,   daughter of H. Ch. Vilé and A. M.
     born in Stratum, 16 September 1918, J. Hezemans, living Boschdijk 28
133 Joannes H. S. van Luijt,   husband of Jacoba C. van Dooren,
     born in Stratum, 4 August 1890,   living Bondstraat 11

[*Dagblad van het Zuiden*, 12 December to 17 December 1942]

In addition there are names of two children who were not mentioned in the original newspaper publication (above). When preparing the monument these names were added to the scroll within the monument.

134 Theodorus H. G. M. Heldens
     born in Eindhoven, 4 June 1938
135 Hermanus G. M. J. Heldens
     born in Eindhoven, 16 March 1940

Appendix VII: List of German soldiers killed

All photographs by Paul Schepers

German soldiers killed in the raid

All listed soldiers are buried at Ysselsteyn German war cemetery in the county of Limburg, The Netherlands.

Name	Born	Killed	Rank	Grave-stone
Friedrich Flint	20-03-1915	06-12-1942	Obergefreiter	Z 3-62
Paul Bäcker	08-01-1914	06-12-1942	Obergefreiter	Z 3-63
Walter Lagershausen	18-01-1916	06-12-1942	Kanonier	Z 3-64
Otto Dütsch	29-11-1923	06-12-1942	Kanonier	Z 3-65
Andreas Merz	14-04-1901	06-12-1942	Gefreiter	Z 3-66
Michael Denzler	10-07-1923	06-12-1942	Kanonier	Z 3-67
Günter Mentzel	06-07-1923	06-12-1942	Gefreiter	Z 3-68

Graves of German soldiers at Ysselsteyn German war cemetery.

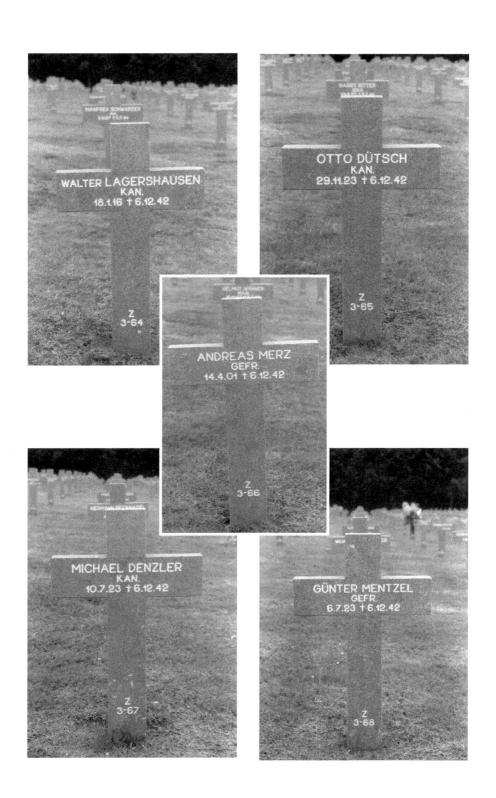

WALTER LAGERSHAUSEN
KAN.
18.1.16 † 6.12.42

Z
3-64

OTTO DÜTSCH
KAN.
29.11.23 † 6.12.42

Z
3-65

ANDREAS MERZ
GEFR.
14.4.01 † 6.12.42

Z
3-66

MICHAEL DENZLER
KAN.
10.7.23 † 6.12.42

Z
3-67

GÜNTER MENTZEL
GEFR.
6.7.23 † 6.12.42

Z
3-68

Appendix VIII: Philips Fire Service Report

(Translated from Old Dutch by Paul Schepers.)

<u>Report of the air raid on the Philips factories on Sunday 6 December 1942</u>

Around half past twelve the switchboard operator on duty in the telephone exchange (Mrs Crommetuyn) received from the LSWK in 's Hertogenbosch (den Bosch) the pre-warning 'Berta'. Directly after this the conversation was jammed, mainly due to a very loud racket from outside. This was caused by British planes, flying overhead at very low level and meanwhile firing everywhere. At the same time the anti-aircraft guns came into action, while bombs were dropped.

It was not possible anymore to provide timely air raid warning; most likely caused by mains electricity failure. Since no air raid warning was to come from the local air defence organization either, the raid came as a complete surprise and had the character of an assault.

A great many demolition and incendiary bombs were dropped, hitting various buildings and causing fires to develop in many places. The attack, carried out by at least fifty to sixty aircraft, took place in two waves following shortly after each other, followed by a smaller third wave that was shorter in duration. The aircraft flew very low and, as observed from the Strijp complex right across the plant from the laboratory in the direction of the railway, this made it possible that incendiary bombs were dropped on virtually every storey of the tall buildings.

The fire brigade and air raid wardens were gathered together for lunch. This was normal, since no air raid warning was received nor was there any expectation of an impending attack. Several members of the aforementioned personnel barely escaped death when demolition and incendiary bombs struck very nearby while the fire brigade had tried to rush to the scene after the first two waves had passed. Remarkable was the calmness of these people and their willingness, despite the grave danger, to put up a good fight.

When I took charge on the Emmasingel complex, around 12.50hrs, in between the second and third attack waves [from the arrival time it seems the third attack wave mentioned must have been the sole Mosquito reconnaissance aircraft] the situation was roughly as follows:

Both head offices were fully enveloped in flames, building D [offices] was heavily damaged as well as buildings E and F, while the paint shop had received a direct hit.

The air raid wardens were sent into the buildings in squads to look for shift workers possibly still present in the buildings and to extinguish fires. Two wounded were administered first aid. Ir v.d. Hoeven, very quick to be on location, contributed substantially in organizing this.

The difficulties were further increased due to the telephone exchange, lighting and emergency lighting having become unserviceable. This necessitated working with Hellesens-lighting [battery hand lamp]. The fire brigade showed much determination in extinguishing fires to their fire station, caused by three incendiary bombs, as well as in the vicinity of the aforementioned paint shop. In the meantime it became clear that mains water supply was also affected, complicating the work of the fire brigade even more. I ordered the fire commander Arends to proceed with a fire engine to the head office via the Willemstraat.

The fire brigade, ably assisted by air raid wardens were busy the rest of the afternoon and evening extinguishing fires to the head office (building D), the warehouse and the 5th floor of building C [Gas Manufacturing Plant]. Due to the lack of water a fire engine was forced to use a local stream 'de Gender'.

Various commanders of the air raid wardens who were not on duty, volunteered to assist so workload could be spread evenly. Nearly the full fire brigade night shift also volunteered. After having put his family in safety while preparing to go the Philips factories to assist, Fire-fighter v. Helvoirt was killed when a time-delayed bomb that had hit his house detonated.

Soon Mr Schussel was ordered to take charge of the proceedings at the Emmasingel Complex, while Fire Commander Boxsem contacted 's Hertogenbosch (Dienststelle of Major Welk) and the *Luftgaukommando Aussenstelle Rotterdam* [respectively organization and outdoor unit of the Luftwaffe in The Netherlands]. Hence it was possible to get outside help from five German fire engines. These were mainly utilised to assist the extinguishing of fires to civilian property.

When it became clear to me that activities on the Emmasingel complex were ongoing in full swing I proceeded to the Strijp complex to get an impression of the situation there, for it was impossible to get in touch via telephone. Also here fires were raging in many places: the Company school, the equipment factory, the Wouters warehouse, the paper factory and many other locations. Everywhere explosions from bombs and ammunition.

Right from the beginning dense smoke and flames forced the Command Post to have to be evacuated. Commandant Buys had retreated to the fire station and was sending first aid patrols from there. The medical station in the Equipment factory was lost, the dressing station of the glass factory being used instead while soon the medical staff opened a station in the Philips Recreation building. Dr Burger, Nurse Kleinod and several other medical personnel assisted in looking for wounded employees. Later on it turned out that two men had been killed in the boiler house, and a car mechanic had also died. Since only a few employees were working at the time of the bombardment the number of casualties and injured was limited.

The fire brigade with Officer Jamin in charge was called to the first Equipment factory. It turned out that the water main was interrupted and the filter building had received a direct hit. The firemen barely escaped with their lives when the second attack wave arrived. Fireman v.d. Mark got severe wounds to his hand but could be treated.

Due to limited amounts of water available and unexploded bombs Commandant van Zetten who was in charge now decided to withdraw all the firefighting material to just outside the factory plant along the Kastanjelaan and continue the efforts from there. A running battle lasting through the night to save the factories succeeded in saving the paper factory, part of the Wouters warehouse and the Etos bakery.

The limited fuel rationing became noticeable, rendering the fire engine non-operational. Fortunately the civil fire brigade came to the rescue. Ir Roeterink, quickly on location, went to great efforts to repair the water and electricity mains assisted in this task by engineers of the Technical Departments, to no avail, however.

After having gained an impression of the conditions on the Strijp complex I returned to the Emmasingel complex. It was already dark when I paid a second visit to the Strijp complex and met Major Hertel and Chief Inspector van Boven who had come to have a look at the situation. Everywhere the fire brigade was fully engaged combating the fire. Also buildings surrounding the factory sites were heavily hit, particularly so in the city centre causing fires till late in the evening.

At present an overview of the damage and the number of dropped bombs cannot be provided. It must be concluded that the numerous delayed action bombs and duds caused severe delays to the operations and continued to do so over the next few days.

Hard work under difficult conditions has been delivered by the personnel. A report has been assembled by Mr Vogels relating the experiences of various air raid wardens and firemen to provide a better picture of the many simultaneous events.

Eindhoven, 17 December 1942.
Department Fire Brigade and Air Raid Protection.

Ir A. P. T. Advokaat.

Detailed description of the activities employed by the Philips fire brigade and air raid defences in the aftermath of the bombardment on the Philips factories on Sunday 6 December 1942

<u>Report of the aerial bombardment on the Philips factories on</u>
<u>Sunday 6 December 1942.</u>

It was without any doubt a big surprise for everybody in Eindhoven when on Sunday 6 December 1942 in the afternoon at around 12.30 hours from the fairly low hanging clouds suddenly a large number of aircraft emerged whose shapes and way of flying deviated from those of the German aeroplanes which circled daily overhead the city and hardly caused any special attention anymore.

As if by intuition those who first observed the swarm of bombers felt that something unusual was about to happen. It took not a long time to guess, since the firing of the German anti-aircraft guns and heavy explosions of bombs dropped made it obvious that the English air force was undertaking a large-scale attack on the city of Eindhoven and in particular on the Philips factories.

Since the mains electricity was disturbed it was not possible to activate the air raid warning sirens. Even so the population and the few Philips employees who were at work in the factory were startled enough to realize that grave things were about to happen.

The factories were hit by three attack waves, amongst two of which were heavy; the bombers flew just above roof level and sometimes even between the buildings dropping various sorts of bombs like incendiaries, high explosive and delayed action bombs. The resulting damage was enormous; various buildings caught fire or were severely damaged by bomb blast.

Both the Philips fire brigade and the ARP saw before them a near impossible task, the more so because in many critical locations no water was available due to damaged water mains. The organization of both departments was solid, however, and as far as conditions allowed they could work according to predetermined procedures.

To have a clear overview of the work, it is necessary to divide and subdivide the work as follows:

A. The work of the fire brigade
I.   On the Emmasingel complex
II.   On the Strijp complex
III.   Outside the factory plants

B. The work of the air raid wardens
I.   On the Emmasingel complex
II.   On the Strijp complex
III.   Outside the factory plants

A. THE WORK OF THE FIRE BRIGADE

I. On the Emmasingel complex.

The duty firemen were barely sat down to lunch when continuous shooting and overwhelming sound of engines roused their curiosity. Even before they left the tables to go outside and have a look, however, the first bombs were already coming down. Hastily they took shelter. Just after the first attack wave left the firemen returned to their fire station to get the old Magirus fire engine out of the garage. The incoming second attack wave forced them again into shelter, partly in the cellar, partly lying flat on the ground along a wall of the fitting shop. Dozens of incendiary bombs came down in the vicinity causing fires to erupt at many different locations. Also the fire station was hit, necessitating turning out the remaining fire engines in the station as soon as possible. To make matters worse, the new Magirus engine refused to start and had to be pushed outside where it was soon started and able to leave the station under its own power. The situation with the material engine, however, was more difficult since an incendiary bomb was burning underneath it, though the firemen eventually succeeded in extinguishing it. Meanwhile, one of the

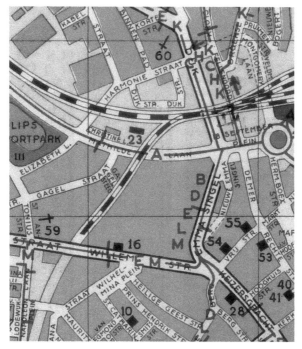

Map 9. Map of the area surrounding the Emmasingel complex. *(Paul Schepers)*
(To assist the reader with street-name locations, The Emmasingel complex itself is located in-between the Mathildelaan to the North, the Emmasingel to the East and Willemstraat to the South of it.)

firemen managed to throw six more incendiary bombs in the Gender stream with his hands, preventing further spreading of the fire.

The old Magirus fire engine was put to good use in the meantime; the fires from the garage, the paint shop and the fitting shop were soon extinguished upon which the Commandant, Mr Arends, directed this fire engine to the Emmasingel to direct water into the burning headquarters. Directly after the second bombardment the new Magirus engine was also relocated here via the fire station gate. The lock keeping this gate closed was quickly taken care of by using a big hammer. First job was to place a hydrant which was underway when the third attack wave [this must have been the photo–reconnaissance mission] came over. The crew of this engine found shelter with utmost speed by lying flat on the ground next to the lower front of the purchase department to protect themselves against shell fragments stones and shattered glass. When this last wave departed it was realized that the headquarter building was beyond salvation despite the full collection of the Emmasingel complex firefighting equipment at hand.

At various places hydrants were placed but the water mains turned out to be severely hit; at only few of the places sufficient water was available. For the firemen who were installing a hydrant behind a wooden canteen this turned out to be an amazing coincidence. Only five meters away, as it turned out later, an unexploded bomb was located.

Only when one of the engines was connected to the council water mains was it possible to provide water with adequate pressure to be able to extinguish fires in the light tower and later wooden shed L. and U.U. Heat here was so enormous that the firemen had to shield their faces with wooden boards and even lie on the ground to prevent being scorched. For the other engine inadequate water pressure was available; by locating it to a water source at the back of the gas factory it was possible to combat the fire raging in building D (office) with six hoses. In the meantime the headquarter building was not forgotten. Firemen put a lot of effort into rolling out a long hose in order to extinguish the fire from inside the headquarters hall. Unfortunately a message was received that all fuel had been consumed, rendering the engine non-operational. The council was able to source an amount of fuel some time later but in the meantime the flames had continued their destroying nature. Ir F.J. Philips [Frits Philips, Director General of the company] requested several of the firemen to try to save various important items from his private office. By hacking away blinds, entry was gained from the street. Apart from a silver smoker's set, a pretty antique cabinet, a big standing clock and various books and documents, many cigars were brought to safety. The cigars were distributed among those present.

Firemen including several volunteers were fighting a losing battle. Through determined action the flames in the delivery and packing shed were extinguished. However, it could not be avoided that the proud headquarter and a substantial part of the light tower were consumed by the fire.

The engine located at the back of the gas factory had been in action uninterrupted since 22.00 hours. From then on the engineer was not able to maintain pump pressure preventing further action. Around 01.30 hours the order was given to make the engine operational again by positioning it along the Gender and tapping water from this stream for mopping up operations on building E.D. Once more, however, inadequate pressure on the pump could be achieved and the other engine was requested to assist. The mopping up operation lasted until 8 o'clock on the Monday morning.

II. On the Strijp complex.

Like on the Emmasingel Complex the Strijp firemen left their lunch when the first English air attack started to seek shelter as soon as possible. As soon as the first bombs were dropped (virtually every building was hit except the fire station) it was decided to have the Fiat fire engine turn out. This truck was just driven out of the garage when again aeroplanes roared overhead the complex, dropping dozens of bombs of various shapes and calibres. At great personal risk the reserve engineer managed to get the Fiat inside the garage again.

Bombs had come down on numerous locations. The boiler house was hit, just like the Philite factory (production of Bakelite), the Equipment factory, the Paper and Cardboard factory, the Wouters warehouse and the Company school. Fires were erupting everywhere, making it very difficult for the fire brigade officers to determine the best location from where to start combating the fires. The more so since the factory site was full of unexploded bombs.

The Fiat engine was positioned next to the second Equipment factory but it soon turned out that no water was available: the water mains had become damaged. At that moment, around 12.50 hours, unexpectedly the third attack wave came in during which one of the firemen was severely wounded to his right arm [from the time the mentioned third wave took place it must have been the lone photo-reconnaissance Mosquito that arrived over Eindhoven instead of an actual bombing attack]. Seeing the circumstances in which they had to work it was a miracle that the number of casualties was not much higher. For the second time the reserve engineer revealed himself as a real fireman by driving the Fiat during the midst of the attack to a secure place.

With the third wave gone the deputy chief fire brigade officer gave order to remove all fire engines, the Fiat, the Magirus and the Laffley (towed fire engine by a Ford AA) from the factory site at once and to relocate them to the Philips Recreation building. The Fiat was then upon urgent request further relocated to the Glaslaan-Kastanjelaan crossing in order to provide water on:

a. Houses along the de Jonghlaan 6 and 8
b. The Company school
c. The Etos bakery

Philips fire brigade around 1928 (left to right: Magirus engine, Fiat engine and Ford AA ladder engine. *(Philips Company Archive ref. A50530-10)*

Since topics a. and c. will be discussed in Chapter III, focus now will be on the efforts to extinguish the fire from the Company school. This large new building was fully ablaze; licking flames from windows at all levels rendered the efforts to combat the fire no more than a drop in the ocean. Upon indication of Ir Roeterink the main effort was in saving the archive from the blaze. This was crowned with success and, assisted by the school's personnel, a valuable collection of the archive was saved. Due to the changing wind direction there was a severe risk of the fire that had already consumed the Company school now threatening surrounding buildings. For that reason the Fiat engine was now relocated to the Lijsterbeslaan next to the Etos bakery (see chapter III).

The Ford AA ladder engine was used to combat the fire in the Company school and to save people who had climbed on its roof. This was not successful, unfortunately, since the roof collapsed soon after. On order from the commandant Strijp the efforts to put out the fire at the Company school were stopped. Instead the hoses were moved to the Cardboard and Paper factory to save them from the real danger of spreading fire. Also the fire raging in the Wouters warehouse was combated in a spirited way. The crew of the Magirus engine, positioned in the Kastanjelaan, where fires in several houses had to be extinguished also managed to put out the fire in the Paper factory. Through this an entrance was gained to other parts of the factory site and assistance was offered to control the fire in the blazing Wouters warehouse.

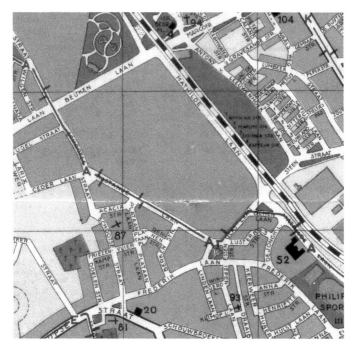

Map 10. Map of the area surrounding the Strijp complex. *(Paul Schepers)*
(To assist the reader with street-name locations, The Strijp complex itself is located in-between the Beukenlaan/Mathildelaan to the North, the Glaslaan to the East and Schootsestraat/Kastanjelaan to the South of it.)

For seven long hours the men of the professional fire brigade, who nearly all turned up, combated the fires on the Strijp complex with a hose from the roof of the Sobu [*Sonderbüro* - German expression for special development department; this department was created by Philips to save technically highly-skilled Jews from certain deportation. It was stated that the products originating from this department were important for German war effort], then with various water jets from the opposite side. Audacious was the action of several of them to kick open a door and enter the warehouse to attack directly the heart of the fire itself with two hoses in suffocating smoke. After one hour these men were ordered out due to the risk of the building collapsing. The flames had not abated in all this time. The reason became obvious when, next to a partition wall, a number of blazing barrels were found, some filled with paraffin and others with carbide. Initially they tried to drench the carbide barrels without any success. The fire brigade officer urged the firemen to prevent spreading of the fire at all cost. To this effect the partition wall was kept wet for hours. One fireman had the idea of putting out the barrels using sand, which was tried after consent from the officer. This turned out to do the job, and it was only two more hours before the whole fire was extinguished. By then it was Monday morning, 5 o'clock. At the S.A.S. shed, the rag warehouse and the waste shed damping down actions continued. Most firemen left the factory site only in the afternoon; one of them was requested by a German soldier to make available a lamp to look for dead soldiers.

Commander in charge on the Strijp complex was Mister van Zetten. Damping down continued on Tuesday as well as on Wednesday; especially the rag warehouse of the paper mill.

III. Outside the factory plants.

Also outside the factory site the Philips fire brigade had a strong presence. The Fiat engine assisted in fighting fires in houses located in de Jonghlaan 6 and 8. Both premises were so damaged that saving them was out of the question. Within two hours the fire was under control and the neighbouring premises could be saved. From the ruins only the bodies of the inhabitants could be secured.

Due to risk of spreading fire from the burning Company school several jets from the Fiat engine were directed onto the Etos bakery very flammable roof. Two hoses have been in action here for eighteen hours.

The Magirus fire engine, while situated in the Kastanjelaan, fought with two hoses against the fires in the paper mill while two other hoses were directed on a few houses. Some time later, however, the fire engine's motor was running hot, requiring it to be put out of action for two hours. The Laffley replaced her during that time.

Upon urgent request from a clergyman the commandant released four firemen to assist in excavating people buried under the debris of a house along the Mathildelaan. After the successful excavation, further medical care was left to a doctor who had arrived in the meantime and first aid members.

Various firemen, through their knowledge of first aid, offered creditable services in the Philips Recreation building where many wounded were accommodated in the afternoon. Fireman v. Helvoirt perished while preparing to go to the factory; after having put his family in safety he shortly returned to his house where right at that moment a delayed action bomb exploded.

B. THE WORK OF THE AIR RAID WARDENS

I. On the Emmasingel complex.

The members of the Philips Air Raid Precautions were called to action in a very unexpected moment. Many of the air raid wardens happened to be in the Command Post, since it was lunch time, when the anti-aircraft guns were heard going into action. Since no air raid alarm was given, on account of reasons already previously mentioned in this report, some wardens went outside to have a look at what was going on. The idea of an exercise by the Germans soon vanished when heavy bomb explosions made clear that the Royal Air Force was attacking the factory. Instantly adequate measures were taken and the ARP commander of the complex tried to get in touch by telephone with the various block leaders, amongst them the Strijp complex ARP commander and the fire brigade. After only a few words, however, the call was interrupted. The situation in the Command Post at that time was far from convenient with everything shaking and rumbling due to the exploding bombs which also caused the electrical lighting to fail.

Immediately after the first attack, ordered so by an inspector of shift II, two wardens went to investigate the gas factory and the boiler house since it was known that employees had been working there. The buildings were still undamaged although one of the stokers had grazed his wrist and was administered first aid on the spot. During that period the second attack wave came in. Once also this wave has passed the commander received the message that a bomb had landed in the boiler house behind building B (valve and lamp factory) but had not exploded. Immediately the order was given to move away from the building as soon as possible. Meanwhile fires erupted everywhere and many of the air raid wardens offered valuable services to the fire brigade in combating the fire.

During roll call of shift II it was discovered that one of the wardens who did not turn up in the Command Post at the beginning of the attack was still missing. A patrol was sent out duly to look for the missing man and observe any possible damage. Luckily, he was found unharmed though he was buried under dust and debris due to a direct bomb hit next to his shelter. During the less heavy third attack most of the wardens retreated to their Command Post the doors of which were closed shut.

When the raid was considered finished the ARP started their work in an organized way. Some of the air raid wardens were sent into the buildings to look for victims as well as dud bombs and to locate blazes. Others were requested to assist the fire brigade. Dressing aids and medicines were also brought to safety from the polyclinic which was surrounded by buildings that were ablaze. Upon completion of this hazardous job, the wardens learned to their consternation that just outside the clinic either a delayed action or a dud bomb was located.

Doctor van Alphen de Veer had arrived in the meantime on the Emmasingel complex upon being summoned. A wounded employee from the head office was treated on the medical post, while a second had such nasty head wounds that he had to be transferred to the Diaconessen hospital via ambulance.

Wounded were carried on stretchers to the medical posts where ARP first aiders ably assisted the doctors. Though the raid was heavy, the death toll was relatively minor, mostly because it was Sunday and only few people were present on the site. But above all the Emmasingel complex ARP has proved to be an invaluable asset during such an event.

II. On the Strijp complex.

Startled by the firing of the anti-aircraft guns and several explosions, the ARP commander hastily left his office for the Command Post. He was barely outside when a bomb exploded which demolished his very office. At the Command Post itself wardens realized what their oncoming jobs were to be and were awaiting orders in orderly fashion. Telephones as well as electrical mains were out of order.

During the second and third attack waves, bombs were dropped by the dozen and a tremendous shock made them realize that a bomb had hit directly overhead. Fires were erupting everywhere; the Philite factory was fully enveloped in flames and was not visible anymore from the Command Post due to dense smoke. There was considerable fear for the safety of the air raid warden at their various posts and not mistakenly so.

The first bombs caused the walls of post 15 (garage) to develop severe cracks. The post's air raid wardens tried to escape the building which was in danger of collapsing via the front door which proved to be stuck and could not be opened with whatever means. Then the back entrance was tried, also unsuccessfully since at that very moment several more bombs hit nearby causing chaos, flames and smoke as well as blocking this path of escape. A final attempt to escape via a window succeeded, though not without one of them being hit by falling debris that rendered him unconscious. After a short while he came to and he, too, escaped successfully via the window. With a colleague, he made his way to the Command Post, barely reaching it alive when a wall they were just passing collapsed. The bomb blast knocked down one of them, thereby wounding him yet again.

Due to heavy smoke from the rapidly spreading fire, conditions in the Command Post became untenable, the more so because steam was escaping from ruptured pipes and further reducing visibility. The Command Post was moved to the undamaged fire station where, shortly after, also Nurse Kleinod and Doctor Ebeling Koning arrived. The fire that caused the Command Post evacuation was mainly concentrated in the adjacent packing building. Using a skeleton key, entry to the building was gained in order to to put out the fire using hand fire extinguishers, sand and water. Undoubtedly, this would have been achieved if the water mains had not gone out of order after the initial bomb explosions. This proved a big handicap for both the fire brigade and the ARP.

Meanwhile, patrols were sent out in all directions to look for wounded and get a general idea of the situation at the various posts. Thus it could be determined that though many had felt the 'heat' not one of the employees had sustained serious injuries.

Many employees were taken by surprise when the attack started while returning from the Philips' mess. One of them was trapped under the debris but, miraculously, this debris was removed largely by bomb blast from a second bomb and he was able to free himself. Going on all fours he hid behind some barrels stored next to a garage. A bomb fragment, however, punched a hole in one of these barrels and leaking oil forced him to seek yet another safe shelter. He tried Post 15 which was completely ruined, however. Desperately now he dropped to the ground next to the garage under a metal plate, this all within a few minutes. Two men from Post 13 also took their share of harassing moments, while seeking shelter together with five civilians in the Philite factory stairwell. Near to them a heavy bomb exploded, blasting away the walls and sandbags protecting the windows dropped down. Through heavy clouds of smoke and dust they managed to leave the plant in between the first and second attack waves in the direction of the Beukenlaan.

Unfortunately it turned out later that a fitter from the car workshop, H. van der Meulen, had not been able to get outside and was killed. Even worse, there were two more casualties from Strijp complex. The boiler house was severely hit, and boiler operators van Kasteren and van Hal were found dead under the debris.

From all this it shows that the task of the Philips ARP on the Strijp complex was not inconsiderable. As well as assisting the fire brigade, they were required to stretcher casualties and provide a continuous supply of first aid dressings. A few of them were working under Ir Roeterink when contributing to the attempts to get the Bedrijfsschool rescued from the flames. Others screened off a dud bomb and ensured that nobody came too close to it.

The fire station was soon too crowded, however, to shelter both the fire brigade and the ARP. Therefore, and for reasons of limited protection offered by the building and its defective lighting, it was decided to move the Philips ARP post to building L.

Special mention must be made of those Philips employees who were working at the glass factory and first put out the glass ovens, according to procedure, before seeking cover in their air raid shelter (when not properly put out the solidified glass would render the ovens non-operational until the glass was removed; this glass was used in the manufacturing of the radio valves).

III. Outside the factory plants.

Those Philips air raid wardens who were put in a very difficult position as a result of the raid were surely those who were on duty outside the plant at the Philips Recreation building. Here were gathered some 650 people dining on casserole. When the anti-aircraft guns went into action and the first bombs started to explode many wanted to leave the building. The air wardens, assisted by the doorkeeper, prevented panic and directed them to the corridors. Upon the second wave of the bombardment, however, panic rose rapidly and many went outside, resulting in three heavily and seven lightly wounded. After the attack the Recreation building became the central location where victims were taken. Under the leadership of Dr Burger, many first-aiders went into action to assist. For some of the victims any help was to no avail, however.

Nearly everywhere bombs had come down outside the factory plants the Philips air raid wardens could be seen in action, like in the de Jonghlaan, de Frederiklaan, de Mathildelaan and even on de Demer and Fellenoord. Many injured were rescued from under the debris, were administered first aid and thereafter taken either to the Philips Recreation building or a hospital. One of these wardens, upon request of the communal ARP, while on his way from home to the Philips factory, assisted effectively in an effort to rescue victims from a building on the street corner of Demer and Parallelweg. Another warden was able to administer first aid to those who received cuts, abrasions and splinter wounds, here and elsewhere in the Philipsdorp.

Last, but not least, the orderlies should be mentioned whose important tasks they fulfilled with great devotion to duty.

Eindhoven, December 1942.
RV/BR.

Glossary

AA	Anti-Aircraft
A&AEE	Aeroplane & Armament Experimental Establishment
AFC	Air Force Cross
AG	Air Gunner
CD	Compact Disc
CO	Commanding Officer
DAF	van Doorne's Automobiel Fabriken
DELA	Deelt Elklanders LAsten
DFC	Distinguished Flying Cross
DFM	Distinguished Flying Medal
DSO	Distinguished Service Order
DVD	Digital Versatile Disc
E	East
ETA	Estimated Time of Arrival
Flak	*Flugzeugabwehrkanone* (anti-aircraft gun)
FW	Focke-Wulf
GP	General Purpose
HE	High Explosive
hp	horse power
HQ	Headquarters
IAS	Indicated Air Speed
JG	*Jagdgeschwader*
Kg	kilogram
lb	pound
LOCOS	LOCal Oxidation of Silicon
MC	Medium Capacity
MO	Medical Officer
mph	miles per hour
MRI	Magnetic Resonance Imaging
N	North
NA, Kew	National Archives, Kew, Surrey
Nav	Navigator
NNE	North-North-East
ORB	Operational Record Book
PoW	Prisoner of War
PR	Photo Reconnaissance

PRO	Public Record Office (now part of the UK National Archives)
psi	pounds per square inch
PSV	Philips Sport Vereniging
RAAF	Royal Australian Air Force
RAF	Royal Air Force
RAFVR	Royal Air Force Volunteer Reserve
RCAF	Royal Canadian Air Force
RNZAF	Royal New Zealand Air Force
rpm	revolutions per minute
SE	South East
Sqn/Sqdn	Squadron
TD	Time Delay
TNA	The National Archives (London)
Uffz.	*Unteroffizier* (equivalent to corporal)
UK	United Kingdom
USA	United States of America
USAAF	United States Army Air Forces
VC	Victoria Cross
W/OP	Wireless Operator

Bibliography

Further Reading and Documents Consulted
In addition to notes kept by the authors, and especially Kees Rijken, over a period of years, the following are the principal books and records drawn upon for information on Operation OYSTER. Not all these documents have been quoted in this concise account of the operation, but this list does serve to illustrate the extent of the material consulted.

Bowman, Martin W., *Low level from Swanton: The History of Swanton Morley airfield from World War Two to the Present Day* (Air Research publications, Walton-on-Thames, 1995)
——, *Mosquito Bomber/Fighter-Bomber Units 1942-45* (Osprey Publishing, Botley, 1997)
——, *The Reich Intruders: dramatic RAF medium bomber raids over Europe in World War 2* (Patrick Stephens Limited, Sparkford, 1997)
Bowyer, Chaz, *The History of the RAF* (Hamlyn Publishing Group Ltd., London, 1977)
Bowyer, Michael J. F., *2 Group RAF: A Complete History 1936-1945* (Faber and Faber Ltd., London, 1974)
Chant, Christopher, *The History of the RAF from 1939 to the present* (Regency House Publishing Ltd., London, 1993)
Chorley, W. R., *RAF Bomber Command Lossed of the Second World War 1942* (Midland Counties Publications, Earl Shilton, 1994)
Clark, G. N., *Holland and the War* (Oxford Pamphlets of World Affairs No. 49, 1941, Michelin Green Guide – Netherlands, 2001)
Delve, Ken, *RAF Marham: The operational history of Britain's front-line base from 1916 to the present day* (Patrick Stephens Ltd., Sparkford, 1995)
Ethell, Jeffrey L., *Warbirds fotofax P-51 Mustang* (Arms and Armour Press, London, 1990)
Freeman, Roger A., *Mighty Eighth War Diary* (Jane's Publishing Company Ltd., London, 1981)
——, *Mustang at War* (Ian Allan Ltd., London, 1974)
Goulding, James & Moyes, Philip, *RAF Bomber Command and its aircraft 1941-1945* (Ian Allan Ltd., London, 2002)
Gunston, Bill, *British Fighters of World War II* (The Hamlyn Publishing Group Ltd., Feltham, 1982)
Hardy, M. J., *de Havilland Mosquito Super Profile* (Haynes Publishing Group, Sparkford, 1984)
——, *The de Havilland Mosquito* (David & Charles PLC, London, 1977)

Hess, William N., *A-20 Boston at War* (Ian Allan Ltd., London, 1979)

Holliday, J. E. & Radke, D. A., *The RAAF PoWs of Lamsdorf* (Lamsdorf RAAF POWs Association, Holland Park, Australia, 1992)

Mason, Francis K., *The Hawker Typhoon and Tempest* (Aston Publications Ltd., Bourne End, 1988)

Middlebrook, Martin & Everitt, Chris, *The Bomber Command War Diaries: an operational reference book 1939-1945* (Richard Clay Ltd., Bungay, 1985)

Moyes, Philip J. R. & Goulding, James, *British Bombers of world war two: volume one* (Hylton Lacy Publishers Ltd., Windsor, 1969)

——, *RAF Bombers of world war two: volume two* (Hylton Lacy Publishers Ltd., Chalfont St. Giles, 1968)

Pelly-Fry, James, *Heavenly Days* (Crecy Publishing Ltd., Manchester, 1994)

Philips, Frits, *45 Jaar met Philips* (Ad Donker BV, Rotterdam, 1976)

Price, Alfred, *Spitfire: a complete fighting history* (Productivity Press, 1991)

——, *Spitfire at war: 2* (Ian Allan Ltd., London, 1985)

Reed, Arthur & Beamont, Roland, *Typhoon and Tempest at War* (Ian Allan Ltd., London, 1979)

Sanders, Bruce, *Bombers Fly East* (Herbert Jenkins Ltd., London, 1943)

Sanders, James, *Venturer Courageous: Group Captain Leonard Trent VC, DFC* (Hutchinson, Auckland, New Zealand, 1983)

Scott, Stuart R., *Mosquito Thunder: No. 105 Squadron RAF at war 1942-1945* (Sutton Publishing Ltd. Stroud, 2001)

Scrivner, Charles L. & Scarborough, Captain W. E., *Lockheed PV-1 Ventura in action* (Squadron/Signal Publications Inc., Aircraft No. 48, Carrollton, USA, 2004)

Smith, Graham, *Norfolk Airfields in the Second World War* (Countryside Books, 1994)

Stanaway, John C., *Vega Ventura: The Operational History of Lockheed's Lucky Star* (Schiffer Military/Aviation History, Pennsylvania, USA, 1997)

Terraine, John, *The Right of the Line: The Royal Air Force in the European War 1939-1945* (Wordsworth Editions Ltd., Ware, 1998)

Thetford, Owen, *Aircraft of the Royal Air Force since 1918* (Putman & Company Ltd., London, 1976)

Thomas, C. H., *The Typhoon file* (Air-Britain Historians Ltd. / British Aviation Archaeological Council, 1981)

Younge, John, *The area of Methwold and its people* (John Younge, Methwold, 2001)

Journals and magazines

Edinborough, Kenneth, 'Men behind the medals: Keen to Serve', *Flypast* magazine, November 2000, pp.32-4

Graham, Ralph, 'Low Level Attacker', *Flypast* magazine, January 1997, pp. 59-63

Ransom, D. C., *Aden and Thorney Island: 1966-67* (RAF Marham Archives)

Stapfer, Hans-Heiri, 'Stalin's Mosquito', *Flypast* magazine, February 2001, pp.56-9

Zunder van, A. C., *History of Woensdrecht aerodrome*

de Havilland Mosquito Handling Notes, A.P. 2653Q – P.N.

Douglas Boston Handling Notes, A.P. 2023D – P.N.

The AIR Britain Military Aviation Historical Quarterly (*Aeromilitaria*, No. 1, 1982)

The Canadian Corner, 2nd Tactical Air Force Medium Bombers Association (Issue 53, 1999)

Internet web pages
http://www.csd.uwo.ca/~pettypi/elevon/baugher_us/a20-05.html (Boston III)
http://www.csd.uwo.ca/~pettypi/elevon/baugher_us/b034-01.html (Ventura I/II)
http://www.csd.uwo.ca/~pettypi/elevon/baugher_us/p051.html#RTFToC2
  (Mustang I)
http://www.research.philips.com (Philips post war)

The National Archives, Kew, London
AIR14, Bomber Command
No. 2 Group Summary of events, December 1942   AIR14/523
RAF Station High Wycombe, 12 January 1943   AIR14/523
AIR25, Operations Record Books: Groups
2 Group RAF   AIR25/23   & AIR25/35
               AIR25/194
               AIR25/204
AIR27, Operations Record Book: Squadrons; all records available on micro-film

21	Squadron (Ventura)	AIR27/263	& AIR27/266
56	Squadron (Typhoon)	AIR27/530	& AIR27/536
88	Squadron (Boston)	AIR27/716	& AIR27/718
105	Squadron (Mosquito)	AIR27/826	
107	Squadron (Boston)	AIR27/843	
139 (Jamaica)	Squadron (Mosquito)	AIR27/960	& AIR27/965
167	Squadron (Spitfire)	AIR27/1092	
226	Squadron (Boston)	AIR27/1406	& AIR27/1408
268	Squadron (Mustang)	AIR27/1563	
411 (RCAF)	Squadron (Spitfire)	AIR27/1804	
464 (RAAF)	Squadron (Ventura)	AIR27/1924	
485 (RNZAF)	Squadron (Spitfire)	AIR27/1933	
487 (RNZAF)	Squadron (Ventura)	AIR27/1935	

AIR28, Operations Record Book: Stations; all records available on paper

Coltishall	56 Squadron (Typhoon), 167, 411 and 485 Squadron (Spitfire)	AIR28/168
Feltwell	21, 464 and 487 Squadrons (Ventura)	AIR28/269
Marham	105 and 139 Squadrons (Mosquito)	AIR28/517
Oulton	88 Squadron (Boston)	AIR28/606 (no relevant info found)
West Raynham	107 Squadron (Boston)	AIR28/909

AIR29, Operations Record Book: Unit   AIR29/259   & AIR29/260

AIR40, Operations undertaken 6 December 1942   AIR40/372
by USAAF and RAF

Index